Technology-mediated Learning During the Pandemic

This volume discusses the emergence of information and communication technology (ICT)-based teaching and learning during the Covid-19 pandemic as a potential alternative to traditional classroom-based learning. It presents a collection of theories, practices, and case studies from across the globe and covers different aspects of education from a multidisciplinary perspective.

While focusing on the various opportunities that surfaced while carrying out innovative experiments in the online learning space, the book discusses pedagogical challenges and the need for a shift in teaching pedagogy towards online learning. It outlines the existing learning theories, reasons behind their failure, and new theories that emerged to fill the need for new methods for delivery of content and pedagogy. The book discusses the issues faced by stakeholders, including institute administrators, students, and teachers to prepare for this new method of teaching and learning. It highlights the role of virtual laboratories in supplementing the needs of students in the remote learning environment. The book also discusses the role and impact of social media as a powerful tool of learning and educational communication.

This book will be of interest to teachers, students, and researchers of education, higher education, digital education, information technology, educational psychology, and media studies. It will also be useful for courses on e-learning, educationalists, policymakers, educational institutions, online education centres, and practitioners working in the related areas.

Jitendra Singh is Assistant Professor in PGDAV College, University of Delhi. He is an engineering graduate in Computer Science and Engineering (CSE) and pursued PhD in the area of cloud computing. With a deep interest in Cloud Computing, Educational Technology, and Machine learning, he has contributed over 40 articles as principal author which are published in leading research journals and conference proceedings. In addition, he has authored three books, namely *Cloud computing for beginner to researcher*, *Data structure simplified: implementation with C++*, and *Python principles and practice*, all of which can be well accessed from Amazon.

Vikas Kumar received an MSc and PhD from Kurukshetra University, India, and this was followed by an MBA. Along with 15 books, he has more than 100 research papers to his credit in various national and international conferences and journals. Dr Kumar is presently serving at Central University of Haryana, India, and is a visiting professor at the Indian Institute of Management Indore and University of Northern Iowa, USA. His areas of interest include information systems, business analytics, and ICT for development.

Technology-mediated Learning During the Pandemic

Challenges vs Outcomes

Edited by Jitendra Singh and Vikas Kumar

Routledge
Taylor & Francis Group
LONDON AND NEW YORK

First published 2024
by Routledge
4 Park Square, Milton Park, Abingdon, Oxon OX14 4RN

and by Routledge
605 Third Avenue, New York, NY 10158

Routledge is an imprint of the Taylor & Francis Group, an informa business

British Library Cataloguing-in-Publication Data
A catalogue record for this book is available from the British Library

ISBN: 978-1-032-20439-0 (hbk)
ISBN: 978-1-032-79377-1 (pbk)
ISBN: 978-1-003-49171-2 (ebk)

DOI: 10.4324/9781003491712

Typeset in Sabon
by Apex CoVantage, LLC

Contents

Notes on contributors

Editors

Jitendra Singh

Jitendra Singh is serving as Assistant Professor in PGDAV College, University of Delhi. He is an engineering graduate in Computer Science and Engineering (CSE) and pursued PhD in the area of cloud computing. With deep interest in cloud computing, educational technology, and machine learning, he has contributed over 40 articles as principal author which are published in leading research journals and conference proceedings. In addition, he has authored three books, namely *Cloud Computing for Beginner to Researcher*, *Data Structure Simplified: implementation with C++*, and *Python Principles and Practice*, all of which can be well accessed from Amazon.

Vikas Kumar

Dr. Vikas Kumar received MSc in electronics from Kurukshetra University, Haryana, India. This was followed by MSc in computer science and further PhD from the same university. He is a life member of Indian Science Congress Association, Computer Society of India, IETE, ICEIE, IPA, VEDA, IVS, and Magnetic Society of India. Dr. Kumar has designed and conducted number of training programmes for the corporate sector and is a trainer for a number of Govt of India departments. Along with 15 books, he has more than 100 research papers to his credit in various national and international conferences and journals. Out of this, 92 are with the Scopus-indexed international journals. He was the Editor of International Quarterly Refereed Journal *Asia-Pacific Business Review* during June 2007–June 2009. Dr. Kumar is presently serving at the Central University of Haryana, Mahendergarh, India and is a visiting Professor at the Indian Institute of Management, Indore and University of Northern Iowa, USA.

Contributors

Ritu Bajaj

Dr. Ritu Bajaj is a Master's in business administration and Doctorate of Philosophy from Kurukshetra University, Kurukshetra. Her area of specialization is marketing and retail. She has an experience of more than 18 years in the area of academics and administration in institutes of higher education of repute. She has published more than a dozen of research papers in international and national journals of repute. She has presented various papers in international and national seminars. She has delivered more than 60 talks at prestigious educational institutions. She has a few books as an author to her kitty too. She has supervised theses of several students for the award of doctorate of philosophy. She has designed and conducted several training programmes on communication, service marketing and retail for middle and lower level executives of both public and private sectors. She is a member of various statutory bodies like the court, executive council, academic council, and board of studies of different universities.

Shafila Bansal

Dr. Shafila currently holds the position of Jr. Data Scientist at Sabudh Foundation, Mohali while pursuing master's in data science from IIITB. Previously, she dedicated 8 years of her career as an assistant professor in the Department of Environment Science, MCM DAV College, Chandigarh.

Aashish Bhardwaj

Dr. Aashish Bhardwaj is working as Head of Department (Computer Science and Engineering) at Guru Tegh Bahadur Institute of Technology, New Delhi. He is recipient of NPTEL Star in the categories of NPTEL Believers and NPTEL Enthusiasts. He is a life member of Indian National Science Congress Association, Indian Society for Technical Education, Fellow of Institute of Electronics and Telecommunication Engineers, and Computer Society of India. He has published research papers in IGI Global journals (IJSSMET, IJSDS), Inderscience journals (IJCC), IIJCS, IJRECE, IJCMS, etc. He has published papers in international conferences such as IPMC-2006 at Quaid-i-Azam University, Islamabad, IEEE Conference ICCIT-2011 at Dhaka, M4D-2012 at New Delhi, ICPE-2008 at New Delhi, and Indian Science Congress 93rd at Hyderabad and 101st at Jammu. He is an IBM-Certified Deployment Professional Tivoli Directory Server V6.1, Rational Functional Tester for Java, and DB2 9 Fundamentals and Rational Application Developer for WebSphere Software 6.0.

Babita Bhati

Dr. Babita Bhati is Associate Professor and Area Chair at the Army Institute of Management and Technology, Greater Noida. She has diverse experience spanning over 17 years in management teaching. She is a certified NLP practitioner and has completed an executive program in HR analytics from XLRI Jamshedpur, India. She was awarded a Ph.D. from the School of Management, Gautam Buddha University, on the topic "Role of Entrepreneurs' Competence in Managing Firm Performance". Her research interests include human behavior, entrepreneurial traits, and performance management. She has published research papers in journals of national and international repute. She is a certified trainer from ISTD Delhi and has done several corporate training assignments with the Indian Industries Association, Anmol Industries HO and manufacturing plants, Daurala Sugar Mills Meerut, the Government Institute of Medical Sciences, and so on, on topics like interpersonal behavior, emotional intelligence, team building, stress management, conflict handling, leadership, psychometric testing, and compassionate discipline.

Santosh Bhukal

Dr. Santosh Bhukal is working as Assistant Professor in the Department of Environmental Science and Engineering at Guru Jambheshwar University of Science and Technology, Hisar. Dr. Santosh Bhukal completed her PhD in the year 2015 from Panjab University, Chandigarh. She was awarded Post-doctorate fellowship for women. Dr. Bhukal has significantly contributed to the field of nanotechnology and wastewater treatment. She holds experience of 8 years in teaching and research in Environmental sciences and has attended 48+ International and National seminars and conferences. She has authored ~30 research articles in reputed national and international journals. Her h-index is 13.

Sujana Chamarty

Ms. Sujana Chamarty pursued a master's degree in business analytics from the University of Central Oklahoma and has a bachelor's degree in mechanical engineering from Jawaharlal Nehru Technological University, India. Prior to her master's degree, she worked in the IT industry for over 5 years. She is currently employed as a Data Scientist in the IT industry. Her experiences range from working with IT support to computer programming, analytics, project management, and machine learning.

Archana Choudhary

Dr. Archana Choudhary is working as Associate Professor, Birla School of Management, Birla Global University, Bhubaneswar, India. She has 20 years of experience in teaching and research. She has a number of publications to her credit. She has reviewed a number of papers of different publication houses. She has conducted a number of MDPs and FDPs. Dr. Choudhary has been invited to chair sessions in HR and OB conferences. She teaches human resource management, organizational behaviour, training and development, HR analytics, compensation management, etc. to the management students. Her research interests are in the area of turnaround management, learning and its implications, organizational change, and career management. She has presented a number of papers at national and international conferences. She has also guided a few PhD scholars.

Leszek Cichobłaziński

Dr. Leszek Cichobłaziński is the Deputy Head of the Department of Applied Sociology and Human Resources Management at the Częstochowa University of Technology, Poland. He has demonstrated history of working in the alternative dispute resolution industry. He is skilled in cooperation, alternative dispute resolution, intercultural skills, Russian, and Polish. He is a strong education professional with a master's degree focused in sociology from Jagiellonian University.

Bhaskar Das

With 30 years of academic and industry experience, Bhaskar brings excitement and learning to his classroom as he encourages his students to think out of the box, take risks, try to solve real-world problems through projects, bring industry conversations alive through a deep knowledge and understanding of the concepts of fashion design, fashion and lifestyle business. He specializes in teaching sourcing, compliances – social/technical, Lean concepts, retail management, textiles, internship mentoring, industry project mentoring, major project mentoring, E-Com compliance, and vendor management. Bhaskar's academic qualifications include Mechanical Engineering Diploma, Master of Arts in Education, PhD in Education (pursuing with 2019 enrolment), Certificate in Teaching and Learning in Higher Education (TLHE), Certificate in Online Hybrid Blended Education, among others. His areas of interest in research include academic management, E-learning, Lean manufacturing, mentoring and EdTech. He was conferred the Best Researcher Award at Pearl Academy in 2020.

Anu Gupta

Dr. Anu received BTech in chemical engineering from Punjab Technical University, Jalandhar, India and MTech in polymers from Panjab University, Chandigarh, India. She has worked in the area of sustainable composite materials for her doctoral thesis at Indira Gandhi National Open University, New Delhi, India. She also holds a Master's degree in business administration and has been a recipient of the prestigious NFP and DAAD fellowships. Dr. Gupta has been an active member of the International Union of Pure and Applied Chemistry, Indian Society for Technical Education, Society for Education and Research Development, Electrochemical Society (USA), and the International Association of Engineers. She has received Early Carrier Award by American Chemical Society, USA and received project grant from Department of Science & Technology, India under the Fast Track Proposals for Young Scientists in Engineering Science in 2013. She has published more than 30 research papers in journals and periodicals of international and national repute. Her areas of interest include sustainable composite materials, sustainable building structures, waste management, and climate change.

Sangeeta Gupta

Dr. Sangeeta is currently working as Professor in Department of Management in Management Education and Research Institute (MERI), Delhi and has an experience of 29 years in teaching, research and administration. She has co-authored a book on MIS. She has published more than 30 papers in journals listed in ABDC, Scopus, and UGC Care list. Under her supervision, four students have completed and three are pursuing their PhD in the field of IT, marketing, and HR.

Shivangi Jain

Shivangi Jain is a PhD researcher at IIT Jodhpur, embarking on a journey to explore the captivating fields of nanomaterials and nanoscience. With a genuine passion for learning and discovery, she is dedicated to contributing to the advancement of nanotechnology.

Nitika Kapoor

Nitika has 12 years of cross-functional experience in areas including academia, training, and marketing. She is currently pursuing MA in Education and has already done her Master's in luxury brand management from Polimoda, Italy. After working as a fashion designer initially, she ran a buying house specializing in denim in Germany for a couple of years. Her quest for knowledge of the luxury retail industry led her to work in strategic management with Reliance Brands Ltd in the CEO's office. With a blended exposure to European and Indian fashion, she joined academia and continues to teach subjects such as business communication, luxury branding, and marketing and visual influences on luxury.

Jaspreet Kaur

Dr. Jaspreet has 19 years of academic and industry experience and she encourages her students to be collaborative and adaptive and to develop a problem-solving mindset. She specializes in teaching marketing fundamentals, CEM, entrepreneurship, marketing research, data analytics, digital marketing, advertising, strategic management, E-commerce, brand management and consumer behaviour, digital marketing, meta-analysis, qualitative research. Her academic qualifications include a PhD in management (marketing), MPhil (management), PGDM (management, marketing, and IT), a BSc degree in textile design and a Diploma in digital marketing. Dr. Jaspreet is a recipient of GRABS Teaching and Research Excellence Award 2015, Best Researcher Award by ITSR 2020, and Best Researcher's Award in SAMMAN 2021. She has published 12 articles in Scopus and indexed journals from ABDC list. In research, her interest areas include consumer behaviour, digital marketing, meta-analysis, and qualitative research.

Simranjot Kaur

Simranjot Kaur is a student of Chemical Laboratory Analysis Course, Toronto, Canada, and is currently working as analyst in college.

Raj K. Kovid

Dr. Raj K. Kovid is Professor and Head-Research at School of Business Studies of Sharda University, India. He has working experience of over 27 years in academics, research, and industry. His teaching and research area includes corporate strategy, M&A, entrepreneurship and innovation, technology adoption, and corporate governance and CSR. He has published research papers and book chapters in Scopus/ABDC indexed journals such as *Management Decision* and *Management Research Review* and in edited books published by international publishers such as IGI, USA. He is involved with some journals in the capacity of guest editor, board member, and reviewer. His cases are available at Harvard Business School Publishing portal and Emerald Publications, and he has also conducted case method workshops. He has consulted firms with respect to their growth strategies.

Manju Lata

Manju Lata received her MTech in computer science and engineering from Gautam Buddh Technical University, Lucknow, India. This was followed by PhD in computer science and engineering from Shri Venkateshwara University, India. Currently, she is serving as an Associate Professor at Chandigarh University, India. She has designed and conducted a number of training programmes for the non-teaching employees for ICT skill enhancement. She has published book chapters and research papers in a number of reputed journals and participated in many international conferences. Her areas of interest include cloud computing, fog computing, Internet of Things (IoT), and smart city applications.

Ayu Maria Lestari

Ms. Ayu Maria Lestari studied in the Master of Business Management program in The Hang Seng University of Hong Kong.

Eko Liao

Dr. Eko Liao graduated from the University of Hong Kong with a PhD degree in management. Her research interests include optimizing employees' personal thriving and work experiences at workplace, and how leaders and organizations facilitate building a contemporary work environment to enhance such experiences. Dr. Eko Liao teaches management-related subjects in undergraduate and postgraduate levels (e.g., MBA, MSc, PhD) and in executive training programmes.

Cheuk Hin Mark Ng

Mr. Cheuk Hin Mark Ng studied in the Master of Business Management program in The Hang Seng University of Hong Kong.

Sivashnee Paragoo

Dr. Sivashnee Paragoo obtained her PhD from the University of Kwa-Zulu Natal, South Africa. She has 11 years of teaching experience. She is a high school curriculum leader at an independent school in South Africa. Her research interests include technology-enabled learning in secondary education schooling.

Parul

Parul is a PhD researcher at Department of Chemistry, Panjab University, Chandigarh. She is working in the fields of silanes appended click chemistry and nanoparticles and looking forward to enhancing the knowledge about the field.

Ayushi Pathak

Ayushi Pathak is currently working as a chemistry faculty at ALLEN Career Institute Pvt Ltd Ahmedabad, teaching students of IIT/NEET level.

C.L.V.R.S.V. Prasad

Dr. C.L.V.R.S.V. Prasad is currently working as Professor in the Department of Mechanical Engineering at GMR Institute of Technology, India. He is presently serving as Principal of the Institute. He has obtained PhD from Andhra University of Visakhapatnam, India. He holds more than 30 years of experience in the teaching profession. He has successfully guided more than two research scholars for attaining their PhD degrees and has his research papers published in indexed journals.

Yang Pu

Yang Pu is working at the Hang Seng University of Hong Kong.

Sandhya Rai

Dr. Sandhya Rai is currently working as Associate Professor at Bennett University, Greater Noida. A postgraduate in mathematics and management and a PhD in Management, Dr. Rai has more than 19 years of experience in teaching, consulting, research, and training. Dr. Rai has nine books to her credit in the domain of operations, decision sciences, entrepreneurship, and project management. She had published many research papers in reputed Indian and international journals. Her areas of expertise include data analytic, decision science, and AI- and technology-enabled learning. Dr. Rai is also a reviewer with reputed journals from India and abroad.

V. Rambabu

Dr. V. Rambabu is currently working as Professor in the Department of Mechanical Engineering at GMR Institute of Technology, Rajam, India. He holds more than 25 years of experience in the teaching profession. He pursued his PhD from Andhra University, Visakhapatnam, India He is presently serving as Associate Dean, Student Affairs at GMR Institute of Technology. He has his research papers published in several popular indexed journals.

Priya Saharan

Dr. Priya Saharan is working as INSPIRE Faculty in Centre of Excellence for Energy and Environmental Studies at Deenbandhu Chhotu Ram University of Science and Technology, Murthal, India. She has obtained her

Master's as well as PhD in environment science from Panjab University, Chandigarh. She has more than seven years of research/teaching experience. Her specialization is in the field of semiconductor and metallic nanotechnology, which includes synthesis, growth, properties, and their various environmental as well as energy storage applications.

G. Sasikumar

Dr. G. Sasikumar is currently working as Professor in the Department of Mechanical Engineering at GMR Institute of Technology, Rajam, India. He holds more than 20 years of experience in the teaching profession. He pursued his PhD from Anna University, Chennai, Tamil Nadu, India. He is presently serving as Head of the Department at GMR Institute of Technology. He has his research papers published in several popular indexed journals.

Kershnee Sevnarayan

Prof. Kershnee Sevnarayan obtained her PhD from the University of KwaZulu Natal, South Africa. She has 14 years of teaching experience. She is an associate professor in the Department of English Studies at the University of South Africa. She is also a Shanghai Open University visiting scholar. Her research interests include open distance e-learning, technology-mediated teaching, learning, and pedagogy in higher education.

G.V.S.S. Sharma

Dr. G.V.S.S. Sharma is currently working as Associate Professor in the Department of Mechanical Engineering at GMR Institute of Technology, Rajam, India. He is a mechanical engineer with double postgraduate in the fields of tool design and CAD/CAM. He pursued his PhD from GITAM Deemed to be University of Visakhapatnam, India, in the field of process capability. He holds 6 years of industrial experience and 16 years of teaching experience. He has his research papers published in popular indexed journals.

Divya Siwach

Divya Siwach is a doctoral scholar in the Department of Environmental Science and Engineering at Guru Jambheshwar University of Science and Technology, Hisar, India. She received a bachelor's degree in zoology from Miranda House, Delhi University and a master's degree in environmental science from Guru Jambheshwar University of Science and Technology, Hisar, India. She has keen interest in nanotechnology, waste management, and waste utilization. Her research focus for doctoral work revolves around agriculture waste management and its utilization as a resource for sustainable applications.

M. Srinivasa Rao

Dr. M. Srinivasa Rao is currently working as Professor in the Department of Mechanical Engineering at GMR Institute of Technology, Rajam, India. He is a mechanical engineer with postgraduate degree in the field of industrial engineering. He pursued his PhD from Indian Institute of Technology Kharagpur, India, in the field of reliability. He holds 21 years of teaching experience. He has his research papers published in several popular indexed journals.

Subagyo

Dr. Subagyo is an associate professor at University of Nusantara PGRI Kediri, Indonesia, and was Dean of the Faculty of Economics and Business at the same university for the period 2015–2023. His research areas and teaching interests are entrepreneurship, business management, empowerment, and the development of MSMEs. Apart from teaching and conducting research, he is very much active in the MSME community, as a business consultant, as a speaker, and have participated in several conferences in the fields of economics and business. He has published several reference books and papers on business management and MSME development.

Bala Subramanian

Dr. Bala Subramanian R., FPM (XLRI, Jamshedpur), is currently working Assistant Professor (OB & HRM) with Rajagiri Business School, Rajagiri College of Social Sciences, Kochi, Kerala. He has 15 years of work experience. His research interests are in the area of positive psychology, personality, and writing business cases.

Danping Yu

Ms. Danping Yu graduated from the Hang Seng University of Hong Kong with a Master's degree in Business Management Programme in Global Finance stream. She works for Bank of China Group as private wealth management manger. Ms. Danping Yu worked in Beijing, London, and Hong Kong. She owns extensive hands-on experiences in the field of private wealth management and financial planning.

Foreword

The Covid-19 pandemic has so far been one of the most important human experiences of the 21st century, which has irreversibly changed many areas of social and economic life. One of these areas is education. So far, teaching and education have been associated primarily with the direct contact between teachers and pupils, at every level, not excluding the university education. The sudden necessity to switch from the previous mode of education based on direct contact between teacher and pupils to contact via electronic media has given rise to a number of challenges but has also opened up new possibilities that were previously known only at a theoretical level. The new way of imparting knowledge required the mastery of not only new technologies, both by students and by lecturers, but also new interpersonal skills to control the perception level of the audience determining the absorption of new information. In particular, the inherent contact with information technology was for some a source of so-called tech-stress.[1]

All of these problems and challenges are addressed in the book *Technology-mediated Learning During Pandemic: Challenges vs Outcomes*, which is a collective work by a number of authors from different countries and cultural backgrounds, representing very diverse academic disciplines and conducting their research in many areas of education. This provides the reader with a comprehensive picture of the issues under study.

The pedagogies, experiments, methodologies, frameworks, and experiences related to learning during pandemic have been presented in the book from a multidisciplinary perspective. Indeed, the experience in this area gained during the Covid-19 pandemic shows a wide spectrum of possibilities for future use. During the enforced change in the form of teaching, it became apparent that in many cases, remote learning can be quite effective and can allow students living far from academic centres to access knowledge. It seems, however, that the forms of teaching known for centuries and

1 The "tech-stress" concept was presented at the 23rd European Conference on Knowledge Management, University of Naples Parthenope and Federico II University in Naples, 1–2 September 2022.

based on face-to-face master–student contact will not be completely a thing of the past, so the question of the limits and possibilities of distance learning requires further in-depth research.

This book fills an important gap in the knowledge of the use of electronic tools in education, making it not only of significant cognitive value but also of practical value. The book can be addressed to teachers of schools of all levels, pupils, and students as well as professionals involved in the preparation of electronic tools for remote teaching.

Leszek Cichobłaziński
Department of Applied Sociology and Human Resources Management, Częstochowa University of Technology, Poland

Foreword

The Covid-19 pandemic that has struck the world brought rapid changes in various areas of life, one of which is education. The policy of working from home and physical distancing significantly impacted the shift in learning methods from face-to-face to online. This condition requires educators to innovate the learning process, including the learning at home through different applications, online seminars, online guidance, online practical laboratories, and an online community service programme. All these activities certainly require the support of technology in the education field.

Online learning was initially just a concept, the pandemic made its implementation necessary with its various barriers and challenges, both regarding the availability of means and facilities and the ability to use learning technologies. The challenges are perceived not only by educators but also by students and their parents. These challenges led to the changes in the system, syllabus, and learning process. The challenge for students is that they must accept the burden of learning without the school environment while studying at home. At the same time, parents must be stressed while accompanying their children in the learning process, along with their own jobs during the pandemic crisis.

Online learning is not just about changing face-to-face learning to online learning by using applications or giving more assignments to students. In fact, the online learning should encourage students to be creative in accessing as many sources of knowledge as possible, exploring the more productive skills, honing insights, and ultimately shaping themselves into lifelong learners. Behind the challenges that arise, the Covid-19 pandemic must be recognized as a significant catalyst that encourages the world of education to use information technology in learning.

The book titled *Technology-mediated Learning During the Pandemic: Challenges vs Outcomes,* edited by Jitendra Singh and Vikas Kumar, is a highly recommended resource for teachers, researchers, and policymakers. It provides a comprehensive coverage of the insights and good practices for learning during and after the Covid-19 pandemic. This book certainly inspires educators to be more creative and innovative towards the teaching–learning practices to improve the quality of education. At the same time, it offers challenges to the policymakers to integrate the innovative teaching pedagogies as part of the regular teaching–learning practices after the pandemic.

Subagyo
Faculty of Economics and Business, University of Nusantara, PGRI, Kediri, Indonesia

Preface

With the spread of the Covid-19 pandemic, the world came to a standstill. Lockdown was imposed by many countries across the world that led to the halt in commercial, political, and educational activities. Despite several locking and unlocking, the situation didn't come in full control. The Covid-19 apprehension prevailed for a long time, putting up challenges to the health systems. Under the pandemic scenario, students and teachers remained at distant locations, and face-to-face teaching–learning got halted. More than a billion students were directly affected by the pandemic as they were not able to go to educational institutions. To continue the learning and to avoid adverse impact on students' careers, ICT-based learning had emerged as a potential alternative to traditional classroom-based learning. With social distance in place and lockdown dilemmas, online learning is set to emerge as new normal learning. Experts also perceive that the emergence of new variants will further force online methods to continue in place of regular face-to-face learning.

For the effective delivery of online learning, technological resources are needed for all the stakeholders including teachers, students, and administrative personnel. However, generally, large-scale educational infrastructural development is the responsibility of governments, and it cannot be developed overnight. Developing and least developed countries have certainly minimal infrastructure to support ICT-based learning. Along with the basic infrastructure, challenges were also faced in developing new pedagogies to shift to online learning and make this more effective for learners. The control of online classes became another issue as unknown disguised users entered the online classroom and created a nuisance. To prevent such incidences, subscription to the application with the advanced features became a requirement. A lot of new applications were developed and many existing ones changed their features. The conduct of examination in online mode also came up as a challenge, since students need to demonstrate a high degree of integrity during examination for fair ranking. To offer a similar platform to all the students during the examination and to avoid any hassle, many universities have introduced the open book examination. However, teachers were ill-prepared to frame the question paper that can prevent the usage of unfair means yet promising enough to evaluate the student's strength.

Hence, a lot of challenges emerged with the shift towards online education, and this also offered a bouquet of opportunities for innovative experiments in the learning environment. This is what the book talks about. The book covers the existing learning theories, explains why they have failed, and discusses what new theories and new initiatives have emerged and how they have contributed to the teaching–learning processes. The book presents several cases studied from the recent experience across the globe. It covers the experiences and thoughts of leading researchers from across the world and offers perspectives from the point of view of different stakeholders.

Chapter 1 by Archana Choudhary and R. Bala Subramanian discusses the problem of online education during the pandemic, highlighting how the online learning was a kind of experiment conducted on the living organism of a school and a university. This chapter studies the motivational factors leading to these experiments and their difficulties while experimenting. It also discusses the outcomes and challenges faced by teachers in tackling the situation. Authors have taken six different case studies to identify the impact of online education on teachers in India. The discussion highlights the crucial need of people with creative skills during a crisis. The outcomes have been related to the existing theories to establish their relevance.

Raj K. Kovid and Babita Bhati have contributed the chapter "Evolution of online learning platforms during and post pandemic: insights from an emerging market", indicating the changes that e-learning tools have undergone with the emergence of the new technology market. This chapter explores how EdTech industry in India has evolved during and after pandemic; how it has gone through consolidation and what challenges it faces in the post-pandemic era. The chapter unfolds the futuristic outlook for the EdTech industry including the innovative hybrid model of education, venturing into Indian languages medium of instruction, reaching out to tier II and tier III cities as well as the scalability and lay-offs. The chapter provides a comprehensive insight about the Indian EdTech industry and how the EdTech firms are going to overcome a lot of obstacles to adapt to the new normal after the pandemic. Authors have recommended to proceed with caution to strike a balance between the conflicting goals of scalability and profitability for the EdTech firms.

In Chapter 3, Sivashnee Paragoo and Kershnee Sevnarayan have presented a case of flipped classrooms from a South African high school and highlighted the student engagement during online learning. The chapter explores teachers' perspectives and challenges of employing the flipped classroom approach for engaged learning in a semi-rural high school. The study is based on primary data, and authors have found that learners may remain disengaged due to pedagogy used by their teachers. The chapter has revealed that teachers continue to use the chalkboard- and textbook-only methods, which seems less interesting to the new generation students. The findings show that the pedagogy of flipping the classroom for engaged learning had a positive effect on students. The results of this study have implications for learners, teachers as well as the higher education institutions. It is recommended that there should be support from the various stakeholders (learners, school governing body, parents, school management team, and government departments) to ensure that the needs of facilitators are accommodated.

Bansal et al. have dedicated their study to outline the "Challenges in conducting practical courses during Covid-19" in Chapter 4. The chapter gives an account of the challenges faced by educators and students in conducting practical classes in different resource-strained situations. Along with the challenges, authors have also presented the best practices from across the globe to overcome those challenges. The literature studies have shown that unequal access to digital resources and technical issues like poor internet connection, low bandwidth, and power failure were among the major common challenges for mentors and learners. However, students encountered the lack of hands-on practice in e-learning, which is requisite to attain laboratory skills. On the other hand, teachers faced issues in developing traditional laboratory practical classes in virtual mode and under time constraints, where they had to opt out the demonstration of time-consuming experiments. Online methods such as virtual labs, remote control labs, and video-based labs were developed at various levels to conduct practical classes. However, virtual labs were the most popular substitute of traditional laboratories for most of the educational institutions worldwide. They will certainly see an integration with the traditional laboratory design in the new normal.

Chapter 5 by Sangeeta Gupta et al. focuses on the need to understand the role of EdTech apps for skilling and knowledge among students from a developing country with the application of the UTAUT model including new constructs such as Playful and Self-Management. The chapter presents "Gender" as a moderating factor to the pre-existing understanding of behavioural intention. A conceptual model on UTAUT has been presented by the authors. Primary data was collected from a sample of 521 Indian school students enrolled in the EdTech apps for online learning during the Covid-19 period, 2020–2021. A Likert-7 scale questionnaire survey was used for data collection, and SEM-PLS techniques were deployed for analysis. The results have shown that the prevailing UTAUT model, along with the new constructs of self-managed learning and playfulness, forms an extended framework for the model. These findings are novel and pave a way forward for students' online learning for global educational opportunities as well as the future of EdTech companies.

Chapter 6 titled "Constraints and impediments to the conduct of extracurricular activities in engineering education during pandemic: an industrial engineering insight" addresses the use of remote learning in extracurricular activities. Failure modes and effects analysis (FMEA) has been considered for improving the extracurricular activities in engineering institutes. The process improvement has been suggested on the basis of risk analysis considering the constraints and impediments in the conduct of extracurricular activities. FMEA helped in detecting out the loopholes in the educational process under consideration and led to delineating the improvement strategy. The authors have concluded that the concepts of industrial engineering can be applied for proposing improvement in the service sector of education and for the smooth conduct of extracurricular activities in engineering education. This can be of significance during challenging times such as the pandemic situation.

The physical, psychological, and mental distress associated with the e-learning has been presented by Shafila Bansal et al. in Chapter 7. Authors have considered the most important issue of stress associated with students' use of information technology, which they have had to master in a short period of time during the pandemic. The chapter suggests some virtual platforms which could be used for helping students to overcome the psychological and mental health-related issues by organizing webinars on topics like stress reduction, enhancing mental health, importance of physical activities, and so on. The role of parents also becomes important in attending to the queries of their wards patiently and giving them company to relieve their burdens. Similarly, the mental pressure of not interacting with their mentors can be reduced by the introduction of mandatory student–teacher talk time. The chapter concludes that a collaborative effort between parents, educational institutes, and government agencies may be helpful for reducing the mental stress, psychotic impacts, and physical effects on students while acquiring virtual learning.

Chapter 8, titled "Engineering education during pandemic: challenges and best practices" by Divya Siwach and Anu Gupta, takes up the specific issues of engineering education during the pandemic. Engineering education faced enormous challenges as the commonly used engineering laboratory equipment cannot be easily replaced by the best e-learning platforms. Authors have considered a number of interactive mechanisms for improving and thriving the learning experiences of students in the engineering labs. A number of ICT-based tools and methods are discussed in the chapter along with their advantages and limitations. Case studies of successful implementations from different institutions of the world are also presented in the chapter. The suggested tools and methods can be employed by various universities to combat the situation and enrich the quality of engineering education.

Chapter 9 developed by Ayu Maria Lestari et al. presents the learning opportunities and challenges in virtual teams in a very novel way and highlights the learning opportunities for team members working in virtual spaces. The authors present a case study of online learning environment of postgraduate students in Hong Kong to identify the benefits and challenges of the hybrid or fully remote working model. The authors highlight that organizations that possess advanced management experience or techniques are able to fully utilize the benefits of virtual team model, and they can harness it for competitive advantage. Contrary to this, in the absence of direct supervision or physical interaction, learners who are not highly motivated to learn and manage their time effectively will face more challenges in attaining the benefits of the virtual team learning model. Thus, the chapter is a good study on virtual teams.

Bhardwaj and Gupta in Chapter 10 present a model for conducting online laboratory courses during the pandemic. This chapter may answer the problems raised in Chapter 8, namely how to conduct remote laboratory learning. The chapter describes the most popular ICT tools, which could be used for conducting online laboratory courses. The chapter provides a comparison of these tools based on the features, usage during the Covid-19 pandemic, and social analysis through Emplifi social marketing cloud. The authors highlight that with the integration of virtual tools, the students can learn at their own pace, spend less time in traditional classroom activities, and create a customized learning environment. These online laboratory courses encourage the collaborative use of virtual reality models, simulations, and animations. This will help students in technology-enabled learning for online laboratory courses and lead to lifelong self-learning.

And finally, Chapter 11 titled "Futuristic outlook of online learning: the post pandemic" concludes the entire collective study. The authors present the reflections on the future of distance learning. This chapter is aimed at discussing the future of technology-enabled learning and how this is going to revolutionize education in future. The chapter discusses the inclusion of technologies like artificial intelligence, big data, virtual reality, augmented reality, mobile apps as well as chatbots in education. The five stages of learning have been very nicely presented by the author with the integration of cutting-edge technologies. The chapter is a step towards giving a roadmap to the new age of learning.

Thus, the chapters in the book cover the different aspects of learning during the pandemic. Both the pedagogical and application perspectives of learning are presented with specific case studies from different parts of the world. The models presented in the book offer implementation opportunities not only at the time of crisis but also in the regular classroom practices. The interdisciplinary approach of the book makes it useful across different domains in the academia and offers useful insights to both teachers and students. The concepts and applications presented in the book make it a useful resource to the practitioners as well as policymakers for strategic planning of educational resources. We sincerely hope that the book will be liked by everyone interested in technology-mediated learning as well as developing applications for the benefit of human beings.

Jitendra Singh and Vikas Kumar

Acknowledgements

A novel piece of work cannot be created without the support of good people. Efforts and support by all individuals and groups for the wonderful contribution to this book are deeply acknowledged. We are thankful to Prof. Tankeshwar Kumar (Vice Chancellor, Central University of Haryana) and Prof. Sushma Yadav (Pro Vice Chancellor, Central University of Haryana) for their constant encouragement and support to work on this project. Special thanks to Prof. Sunil Kumar (Registrar, Central University of Haryana) for his overwhelming support and guidance.

The support from the Routledge team is also appreciated. The editorial and administrative staff guided us at every stage to compile this volume. We owe an enormous debt of gratitude to all the reviewers who offered detailed and constructive reviews for improving the chapters and helped in improving the quality of this project. We are sincerely thankful to all the authors for their original contributions and working as per the tight deadlines.

Thanks are also due to our colleagues: Prof. Sidney Filho (University of Fortaleza), Prof. Jakob Svensson (Malmö University), Prof. Raj K. Kovid and Dr Rachna Bansal (Sharda University), Dr Christine Schrage (University of Northern Iowa), Prof. Sri Aliami and Dr Gesty (Nusantara PGRI University), Dr Gaurav Gupta (Amity University), Dr Pawan Gupta (Chaudhary Bansi Lal University), and Dr Manju Lata (Chandigarh University), Dr G.K. Sethi (MLN College), Dr Pooja Nanda (Sushant University), Dr Surender Kumar (Jaipuria Institute of Management), Dr Anand Rai (G L Bajaj Institute of Management & Research), and other peers from academia, who have supported this project in different ways.

Finally, we would like to thank our parents, family members, and friends for their constant support and motivation to complete this project in a timely manner.

Jitendra Singh and Vikas Kumar

1 Online education during the pandemic

Teachers' experiments with pedagogy

Archana Choudhary and R. Bala Subramanian

Introduction

The Covid-19 pandemic has wreaked havoc in everyone's life (Kumar and Malhotra, 2021). Education is not an exception. It is also seeing significant upheaval as a result of the closure of educational institutions. Social isolation and lockdown are two of the most often used strategies for controlling the virus's transmission (Kumar and Gupta, 2021). All this has affected the education sector as well and resulted in students missing their physical classes, lesser opportunities to work with peers in groups leading to a reduction in team skills and interpersonal skills. Due to this, they are missing the opportunity of co-learning and co-creating, which were quite normal before the advent of Covid-19 (Kovid and Kumar, 2022). Parents are also having difficulty motivating their children to remain attentive to online classes and maintain the pace of learning. Instructors are also trying their level best to adopt new methods of pedagogy, tools, and techniques to make the teaching–learning process effective and engaging. For this, they are using virtual space and artificial intelligence to sustain the interest of students and help develop the competencies and skills of students (Bhardwaj and Kumar, 2023).

Over 34,337,594 children in India have been affected by Covid-19 and are presently receiving education remotely via digital platforms (this number includes only learners enrolled in tertiary education in Indian universities, as of May 3, 2020). To assist schools and colleges in overcoming the Covid and post-Covid crises, UNESCO has also begun working with education ministries across nations to support students' continuous learning through a variety of channels and in a variety of ways, including technical assistance, webinars, tool selection, and the creation of national learning platforms. Even educational institutions have begun to provide faculty development programmes to help instructors improve their online knowledge by providing hands-on experience with various software and apps and preparing them for the new normal world. Individual teachers also started experimenting with their tools and pedagogy to reach the maximum number of students. The purpose of this study was to examine how the teachers designed innovative teaching methods to overcome the lockdown constraints in reaching

DOI: 10.4324/9781003491712-1

the students during the first wave of Covid-19 during 2020 in India. To the best of our knowledge, there have been no studies to examine the teachers' creative pedagogy during the pandemic, particularly in a developing country like India. The study warrants importance of attention as this may unravel the hidden talent and motivation exhibited by the schools and teachers to resolve students' problems during the pandemic time. Moreover, the study has implications for practitioners and academicians. Documenting such case studies may help policymakers, educationists, and philanthropists to identify the lacunae in the system and provide the best possible solutions for the same. The concerned stakeholders can even adopt some best methodology from amongst the discussed cases. For academicians, it provides scope for applying or formulating the theories that explain the exhibited behaviours. This chapter discusses such case studies and suggests how, if replicated by others, they can be useful and effective for others as well.

Methodology

The researchers have used secondary data resources for the study. They relied on the published reports of reputed journals, magazines, and newspapers of national and international repute. There were a number of reports about school teachers' pedagogy for teaching children. However, the inclusion criteria of these cases are as follows:

a The pedagogy adopted by the teachers should be innovative, less costly, and unconventional;
b The teachers should have been teaching in primary or higher secondary schools of India;
c The published source should be an authenticated one.

After shortlisting all the cases, the six most interesting and relevant ones which have more scope for learning were selected.

Objective

This study intended to examine teachers' innovative pedagogy to reach out to students during the lockdown period that happened in the first wave of Covid-19 (March 2020 to November 2020) in India through secondary sources. Through this, we were also interested to find the relevant theories that explained the exhibited behaviours.

Case 1: Hand in Hand India

"In a time when all schools were shut, we took the schools to the children!" This statement was given by an insider at Hand in Hand India's Satellite Learning Center for the Child Labor Elimination Program (CLEP).

As academic centres were closed owing to repeated lockdowns imposed by the federal and state governments to limit the spread of the Covid-19 virus, everyone began to turn to e-learning platforms. However, as time went on, the harsh truth became apparent, and schools and teachers discovered that not all pupils had access to an electronic device and an internet connection to participate in digital platforms programmes. According to the World Economic Forum, the pandemic lockdowns affected up to 350 million schoolchildren, and many children were unable to attend online classrooms owing to a lack of technological equipment at home. In rural India, just 47% of families have access to electricity for more than 12 hours each day while 36% of schools are without power (www.unicef.org). Because their parents' employment was lost, the children were forced to work in factories and fields to support themselves and their parents. As a result, the progress made in reducing child labour was undone, and India's next generation's fate was in jeopardy.

Detached: rural India

Hand in Hand India saw this gap and worked towards ensuring that the children at their Residential Special Training Centers (RSTCs), which are specifically designed for vulnerable children, were able to keep up with their classes and reading materials. The goal of this expedition was to stop child labour and prevent it from reoccurring. When the Central Government imposed the lockdown, the children staying at the RSTCs were sent home with their parents. Volunteers from the Child Labor Elimination Program (CLEP) and instructors from Hand in Hand India's RSTC administered questionnaires to the children to assess their learning capacities. Since the children were not enrolled in regular sessions at the centre, the surveys were conducted in their communities. They gave the assessment questionnaires to the children and chatted with the parents to learn more about their condition. To ensure everyone's safety, various Covid-19 protocols such as social distancing measures were implemented.

The results of the study revealed that these children's learning levels had returned to where they were before the lockdowns when they first started learning at the RSTCs. They also learnt that the migrants had resumed the practice of taking their children to the farm to receive additional assistance and earn money to augment their income. The parents said that leaving the children alone at home was dangerous, which is why they took them to work.

The solution: taking the school to the children

Considering these factors, the CLEP team decided to build remote Satellite Teaching Centers (STC) for children who were unable to attend online sessions. This allowed the youngsters to resume learning that had been halted owing to the pandemic. The Covid-19 dropouts, that is students who were unable to attend lessons due to a lack of schooling, internet, or electricity, began receiving instruction at the same centres that first provided classes for RSTC students. These institutions also served all other community dropouts, particularly those who were unable to complete their education owing to a variety of personal, social, and cultural factors (https://hihindia.org).

Every day, students were given two hours of instruction and provided teaching and learning materials. Additionally, teachers and volunteers were given training to ensure their proficiency and expertise in their instructional methodologies. Courses were offered in batches throughout the outbreak to ensure that every kid had access to education and safety. Before establishing facilities in and around certain areas, the CLEP team mapped the whereabouts of the youngsters. Some classes were held in government buildings and schools while others were held on open land or beneath the shade of trees. Because there was no public transportation owing to the lockdowns, teachers and volunteers drove themselves to these places. Some went as far as 50 kilometres each way to teach and assist these children. Throughout these, all of the Covid-19 protocols were followed. Before entering the STC for the day, all of the children were given masks and sanitizers and were instructed to wash their hands and keep social distance to ensure the safety of the child and teachers. As a consequence, CLEP team managers from all districts stated that children were eager to participate in classes and that parents encouraged and supported instructors in enrolling additional children and aiding additional adults. At that time, the STCs operated in two states: Tamil Nadu and Madhya Pradesh. There are 114 operational centres in all, with 1,555 youngsters taking instruction in batches every day. The CLEP team also supplied food to households with the assistance of donors to ensure that families and children were not only nourished but they also obtained the necessary nutrients. This effort also helped to ensure that families had enough groceries and food and that they need not put their children to work for extra money. The grocery kit included 5 kg of rice or wheat, as well as pulses, spices, salt, and other items. The CLEP team provided grocery kits to 137 RSTC kids in total (https://hihindia.org).

Fun incorporated into learning

The students at STCs also participated in extracurricular activities to keep their brains stimulated and focus on things other than academics. Students were able to master new abilities and art forms as a result of these activities. To demonstrate their abilities, the children competed in a variety of competitions and tournaments. Extracurricular activities aided in the complete development of students, particularly when they left the classroom and entered the real world. Sports equipment and tools for extracurricular activities were provided to the children. The CLEP team delivered sporting equipment to 13 STCs, benefitting 240 youngsters. These items were also obtained from contributors.

In between classroom sessions, the children were given breaks where they could play a game or indulge in any activity that would help them learn and develop new abilities. This also helped them improve their attendance and attention span. In the districts of Chengalpattu and Tirupur, children were taught how to make greeting cards. They created lovely cards to send to the donors as festival greetings. Apart from this, several new activities were launched in the STCs for the benefit, enjoyment, and learning of children, such as yoga sessions, book festivals, online quiz competitions, puppet plays, pottery classes, and food festivals. Training was also conducted on how to use computers and communicate while writing emails. Students were taught alphabets, poems, and even storytelling using craftworks and cut-outs. Teachers in Kanchipuram and Thiruvallur districts used craft paper to build palm leaf (*Olaichuvadi*) manuscripts of "Thirukural". Additionally, the CLEP team added QR codes on the back of instructional items for students to scan and gain access to additional reading materials and activities as needed. Students were also given access to 3D animal and creature animations (https://hihindia.org).

Case 2: innovative teaching in government middle school in Gumla

Following the implementation of the statewide lockdown in March 2020, Navin Chandra Jha, Principal-in-Charge of Government Middle School in Gumla's Raidih block, made worksheets with sets of questions for numerous courses and personally delivered them to students at their houses. The workbooks were created with the help of a local NGO (Gupta, 2021).

"I was able to obtain the arithmetic, English, and Hindi worksheets and send them to the homes of over 150 students", Jha said. The youngsters turned in their worksheets, which contained home assignments, after a week. This process is still ongoing, and it continues to pique their attention. It also assisted them in settling their uncertainties. Jha, who teaches maths and English, has also launched the "Learn By Trick" YouTube channel. "I've been aiming to teach kids problem-solving skills through my YouTube channel. The channel has been subscribed by over 28,000 students", he said (Gupta, 2021).

Jha sought the help of ex-students from each village's schools to help people who don't have cell phones with the education department's online curriculum, known as "Digi Sath". "When their class timings were fixed, past students who lived in the same village as the current students used to share their phones for a couple of hours to help the kids learn", he said, adding that the students were also taught Covid safety protocols such as hand washing and mask use during the teaching.

"We also formed hand-wash warriors by enlisting the help of a few students who used to visit the homes of their colleagues to raise awareness among other students and their families in each village", he said, adding that their school had established a soap bank by asking all students to donate one soap on their birthdays (Gupta, 2021).

"Several activities started by Mr. Jha helped the kids stay engaged in a positive way during the lockdown while the school was closed for a long time", said Balram Nayak, the school's management committee's chairman.

"Our education proceeded even during lockdown due to Navin Sir", stated Vishal Chandra, a Class VIII student. "We profited from the worksheets because they presented us with practice exam questions, and his YouTube channel assisted us in resolving our issues. He also helped us to remember our birthdays".

Sanjay Oraon, a representative of an NGO that interacts with UNICEF, remarked, "This school has acquired a 5-star badge under the Mukhya Mantri Swacch Vidhyalaya Puraskar. It's a good school with all the characteristics of being clean and sanitary". Gumla extra district programme officer Piyush Kumar commended Jha's efforts as well. "The school has done well in terms of teaching and student accomplishment under his leadership".

Navin Chandra Jha was honoured by the All India Primary Teacher Federation (AIPTF) for his exceptional teaching abilities during the Covid-19 pandemic lockdown.

Government schools of Haryana, Himachal Pradesh, and Rajasthan also innovated and engaged stakeholders to tackle educational challenges. While some schools were well-equipped with digital learning tools and infrastructure, others had to devise novel ways to reach kids at home. They also had to support teachers and the students' parents. The Covid-19 pandemic accelerated online education in India, and the state governments were empowered to adapt to technology-enabled solutions quickly. This was the only way through which they could provide normalcy to students. They also wanted to promote physical and mental well-being amongst these children.

Case 3: tech solutions in government schools of Haryana and Rajasthan

In Himachal Pradesh, a recent educational system transition resulted in the creation of a WhatsApp-based home study plan called "Har Ghar Pathshala". Before the pandemic, more than 70% of students were participating in the plan. The instructors used the WhatsApp solution to meet additional educational demands. Additionally, they spoke with parents through WhatsApp and organized an online parents' teacher meeting attended by over 700,000 parents (Bansal, 2020). The government also established "Har Ghar Pathshala 2.0" in May to address these issues and inject the programme with fresh vitality. The primary goals of this initiative were to promote student engagement with various learning content and to facilitate students without cell phones to access learning resources. To achieve the first objective, which was how to increase student engagement, three new components were added to HGP: daily online live classes (for conceptual teaching and doubt resolution); weekly telephonic connections between teachers and students (for a personal check-in with each student); and a fortnightly "break" from conventional academics in the form of "Pratibha Utsav", during which students were encouraged to engage in activity-based learning. To accomplish the first objective, namely increasing student engagement, three new components were added to HGP: daily online live classes (for conceptual teaching and doubt resolution); weekly telephonic connections between teachers and students (for a personal check-in with each student); and a fortnightly "break" from conventional academics in the form of "Pratibha Utsav", during which students were encouraged to engage in activity-based learning like poetry recitation, storytelling, newspaper reading, and singing. To increase access to educational materials, the state government launched the "Digital Saathi – Bachon ka Sahara, Phone Humara" phone donation initiative. To assist students who did not have access to cellphones or online classrooms, the state was also printing and distributing workbooks containing chapter-linked practice questions. All HGP projects were rigorously recorded and reviewed to guarantee accountability (www.samagragovernance.in). As a result of these measures, student engagement with online learning increased. According to the HGP 2.0 monitoring form, a maximum of 45% of teachers reported taking at least one live class each day, and 50% reported connecting with at least one student by phone. Additionally, student engagement in WhatsApp quizzes returned to 2020 levels, hitting 69% (www.samagragovernance.in). However, the state still faces obstacles in its quest to ensure that no pupil is left behind. While students with smartphones were benefitting from HGP 2.0, around 20% of pupils in the state remain entirely disconnected from learning owing to a lack of devices. As schools reopened, the state intends to build on the progress made last year while assuring children's safe return to classrooms. One way to do this would be to gradually make the transition from Har Ghar Pathshala (at-home internet study) to a Blended Learning Model (in-classroom learning complemented with at-home online learning). By adopting a blended learning model, students will benefit from both in-classroom and online learning for conceptual clarity and practice. A gradual shift from Har Ghar Pathshala to a Blended Learning Model would be one approach to accomplish this (in-classroom learning complemented with at-home online learning). A change to a Blended Learning Model would mean that the student would benefit from both in-classroom and online learning for conceptual clarity and practice. Blended learning facilitated by technology would also include tailored remedial instruction and the ability to track granular information about a student's learning experience (www.samagragovernance.in).

In Rajasthan, shortly following the lockdown, the school administration launched the government's DIKSHA platform – an online instructional site for instructors. Over 1.2 million instructors accessed approximately 15 training courses on pertinent themes and how to provide remote help to pupils. Due to the state government's investment in this platform before the pandemic outbreak, it was easy to provide teacher assistance as soon as Covid-19 struck India (www.vikaspedia.in).

Private sector partnerships in remote learning

ConveGenius and Avanti, the EdTech applications also provided their support for remote learning for students across the country. ConveGenius helped all students, parents, and teachers through a WhatsApp-based application having features such as weekly quizzes. The software collected robust information on student and teacher engagement, enabling schools to provide engaging and interesting content throughout the pandemic. By the end of March 2021, ConveGenius's system was able to reach over five million users and enabled the exchange of over two million communications between instructors, students, and parents.

Avanti also contributed by opening its senior-level maths and scientific content libraries for government use. Saksham, a programme in Haryana, also used this content to provide asynchronous learning to over 250,000 pupils in Class 9 through Class 12. Avanti also made its live session films available for free to all government school students bringing the total to over two million by March 2021.

A lasting impact on the education system in India

The pandemic brought attention to the importance of building resilient educational systems and fostering educational innovation. It also gave rise to new challenges, such as learning loss, mental health implications, and financial difficulties. These concerns should be addressed in current and future educational models, which should allow for flexibility in learning in person, at any place, or in a hybrid format. The outbreak, on the other side, offered hope for the future, and the following changes occurred:

- Both teachers and students had a greater understanding of technology.
- Parents were greatly involved in the education of their children and had several one-on-one interactions with teachers.
- For at-home learning, schools and organizations created wonderful tools and support models.
- Effective tools and support models for at-home learning were developed by schools and organizations.

Case 4: innovative learning methods used by educators

Numerous innovative teaching approaches gained popularity, and educators and administrators addressed them. It's intriguing to consider how many of these things existed for a long period (but had received little attention) and were now being acknowledged as critical in today's environment. Academics have time and again said that online education and virtual classrooms powered by technology and artificial intelligence are not novel notions.

Teachers took online classes, listened to podcasts, watched Ted lectures, and browsed the internet all the time, but they didn't anticipate that Covid-19 would mandate teaching only in online mode. The use of digital technology to transform the classroom environment was important, but it was also very challenging. Educators used online platforms like Zoom meetings, Google Classrooms, Cloud Meeting, Udemy, Coursera, and so on.

These educational platforms offered a variety of tools in addition to audio-visual, such as the ability to produce videos, create Excel sheets, PDFs, PowerPoint presentations, whiteboard features to enhance teaching and learning, multiple-choice quizzes with immediate feedback, assignments, exams, and grading, and so on.

Students prefer hands-on experience learning and were attracted to items that presented them with new difficulties. Several gaming companies also started encashing these opportunities and designed simulations that could eventually replace classrooms.

Young people, students, and children were increasingly drawn to artificial intelligence-based games, which provided a plethora of new and exciting experiences. This also helped in enhancing competencies such as risk-taking readiness, critical thinking, decision-making in critical situations, persistence, and the development of intrapreneurial attitudes. Educators were now using this information to create reading materials and virtual classes that provided students with a blend of these experiences, such as simulation exercises based on various stages, situational aspects, and decision-based games/quizzes that helped them earn points towards completing each stage and motivated them to pursue and learn more. This entire story depicted how learning and teaching were both complex and multifaceted (https://eduvoice.in).

Case 5: innovation using ICT: how an education operation in Bihar inspired online application and admission system

Integration of technology into large-scale educational systems is problematic. Incremental innovations, on the other hand, are more likely to succeed due to their non-disruptive nature, in which technology is used to replace routine tasks.

One such smaller-scale innovation was spearheaded by the Directorate of Research and Training (DR&T) of the Department of Education of the Government of Bihar (India), with the purpose of streamlining the application and admission processes for teacher education institutes throughout the state.

Sixty-six teacher education institutes in Bihar offered pre-service teacher training programmes for elementary schools. These institutions get over 300,000 applications each year from young people interested in teaching, and the number continues to grow. These applications were formerly submitted on paper, which presented a variety of administrative challenges (https://blogs.worldbank.org/education).

After receiving applications by mail, administrators would need to enlist the cooperation of all teaching and non-teaching employees to convert the data from application forms to physical registers, distracting teachers and principals from their main academic responsibilities. In the past, manually copying data and computing applicants' scores and merit lists were prone to mistakes, resulting in complaints. Frequently, applications were lost in transit or arrived after the deadline was over. There were also complaints related to corruption, which the administrators were unable to resolve due to lack of resources (https://blogs.worldbank.org/education).

The DR&T responded by implementing a series of reforms over a number of years. At first, data entry operators were recruited at the institution level to feed data from paper applications into a computer. This was done using spreadsheets, which doubled as a register, and a calculator, and they improved efficiency by making computations simpler. Furthermore, the data could be organized, searched, and immediately corrected, allowing for the quick and easy publication of a list of selected applications. The administration decided to take this technique a step further after witnessing some success with it (https://blogs.worldbank.org/education).

Inspired by the World Bank-funded Enhancing Teacher Effectiveness in Bihar Project, teacher education institutes cooperated with local website developers to establish simple websites that enabled candidates to apply and pay application fees online. "We had no trouble submitting online applications because we were used to filling out online forms for our school matriculation examinations". "We also didn't have to be concerned about the application forms arriving late due to postal delays", said a student at a teacher education college. In addition, due to general cost savings at the schools following the introduction of technology, the application fee for students was decreased to one-fifth (https://blogs.worldbank.org/education).

Furthermore, as a result of overall cost reductions at schools as a result of the introduction of technology, the application fee for pupils was reduced by one-fifth. Having a clear application deadline imposed by the online system makes it easier for schools to keep track of the academic year. The online applications were shown to applicants for editing before final submission. Individual applicants, rather than data input employees, improved accuracy and openness by collecting and correcting data. By decreasing the effect of local patronage networks, automatic release of merit lists aided in the development of confidence in the admissions process. The government was able to cooperate with commercial banks to confirm payment information across the state as a result of online fee payments (https://blogs.worldbank.org/education).

This shift can teach us two essential things. To begin, bringing ICT into education demands technology that is highly contextualized. The success rate of "imported" solutions is lower. Understanding the problem from the end-user's perspective is critical, as is establishing concepts and reimagined procedures that can be enabled or expanded/scaled using technology, and ensuring that end-users are involved in the process. Local providers designed the institutional websites in Bihar working directly with users, that is principals, teachers, and applicants, to offer the best user experience feasible in the current situation. The changes were likewise gradual, with data entry operators first "digitizing" their responsibilities before redesigning them online. "The finest element of individual teacher education institutions (TEI) spearheading this process was that there was opportunity to make mistakes and learn from them", said the principal of one teacher education institution. "As issues developed, we were able to work as a team and rectify the problems related to development of website" (https://blogs.worldbank.org/education).

Second, large-scale reforms required all parties to coordinate for reforms to achieve and maintain momentum. By putting users (institution heads) in the driver's seat, the Department of Research and Technology (DR&T) in Bihar was able to assist institutions in recognizing the problem and developing local solutions.

This project demonstrates how a series of small, incremental improvements may free up administrators' time to focus on improving the quality of education provided by their organizations. Such projects will become increasingly significant as we move away from Covid-19 and towards more ICT use in school systems. This change, together with the leadership that facilitated it, can serve as a model for large-scale ICT advancements in education in other regions of the world (https://blogs.worldbank.org/education).

Case 6: teachers at BMC schools developed creative ways to keep students engaged

Teachers at Brihanmumbai Municipal Corporation Schools (BMC schools) adopted innovative ways to engage students in academic activities online while schools were closed due to Covid-19. The activities were being built in such a way that they could be accessed via Android phones, which most parents owned, as well as popular apps. Even though final examinations for Classes I to VIII were cancelled, BMC education officer Mahesh Palkar conducted Zoom meetings to exhort teachers to use technology to ensure frequent communication with students and encourage learning. Some teachers started implementing a slew of ideas since then, and the department increased its use of existing digital platforms. "We reviewed a variety of channels that might be utilised to engage with students", said Madhukar Bhosle, a lecturer and technical assistant. "For a long time, the department was training instructors in the use of technology, and now it had come to their rescue". Many teachers had mastered the art of video production. A repository of such resources was created (Goradia, 2020).

The department started using Telegram, a messaging network where teachers could receive circulars, directives, ideas, and links to various educational resources. A class V teacher of BMC's Pachpaoli School (Powai) made a movie on corona virus with the help of her students which she uploaded on a

YouTube account. She also gave daily homework via WhatsApp, which was shot and shared by classmates. She then marked the responses and offered them comments using photo editing software. She got responses from over 12 pupils in her class, out of a total of 34, to the tests she prepared on Google Forms, and more students were joining every day. Parents emailed her the footage of their children studying and participating in the allocated activities. Another class VI teacher at a corporation school in Govandi started a blog and two YouTube channels for his students. His digital classroom had materials like flashcards on various objects and posts on topics like how to make PowerPoint presentations, how to obtain medical cards, and how to use Digilockers, amongst other things. He also posted a set of question papers on his blog called "Kaun Banega Gyanpati". On the model of Kaun Banega Crorepati, he created multiple-choice questions which had four options. It offered them the correct answers after they submitted all of their responses so that they could see how much they had scored. It also gave them the option of taking the test again. Many teachers recommended studying through connections to instructive E-balbharti classes (Goradia, 2020).

Another teacher at BMC's Bandra east school, Pooja Sankhe, who received the Best Teacher award, made sure that her students kept talking to Alexa, a speaker device of Amazon. She had received accolades for her idea, in which she placed the entertainment device inside a mannequin and connected it to speakers to create a robot. Students used to call her to talk to Alexa, and whenever they did, they were given personalized creative activities to complete. She showed them designs for meditation that could be turned into colourful artwork and music. Since majority of the children lived in slums in tiny shanties, they were accustomed to venturing outside their homes. So they needed to figure out how to keep them occupied at home. Hence, she initiated a Tell Your Mom activity, in which students were encouraged to narrate their day in English.

Nearly 32 kids from BMC's Dahisar East school's class IV took online assessments in all disciplines. Apart from assigning learning-based exercises, general knowledge assessments using Google Forms were also created.

Discussion and conclusion

This study was intended to examine the innovative methods adopted in school education during the pandemic time (2020–2021) in India. The pandemic opened a number of avenues for the future. Teachers and students became highly conversant with technology. Parents got highly involved in the education of their children. They also started frequently interacting with teachers.

There is a saying that "If the mountain doesn't come to Muhammad, Muhammad must go to the mountain", Hand in Hand India, an NGO, did the same thing for the rural children who could not afford and had no access to technology-based education. They created Residential Special Training Centers (RSTC) and took the schools to the children. Navin Chandra Jha, Principal-in-charge of Government Middle School in Raidih, block of Gumla, made worksheets with various sets of questions for different subjects and distributed them to the students at their houses. He also launched his YouTube channel to teach the subjects. The principal approached the ex-students to share theirs for those who didn't have smartphones. Government schools in Himachal Pradesh (HP) started the home study plan "Har Ghar Pathshala" (every home is a school) with the help of WhatsApp. Similarly, teachers of BMC used digital platforms, digital gadgets like Alexa and Telegram, to keep children engaged at home so that they don't venture out of their homes during the lockdown. So there was a common motive amongst all of them. They all intended to do their bit in devising new methods of teaching to help the children learn and remain engaged in their homes.

The behaviour and motivation behind doing this may be attributed to altruism. Altruism can be defined as that behaviour "that is motivated by a desire to benefit someone other than oneself for that person's sake" (Kraut, 2016). The act of the Hand in Hand NGO, other schools, and the principal's efforts fall in the domain of altruism. While the interest of the organization (NGO) may be hidden behind their motive, studies suggest that a behaviour may tend to be altruistic though they are motivated with self-interest. In the same manner, though the school principal's act may be inferred as "in role behavior" (duty to educate his schoolchildren), he went beyond his "role" (going to the house) and took the extra effort of making notes and preparing sheets thus showing the altruistic motive.

The second plausible explanation could be "creativity". The majority of definitions of creative ideas include three elements. First and foremost, such concepts should be unique, innovative, and indigenous. Those concepts should be quality ones. Third, such innovation needs to be related to the core task at hand. As a result, an innovative solution to any issues should be unique, sound, and relevant. However, the term "creative" should be used to describe more than only ideas. A person can also be inventive when exploring in the classroom or with music (Kaufman and Sternberg, 2007).

The problem (lack of access to technology) forces the people and organizations to be creative in reaching out to people. Taking the efforts to make the teachers and worksheets available in the houses of students are some creative ways to make education available to the masses. These ideas meet the abovesaid definition of creativity (new high quality and is also appropriate to the task at hand).

This study is not without limitations. There were several stories about the innovative methods adopted by teachers and institutions. Due to the paucity of time and word limits, we could not include all. Moreover, this study is limited to only India. We have written this based on secondary research. The lack of primary data is another shortcoming of the study.

Our contribution lies in highlighting some case studies of some teachers and educational institutions that addressed the crucial need of people with creative skills during a crisis. We have made a humble attempt to relate with relevant theories. Future studies can expand further in terms of more schools and higher education. Interviewing teachers about the challenges faced in online education and how they overcame the hurdles may throw more light on the creative skills adopted by the teachers.

References

Bansal, A. (2020, May 26). *'Har ghar pathshala': How Himachal govt made online classrooms accessible as schools shut.* News18. Retrieved from https://www.news18.com/news/buzz/har-ghar-pathshala-how-himachal-govt-made-online-classrooms-accessible-as-schools-shut-2637973.html

Bhardwaj, A., and Kumar, V. (2023). Social Media as an Enabler to Combat Misinformation. In *Pandemics in the Age of Social Media: Information and Misinformation in Developing Nations*. Routledge: New York (USA), pp. 1–15.

Goradia, A. (2020, March 26). *In times of COVID-19, teachers find creative ways to engage students online.* The Indian Express. Retrieved from https://indianexpress.com/article/cities/mumbai/coronavirus-india-lockdown-in-times-of-covid-19-teachers-find-creative-ways-to-engage-students-online-6331962/

Gupta, K. A. (2021, January 4). *Gumla teacher gets award for innovative teaching.* Times Of India. Retrieved from https://timesofindia.indiatimes.com/city/ranchi/gumla-teacher-gets-award-for-innovative-teaching/articleshow/80086605.cms

Hand in Hand. (2021, March 19). *Innovation in Education during the COVID-19 Pandemic.* HAND IN HAND INDIA. Retrieved from https://hihindia.org/blog/child-labour-elimination/innovation-in-education-during-the-covid-19-pandemic

Incremental innovation using ICT: How an education operation in Bihar, India inspired the online application and admission systems. (n.d.). World Bank Blogs. Retrieved March 5, 2022, from https://blogs.worldbank.org/education/incremental-innovation-using-ict-how-education-operation-bihar-india-inspired-online

Kaufman, J. C., and Sternberg, R. J. (2007). Creativity. *Change: The Magazine of Higher Learning*, *39*(4), 55–60.

Kovid, R. K., and Kumar, V. (Eds) (2022). *Cases on Emerging Markets Responses to the COVID-19 Pandemic.* USA: IGI – Global Publications (ISBN13: 978-16-6843-504-5, DOI: 10.4018/978-1-6684-3504-5).

Kraut, R. (2016). "Altruism." In *Stanford Encyclopedia of Philosophy.* Stanford: Stanford University.

Kumar, V., and Gupta, G. (Eds) (2021). *Strategic Management During a Pandemic.* USA: Routledge, Taylor & Francis Group (ISBN 9780367646479).

Kumar, V., and Malhotra, G. (Eds) (2021). *Stakeholder Strategies for Reducing the Impact of Global Health Crises.* USA: IGI – Global Publications (ISBN13: 978-17-9987-495-9, DOI: 10.4018/978-1-7998-7495-9).

Remote Learning Initiatives in Rajasthan. (n.d.). Vikaspedia. Retrieved March 5, 2022, from https://vikaspedia.in/education/education-best-practices/remote-learning-initiatives-in-india/remote-learning-initiatives-in-rajasthan

2 Evolution of online learning platforms during and post pandemic

Insights from an emerging market

Raj K. Kovid and Babita Bhati

Introduction

The regular timetable for the school year has been significantly altered during the pandemic (Kumar and Malhotra, 2021). As a consequence of this, the earning potential of a lot of employees in the private sector, which is responsible for providing services to a sizeable percentage of the nation's student population, has been diminished. A comparable influence has been seen at educational institutions that are analogous to one another and which offer students with counselling services. Online education has become the go-to option for students who are unable to attend regular courses due to unforeseen circumstances (Singh and Kumar, 2022). This is done in an attempt to make up for lost educational ground and get back on track. Parents in India have been particularly anxious about making sure that their children do not skip school as a result of the lockdowns. Spending more money on a child's education is seen to be of more priority by Indian parents than spending money on the parents' own healthcare or on any other aspect of their lives. This is done in order to maintain market dominance and keep ahead of the competition (Bhardwaj and Kumar, 2022). Since the epidemic made it clear that this was the way things were going to go in the future, the market for EdTech has risen substantially, and all companies are eager to make investments in it.

The phrase "educational technology" refers to any and all applications of computers, the internet, and associated software and services with the overarching purpose of enhancing students' educational experiences and overall growth as individuals (Sharma and Kumar, 2017). Businesses and organizations, whose primary emphasis is the creation of instructional resources, are referred to as "ed-tech" companies and organizations. It integrates many different kinds of computer-based education, such as online learning, education delivered through mobile devices, and many more (Bhardwaj and Kumar, 2023). It is the systematic approach to using technology in classrooms in a way that helps students learn more effectively. In addition to this, it fosters a multicultural learning environment for students of all ages and from

DOI: 10.4324/9781003491712-2

all over the world (Meraj, 2022). There are many different types of tech-enhanced education, including those that are directed by an instructor, peers, or algorithms. Systems and techniques for algorithm-guided learning have been developed over a prolonged period of time via a progressive process (Reich, 2020).

The focus in education has evolved away from standardized test scores and towards a more holistic approach to student learning that places a greater emphasis on conceptualization and application of previously taught content (Kumar and Sharma, 2017). The aforementioned change in educational philosophy has been somewhat facilitated by the proliferation of EdTech platforms that place a greater focus on the acquisition of practical skills and their effective application. One more significant advantage offered by the educational technology industry is the opportunity for students to participate actively in the educational process from the comfort of their own homes, thanks to various methods of online instruction, rather than being required to travel long distances to do so (Kumar and Bhardwaj, 2020).

A sector in India that is growing at one of the quickest rates is the education sector (Kovid and Kumar, 2022). We can see its development from the illustrious Gurukul, which was based on the chalk-and-talk paradigm, to the contemporary classroom, which is filled with cutting-edge technology and applications. Between the years 2025 and 2030, it is anticipated that the EdTech sector in India would generate revenues between US$4 billion and US$30 billion (Entrackr, 2022). According to the findings of another research, the value of this industry is projected to reach US$10.40 billion by the year 2025 as shown in Table 2.1 (Idea-Briefing, 2022).

The Indian EdTech sector has evolved from traditional classroom settings to completion of some educational degree in fully online model. The corona pandemic provided an extremely favourable market for online learning platforms, like other countries, in India (Kumar and Gupta, 2021). The education technology sector witnessed an unprecedented consolidation through a chain of mergers and acquisitions among the companies during and after pandemic in 2022. This chapter explores how the Indian EdTech industry evolved in terms of growth and consolidation. Based on the analysis of its

Table 2.1 EdTech Market Size

Segment	*2020*	*2025 (Projection)*
K-12	US$1.16 billion	US$4.3 billion
Test preparation	US$0.8 billion	US$3.99 billion
Online certification	US$0.58 billion	US$1.38 billion
Skill development	US$0.26 billion	US$0.73 billion
Total	US$2.8 billion	US$10.4 billion

evolution, the chapter identifies the challenges and future scenario and correspondingly the approaches EdTech companies would need to adopt.

Evolution of Indian EdTech industry

There are evidences that students were being instructed in Indian philosophy, religion, and Vedic mathematics in the ancient Indian schools of Takshashila and Nalanda thousands of years before the birth of Christ. Because of the British empire's colonial authority over India, the conventional Indian educational system was gradually phased out in favour of one that put a greater emphasis on the study of English literature and Western science. Up until the early years of the new millennium, the vast majority of students as well as instructors followed the traditional model of classroom education (Eximius-ventures, 2021). For the greater part of a decade, the EdTech sector has been stuck in a rut due to the broad lack of interest in the products and services it provides. In those days, EdTech companies such as EduComp Solution had no option but to zero in on the business-to-business sector as their primary target audience. The sluggish use of technology in the classroom led to a severe financial challenge for EduComp in 2011. Because of the prevalent assumption among educators and parents that conventional classroom environments are preferable for teaching crucial soft skills like communication, cooperation, and critical thinking, many EdTech businesses went out of business as time went on (Eximius-ventures, 2021).

Driving education – content versus marketing approach

Byju's (www.byjus.com) drove India into the next generation of educational technology and was the first company to bring app-based learning to the international scene. This accomplishment served as an example for a plethora of other enterprises to follow in its footsteps. However, to compete for clients and broaden their bases of subscribers, these firms started offering a greater range of choices. However, at that point in time, nobody was really giving any thought about content. However, they quickly came to the realization that the rigorous examination and evaluation systems implemented by India's central education boards were constraining their creative approaches to classroom instruction and the development of curricula.

They quickly altered their content marketing strategies to separate themselves from their competitors as the demand increased. Byju's started catering to the requirements of Indian students and their families to assist the students in achieving success in entrance examinations that are necessary for enrolment into medical and engineering institutions in addition to other government service examinations. Unacademy was formerly a YouTube channel devoted to preparing students for the Union Public Service Commission (UPSC) examinations. However, the company has extended its offerings to include preparatory classes for medical and engineering colleges. They changed the system in such a way that it is now impossible for the common individual to take classes or read books that might further their education. In addition, with the sole exception of Extramarks, which is geared towards students learning Hindi as their medium of instruction, they ignored those students who did not acquire English as their initial language of instruction and continue to do so (Eximius-ventures, 2021).

EdTech in India in a new avatar

During the lockout, education technology businesses saw a significant increase in the number of people subscribing to their services. The K-12 market had a dramatic increase in subscriptions, going from 45 million in 2016 to 90 million in 2021. Byju's attracted 7.5 million new users while Toppr's premium user base witnessed a 100% rise in growth during the same time period. As a consequence of this, a recent study projected that India's EdTech market will increase to US$10.4 billion by the year 2025 (Idea-Briefing, 2022). EdTech has made its way from the classroom to the boardroom, where it focuses on the creation of material, the teaching of that information, the resolution of doubts, and the transfer of life skills. Additionally, important during this time period was the creation of mechanisms for the delivery of courses based on cohorts (CBCs). It was inevitable that online education would eventually have to catch up to these kind of cooperative, engaging, and social learning experiences at some point in the future. Unacademy is transitioning Graphy into a platform for CBC whilst in the area of online MBA programmes, Stoa School has been making headlines for all the right reasons. The market as a whole has undergone a considerable transformation, and a large amount of money is currently being invested in continuous education. Online learning systems such as Upgrad and Simplilearn provide a major emphasis on enterprise learning, upskilling, and the development of corporate skills. Children of the future generation have access to a broad range of individualized educational opportunities, should they so want. As a direct consequence of this expansion, forward-thinking educational technology like learning management systems (LMSs) and EdTech have found their way into classrooms as well as the administration of schools.

Consolidation in Indian EdTech industry

Consolidation in the EdTech sector in the form of large-scale acquisitions is becoming more common as unicorn companies such as Byju's and Unacademy battle for market supremacy. One such example of this is Byju's acquisition of WhiteHat Jr coding platform. Because of these purchases, Byju's is able to broaden its demographic appeal and increase the number of people it can reach within its audience. In addition to a focus on progressive pedagogical practices such as e-learning and m-learning, the government has taken a number of other initiatives to encourage the growth of the remote education business. It is possible that the corona pandemic is to blame for the recent uptick in the number of mega-deals in the education technology industry.

In this industry, new businesses are aggressively seeking funds, which they put into expanding their operations via mergers and acquisitions as well as strategic investments. Larger companies, like Byju's, are able to get a disproportionately large piece of the mergers and acquisitions activity and, as a result, obtain a disproportionately large amount of the available capital. However, the global scene has been very sluggish on this front, despite the fact that the education technology industry in India has raised a significantly larger amount of money for 2021 than it did in 2020 (Table 2.2). This practice of obtaining capital has been driven, to a significant part, by seed, angel, and Series A agreements for newly established enterprises (Mukul, 2021).

After the pandemic, the education industry, along with a great number of other service-based businesses, was able to capitalize on the digital realm by organizing online fundraising events. Even though the majority of the EdTech explosion that we are witnessing in India is taking place outside of the classroom in the form of private tutoring, there is an opportunity for these start-ups and enterprises to collaborate with governments and education boards to create a curriculum that is more appropriate for the digital age.

We only have to look at the ecommerce boom of 2015 and 2016, which led to the rise of Snapdeal, Paytm Mall, Shopclues, and others besides Flipkart, Myntra, and others, but then only a select few companies survived that boom and stayed relevant in the current e-commerce ecosystem (Kumar and Ayodeji, 2021). The likes of Paytm Mall and Shopclues are a shadow of their former self while Snapdeal has also been consigned to the sidelines in the e-commerce race. Now, investors in the EdTech space contend that a similar fate may await some EdTech players in the Indian market – particularly those that are overburdened with costs or have their hands in various pies

Table 2.2 PC-VC Investment in Education, EdTech Firms

Year	*No. of Deals*	*Amount (US$ Million)*
2021	75	3,772
2020	78	2,224
2019	61	968
2018	57	831
2017	41	191

Source: Mukul (2021), www.indianexpress.com.

with mixed results. As a managing partner of a growth-stage venture capital firm told us, there are lots of operational and financial challenges even with their plans to expand into offline coaching. This pivot will be expensive, and already Unacademy is facing problems on the ground. Competition for talent and space in the offline category is already biting Unacademy hard, particularly, in Kota with Allen Career Institute fighting Unacademy over poaching teachers. In terms of funding over the past couple of years, the EdTech sector has figured among the top five funded sectors – raising US$1.4 billion in 2020, which shot up to US$4.7 billion in 2021, but it has dropped back to US$1.6 billion as of June 18, 2022 (INC42, 2022).

EdTech consolidation: the case of Byju's

The couple Byju Raveendran and Divya Gokulnath established Think and Learn Pvt Ltd in Bangalore in 2011. The company's flagship brand is known as Byju's. Students in high school and college programmes may participate in this online classroom. In addition to that, it offers advice on how to do well in standardized examinations like the Joint Entrance Examination (JEE), National Eligibility Entrance Test (NEET), Common Admission Test (CAT), and so on. After Paytm, Byju's is the start-up company with the second highest valuation in the world. It is a market leader in the EdTech business. Byju's, which is now a decacorn, has more than 115 million subscribers and is estimated to be worth US$22 billion (Byjus, 2022).

Byju's Classes is an online educational resource that helps students of grades 6 through 12 to improve the quality of their education by preparing them for standardized examinations that are necessary for admission to engineering, business management, and medical degree programmes. Students get access to a wide selection of quizzes and tasks, as well as personalized feedback and comprehensive assessments, and they may participate in classes using either a desktop or a tablet computer. In a study of parents who had used the Byju's app, 93% of respondents reported that their children's academic performance had improved as a result of using the programme. There are now 15 million customers registered with Byju's, with 0.9 million paying for an annual membership and an 85% renewal rate for their subscriptions. The company reports that the average amount of time one of its customers spends using one of its applications on a daily basis is 53 minutes (Byju, 2022).

Byju's started its acquisition spree in 2010, when it bought Specadel, a company that developed educational mobile applications that students could use to create their own study materials and then move them to their own personal electronic portable devices. The journey of acquisitions has been shown in Table 2.3 (www.tracxn.com, 2022). In July 2015, the company made the decision to acquire Infinite Student, a website that assists students in grades K-12 in preparing for standardized exams such as the Graduate Record Examination (GRE), graduate management admission test (GMAT), and Scholastic Assessment Test (SAT) by offering online lessons and practice tests. In January 2017, Byju's spent US$7.32 million to acquire Vidhyartha, a firm that assists children in making informed career decisions via the use of hands-on activities (Byjus, 2022). The foundation of its career advising system was built on the pillars of personality examinations, interest questionnaires, and talent assessments. Evaluations are carried out by a team of licensed psychologists, who also give interpretations of the results.

2017 was the year when Byju's made the acquisition from Pearson of both TutorVista and Edurite. The increased worldwide footprint and broader product selection were the intended outcomes of the partnership (Byjus, 2022). Byju's plans to broaden its reach around the globe and engage in smart mergers and acquisitions got a boost from this funding. Every month, TutorVista is visited by millions of individuals from all over the globe, and this is all due to the fact that it is a prominent online tutoring firm that is popular with students in the United States. Edurite offers a broad selection of CDs focused on cognitive learning that may be used for individual study.

Table 2.3 Acquisitions by Byju's

S. No.	*Date*	*Company Acquired by Byju's*	*Valuation of Deal (US$)*
1	May 1, 2010	Specadel	Undisclosed
2	June 1, 2015	Infinite student	Undisclosed
3	January 17, 2017	Vidyartha	7.32 million
4	July 3, 2017	TutorVista	Undisclosed
5	July 3, 2017	Edurite	Undisclosed
6	July 24, 2018	Math Adventures	Undisclosed
7	January 19, 2019	Osmo	120 million
8	August 5, 2020	Whitehat Jr	300 million
9	September 17, 2020	Labinaap	Undisclosed
10	January 12, 2021	Aakash Educational services	1 billion
11	February 18, 2021	Scholr	2.47 million
12	May 29, 2021	Hash learn	Undisclosed
13	July 21, 2021	Epic	500 million
14	July 25, 2021	Great Learning	600 million
15	July 25, 2021	Toppr	150 million
16	August 4, 2021	Whodat	Undisclosed
17	September 7, 2021	Gradeup	Undisclosed
18	September 12, 2021	Tynker	200 million
19	December 8, 2021	Geogebra	100 million
20	March 22, 2022	Hello English	Undisclosed

[1] *Source:* www.tracxn.com (2022).

1 www.tracxn.com (2022). Retrieved from https://tracxn.com/d/acquisitions/acquisitionsby-BYJU'S, viewed on 05.09.22.

Byju's was successful in extending its footprint around the globe thanks to the support of TutorVista and Edurite. Reports indicate that the projected value of the agreements might range anywhere from five million dollars to 30 million dollars.

Through the acquisition of Math Adventures in July of 2018, Byju's expanded its growth efforts. The acquisition was made with the intention of enhancing and broadening the range of possibilities for the subsequent K-3 educational programmes. Math Adventures is a game that makes learning mathematics more interesting by combining traditional forms of play with modern, interactive digital technologies. Young students have the opportunity to profit from the programme's innovative combination of short, captivating videos with an approach that is centred on activities and interactive elements. Byju's made its first acquisition in the United States in January 2019, when it paid US$120 million for educational game developer Osmo. This marked the company's first move into the American market. After the transaction is finalized, Byju's will be able to use the physical-to-digital technology and material that Osmo has developed to better meet the educational requirements of children aged three to eight. Byju's has been emphasizing a mission to provide students with highly individualized educational experiences that submerge them in content that is both captivating and participatory. It is expected that Osmo's use of mixed reality interactions would enable it to attract new users and spark the creation of new applications. When combined with an iPad, the Osmo gaming attachment produces a convincing simulation of the game world for children between the ages of five and 12. The reflecting camera on the iPad, which is included as part of the gaming equipment, scans whatever is in front of it so that the software that is included with the iPad can recognize it and respond correctly (Byjus, 2022).

Byju's, a powerhouse in the Indian e-learning industry, made the acquisition of White Hat Jr., an educational technology company, in July 2020 for the sum of US$300 million. This was done as part of Byju's goal to solidify its position as market leader within the country. All three of these types of coding – sequential coding, structural coding, and algorithmic reasoning – were covered in the class. The cost of a membership to it varied according to both the grade level and the topic area. When it came to instruction in computer programming, WhiteHat Jr was by far the industry leader in the EdTech sector. The fact that there is just one student for every instructor is a selling factor. After the acquisition, Byju's would assist WhiteHat Jr by making significant expenditures and providing the teachers required for the business's anticipated expansion. Byju's now has the opportunity, thanks to this acquisition, to join the highly competitive profession of computer programming in a position of leadership. After that, in September 2020, Byju's made the acquisition of LabInApp. LabInApp was an EdTech company that was sponsored by Unitus Ventures, and it provided licence-based programming that included experiments in mathematics and science for classes 9 through 12 that used 3D simulation. iLab is a virtual 3D laboratory platform that is hosted in the Cloud and is meant for usage in educational settings such as classrooms and other similar environments. Byju's will be able to regain its former prominence among K-12 schools as a result of the many new collaborations it establishes and the flood of new students that it draws as a result of the great services it provides in the form of a virtual laboratory (Byjus, 2022).

Byju's made history in the education technology business by purchasing Aakash Educational Services Ltd. (AESL) for close to one billion dollars at the beginning of January 2021. Aakash is a training centre that was established in the year 1988 in New Delhi. It is a coaching institution that provides training for admission examinations in the fields of medicine and engineering, as well as short-term crash courses. Under the leadership of Byju's group, Aakash maintains its status as an independent organization. The organization that provides test preparation also operates over 200 different tutoring centres around the nation. The market for test preparation in India is already rather competitive, with a number of different businesses trying to establish themselves as market leaders in a variety of subsectors. In addition, Byju's completed the acquisition of a number of educational technology companies in the year 2021. These companies included Scholar, Hash Learn, Epic, Whodat, Gradeup, Tynker, Great Learning, Toppr, GeoGebra, and Hello English (Byjus, 2022).

With the acquisition of Hash Learn in May 2021, Byju's will be better able to maintain its dominant position in the industry where parents often spend significant amounts of money on their children's education. Byju's has acquired the digital reading platform known as Epic for use by youngsters in the United States in a transaction valued at US$500 million. This purchase would help widen Byju's impact in the United States as the company will get access to Epic's huge worldwide user base. Epic's user base is believed to have quadrupled over the course of the previous year and now consists of more than two million instructors and 50 million students. Also, in July 2021, Byju's completed the acquisition of Great Learning, a school located in Singapore, for the sum of US$600 million. To further strengthen its position in the market for higher and professional education, an additional investment of US$400 million will be made. Great Learning will continue to operate independently from the rest of Byju's group and will continue to be headed by the company's original creator. Classes are available in a variety of subjects, including business, software development, cloud computing, cybersecurity, and artificial intelligence, among others. It has collaborated with educational institutions located all over the globe and depends on the expertise of more than 2,800 mentors who are recognized as leaders in their respective disciplines (Byjus, 2022).

The acquisition of Topper by Byju's cost US$150 million. Toppr is an application and software as a service (SaaS) that enables children to better prepare for and perform better on standardized examinations. Byju's position as the industry leader in India's EdTech sector was bolstered significantly as a result of the purchase. Then, in August 2021, Byju's acquired the augmented reality (AR) business Whodat for an undisclosed amount. The augmented reality platform for product visualization is an app that lets users see furniture like couches and chairs in their own homes before they buy them. Whodat's augmented reality technology provides completely immersible experiences since it does not need the use of physical markers to overlay 3D content. The aforementioned technology, which drives applications in mobility and robotics, will be beneficial to the development of Byju's products, which in turn will have an effect on the education that students get (Byjus, 2022).

By acquiring Gradeup in September 2021, Byju's will be able to capitalize on Gradeup's pedagogy and student reach while simultaneously strengthening its position in the rapidly expanding online competitive examination preparation sector. Gradeup is one of the leading online test preparation platforms in India. In the competition to win a portion of the nation's US$180 billion education market, it would offer the firm an advantage over competitors such as Unacademy, Simplilearn, UpGrad, and Amazon Academy, as well as more traditional educational institutions. Byju Raveendran made the following statement on the acquisition of Gradeup: "With Gradeup on board, we will be able to further expand and extend our test-prep products in postgraduate level exams" (ET, 2021).

> It has already shown its usefulness, and we are delighted to be collaborating with such an experienced set of people. Our shared goal is to be able to provide learning experiences that are not only engaging but also specially crafted to meet the needs of each and every person.
>
> (ET, 2021)

With the help of this acquisition, Tynker would be able to make its creative coding platform accessible to an even greater number of individuals, including students, instructors, educational institutions, and summer camps located all over the globe. Tynker is a platform for creative coding that has been used by over 60 million children from 100,000 schools located in 150 different countries. With its engaging, interactive courses that are modelled after games, Tynker is an excellent tool for teaching young people how to code. Byju's made the purchase of the Austria-based company GeoGebra in December 2021 with the intention of further expanding its worldwide online education platform. In excess of 100 million students in over 195 countries and territories utilize GeoGebra, an interactive and collaborative mathematics learning tool that is maintained by GeoGebra. This acquisition is beneficial to Byju's product strategy as a whole, as it moves the firm closer to achieving its goal of making mathematics more engaging. Independent activities for GeoGebra will continue as they have in the past (ET, 2021).

In March 2022, Byju's completed the acquisition of Hello English, a cloud-based language learning start-up that provides customers with the ability to study many languages (both Indian and international). Reading, writing, public speaking, and listening are all skill sets that may be improved via the use of this programme, which includes gamification aspects and interactive courses and exercises. Due to the fact that Byju has never before dabbled in the market for language services, this purchase will represent the company's formal debut into the industry. According to the observations of one industry expert, "Besides India, Byju's also plans to expand Hello English to other countries, particularly the Southeast Asia region" (Varindia, 2021).

Byju's is planning to launch its research and development centre as well as its EdTech services in Doha, Qatar, in 2022 in partnership with the Qatar Investment Authority (QIA), thus expanding its growth story globally. The two organizations have decided to launch a joint venture to give students in the Middle East and North Africa (MENA) with unique educational solutions that are based on extensive academic research. This will help students in those regions (Startup Talky, 2022). Bengaluru, the dominant city in India's EdTech sector, is preparing for the arrival of the next normal after the year 2022. Because of the escalating costs of both online and conventional schooling, many families are finding themselves in a position where they need to consider whether or not their children's education would be best served by a mix of the two approaches now that classes have returned. As a consequence, Byju's confronts a significant challenge. Divya Gokul Nath, one of the cofounders of Byju, said that "there is just no tolerance for complacency" (Raghunathan, 2022).

EdTech industry: post-pandemic scenario

One of the few industries that considerably made profit from the "corona positive" effect is the education technology industry. This traditionally slow growing industry has lately experienced a tremendous development. The present situation is becoming better, and the future seems to be heading towards a lot more positive direction, with potential new chances for early adopters in the business. In addition to the staggering increase in demand for the established leaders of the business, a number of new competitors have emerged, all of whom look to be here to stay.

Lay-offs, cutbacks, and restructuring have become the new buzzwords in the industry replacing words like inflexion point and boom that had become part of the Indian EdTech vocabulary since early 2020. While the pandemic was undoubtedly a massive boost for the sector, now it has come crashing down like a pile of bricks (INC42, 2022). EdTech firms have laid off around 6,000 employees since the beginning of 2022 as depicted in Table 2.4 (Business Today, 2022; INC42, 2022).

With some giants scaling back, the path may open up for newer players and under-the-radar start-ups to grab market share. The primary example here is PhysicsWallah (PW), the newest EdTech unicorn and the only profitable EdTech unicorn, which raised US$100 million while its rivals are struggling. The company claims to be profitable since FY21 and says it acquired over four million app users organically. The EdTech start-ups that will attract

Table 2.4 Lay-Offs in EdTech Industry

Name of EdTech Firm	*No. of Employees*
Byju's	2,500
Lido Learning	1,200
Unacademy	1,150
WhiteHat Jr	1,000
Vedantu	624
Crejo.Fun	170
FrontRow	145
Emeritus	40
Invact Metaversity	20

Source: Business Today (2022); INC42 (2022).

funding are the ones like PhysicsWallah that have a lean acquisition strategy. Early and growth-stage start-ups need to also prove that the pricing is attractive to users, and the model is actually delivering outcomes, if they are looking to fill the gap left behind as Byju's, Unacademy, and others scale back or shake (INC42, 2022).

Post corona pandemic, EdTech and offline businesses throughout the country are reportedly embracing a hybrid strategy consisting of acquisitions and partnerships to develop a business model that is viable over the long run. Both EdTech start-ups and unicorns are turning to the hybrid retail model to figure out how to best serve the future of the EdTech industry in the post-Covid age. This is because the omnichannel strategy is more feasible even going forward (ET, 2022).

EdTech sector: challenges and futuristic outlook

In spite of the high pace at which this sector is rising, its growth in India is being hampered by a number of problems. The burdensome regulations that are imposed by the government in our country slow down the progress that is made in education. Because of the subpar quality of their networks and the internet in rural areas, the decacorn company Byju's has had a difficult time expanding into new markets and gaining customers in such areas. The misconception that conventional forms of education are better is another obstacle that prevents students and their parents from seeing that online education is the way of the future (Kumar and Nanda, 2020). Parents believe that the online system is acceptable for the time being; but, after the epidemic has passed and the lockdowns have been removed, they want their children to return to school since they believe that this is where they will get the best education. It is true that some educational apps have surpassed the quality of traditional schooling, but many parents are still hesitant to put their children's education in the hands of a digital resource.

As venture capitalists vie with one another for investment possibilities, the EdTech 5.0 era in India's history is sure to be an eventful and fascinating period. If India wishes to keep its position as the number two EdTech hub in the world and keep up with the United States, it will need to make significant investments in emerging technologies and hybrid learning environments. Parents who are forward-thinking are starting to examine how their children may benefit from an online education in addition to traditional classroom settings, even if there will always be a place for traditional classroom settings. The most exciting developments in online education technology will include virtual reality (VR)-based learning platforms. These platforms will allow learning apps to provide a full and immersive experience for students of all ages. Future consumer experiences will be driven by uses of virtual reality (VR) for corporate training and simulation, artificial intelligence (AI), and VR-based hybrid teaching (Eximius-ventures, 2021). This does not mean that educational technology programmes do not come with their share of difficulties and inconveniences. The expansion of EdTech is still being overshadowed by insufficient infrastructure, poor accessibility, and our existing digital divide. Recent events have brought to light concerns over deceptive ads and unethical business practices. In response, an EdTech consortium has been trying to eradicate these problems through the use of self-regulation.

More than 4,450 EdTech enterprises in India have a beneficial influence on the country's education system, which serves more than 300 million children who are engaged in formal education programmes. Forty million of them are individuals who were on track to attend college but had their education side-tracked by Covid-19 (Patnaik, 2022). This resulted in a growth in the area of EdTech, which is the use of ICT to the process of facilitating learning in a manner that is open to everyone, engaging for students, and adapted to the specific requirements of each student. In the long run, India's EdTech industry could be able to assist reduce the gap in academic accomplishment that exists between the country's affluent and its poor by making improved educational options available to all Indians. There is a big pool of competent instructors readily available, as well as an abundance of motivated entrepreneurs, all of whom have contributed to India's EdTech boom. Novel products and approaches have also been developed. Students from all over the world are preferring Indian EdTech firms not just due to the inexpensive tuition prices that these companies provide but also due to the excellent quality of the training that these companies deliver.

The Indian education technology sector is facing a more competitive environment as a direct result of the recently implemented National Education Policy 2020. Because it places such a focus on broadening students' access to educational opportunities, the "Education for all" programme that the Indian government is implementing has great potential for the development of educational technology in the years to come. India has already established itself as the global leader in a variety of start-up indicators, including investment (with Byju's firm being the most valued unicorn) and total number of enterprises.

India's success in this arena has led to the creation of a unicorn. This might be bolstered even further if Indian entrepreneurs offered innovative solutions on student-interesting issues that could be included into the NCERT curriculum. To satisfy the expanding demand for this post-corona hybrid learning paradigm, businesses will want partners who are focused on providing services. The key to success is consolidation, which may be accomplished via mergers and acquisitions. Because of this, businesses that concentrate on certain niches will have to make scalability a top priority if they want to be successful.

Despite the fact that initial public offerings (IPOs) and mergers and acquisitions (M&As) are two of the most prevalent exit strategies for start-ups, comparatively few EdTech companies have chosen to go public. This is particularly true with regard to the Indian market. As a direct consequence of this, the EdTech industry is now engaged in a frantic effort to improve and strengthen its standing in the market.

The creation of innovative educational methods is one of the most pressing problems that the organizations that are less well-known have not yet been able to tackle. The majority of players have relied on live learning via the use of an app or a hybrid technique (physical) up to this point, and it is very unlikely that this will change in the near future. When it comes to selling their wares to students, EdTech companies need to make some adjustments to their marketing strategies, as well as their customer acquisition processes, pricing models, and finance models. These are the three areas in which change is most likely to take place, and it is possible that it may cause a commotion in the EdTech business (INC42, 2022).

Upskilling

Because of the unavoidable fundamental shifts that are going to take place in the corporate world over the course of the next several years, specialized training is going to be absolutely necessary (Kumar and Rewari, 2022). During such a time period, there would be an increase in the demand for educational technology. This is due to the fact that both children and adults are becoming more reliant on EdTech start-ups to supply them with the resources they require to attend formal classes and acquire new skills. These programmes are also expanding their linguistic support to provide assistance for the several languages spoken in the United States. Therefore, students whose native language is not English would be able to depend on and make greater use of these tools for expanding their knowledge of new topics and getting ready for tests. According to a study titled "Augmented and Virtual Reality in Education", the market for augmented reality in education is projected to reach US$5.3 billion in 2023, while the market for virtual reality head-mounted displays is estimated to come in at a distant second place with US$640 million (INC42, 2022). As long as this industry is in the midst of the corona-led boom, we can expect to see a great deal of further funding, investment, as well as mergers and acquisitions.

Regulatory framework

What is truly required in India at this time is prompt action on the part of the government in addition to a set of rules that will allow the sector to focus on providing excellent education that is in accordance with government education goals and classroom learning (Singh and Kumar, 2021). In the event that we do not make preparations to promote traditional methods of education, we run the risk of being drawn into a competition that is focused only on material gain. EdTech companies have, for the most part, shifted away from the model of the standard-issue tutorial centre. Several state governments, including those of Manipur and UP, as well as others, have established laws and programmes with the goal of creating an environment that is conducive to the establishment of EdTech enterprises in a manner that is both ethical and secure. They have established and maintained robust regulatory frameworks. Nevertheless, they should have more of a bite to them and incorporate more components of the EdTech industry that are forward-thinking and innovative.

Hybrid business model

The EdTech industry has a huge growth potential to create value for its stakeholders. In line with other industries such as fintech, it witnessed a transformation post pandemic. The sector is further bound to grow fast by 11.6 billion by 2026 (Indianexpress, 2022). Thus, we observe that EdTech revolution is bound to stay the course permanently, and the future outlook for the industry appears to be strong. With reaching to large chunk of students seeking tuitions, coaching and training in online, offline, and hybrid mode in tier I cities, EdTech firms are now looking to expand to tier II and tier III cities which offer an attractive opportunity. However, the medium of instruction may pose a challenge for their sailing these markets smoothly (Sharma and Kumar, 2017). So these firms would need to offer their education programmes – online or hybrid mode – in Indian languages along with the English language. This would definitely create cost pressure and require investment in technology and other support systems.

The momentum and pace of using technology for imparting education after the pandemic are fraught with a lot of challenges and issues related to the substantiality of the EdTech business models. Educators need to keep in mind, while engaging in online education, mental health (Martin, 2020). The stakeholders of education system need to be on constant vigil and keep adapting to the unabatedly evolving learning system in view of uncertainties – natural and man-made as Todorova and Bjorn-Andersen (2011) observed that "the key lesson for others may be to embrace e-learning technology before disaster strikes". So, in panicky situations, EdTech companies would need to tread cautiously to further sustain their growth while imparting education online or in hybrid mode as the interest of so many stakeholders, especially students, are at stake.

Conclusion

The Covid-19 epidemic has caused a lockdown in a lot of nations all over the world, which has led to a shift in the education patterns over the last few years. Because of this, the EdTech business has witnessed an immense surge over the past few years. Byju's, the market leader, became the focal point of a series of mergers and acquisitions that were precipitated by the rapid expansion of the industry. Byju's has reacted to the comparable trend to obtain control and have a market edge to extend its presence in a variety of different elements of the EdTech business. Byju's has gained a competitive edge in the market as a result of its purchase of other businesses that compete with it. This allows Byju's to capitalize on the skills that are unique to their specialty. EdTech firms, on the other hand, are going to have to overcome a lot of obstacles to adapt to the new normal after the pandemic. They would need to proceed with caution to strike a balance between the conflicting goals of scalability and profitability.

References

Bhardwaj, A., and Kumar, V. (2022). Web and Social Media Approach to Marketing of Engineering Courses in India. *International Journal of Business Innovation and Research (IJBIR), 27*(4), 541–555.

Bhardwaj, A., and Kumar, V. (2023). Social Media as an Enabler to Combat Misinformation. In *Pandemics in the Age of Social Media: Information and Misinformation in Developing Nations*. Routledge: New York (USA), pp. 1–15.

Business Today (2022, Aug 8). Edtech Decacorn BYJU'S Multiple Challenges. Retrieved from https://www.businesstoday.in/magazine/corporate/story/edtech-decacorn-byjus-multiple-challenges-343469-2022-08-02, viewed on 08.09.22.

Byjus (2022). Retrieved from https://byjus.com/about-us/; https://byjus.com/companies-acquired-by-byjus/, viewed on 31.08.22.

Entrackr (2022). The rise and fall of edtech startups in 2022: Entrackr report. Retrieved from https://entrackr.com/2022/08/the-rise-and-fall-of-edtech-startups-in-2022-entrackr-report/, viewed on 05.09.22.

ET (2021). Byju's acquires online exam preparation platform Gradeup. Retrieved from https://economictimes.indiatimes.com/tech/startups/byjus-acquires-online-exam-preparation-platform-gradeup/articleshow/86016376.cms?from=mdr

ET (2022). Edtech cos eye hybrid route, mergers for business sustainability. Retrieved from https://economictimes.indiatimes.com/markets/stocks/news/edtech-cos-eye-hybrid-route-mergers-for-business sustainability/articleshow/93417284.cms?utm

Eximius-ventures (2021). Evolution of Edtech in India. Retrieved from https://medium.com/eximius-ventures/evolution-of-edtech-in-india-6cfc86bec5ca, 29.08.22

Idea-Briefing (2022). Retrieved from https://www.india-briefing.com/news/profiling-indian-edtech-industry-us-10-billion-dollar-opportunity-24013.html/, viewed on 05.09.22.

INC42 (2022). How Indian Edtech Startups Can Bounce Back After Slowdown Bump. Retrieved from https://inc42.com/features/how-indian-edtech-startups-can-bounce-back-after-slowdown-bump/, viewed on 01.09.22.

Indianexpress (2022). Education Outlook 2022: Future of EdTech sector, digital learning and beyond. Retrieved from https://indianexpress.com/article/education/

education-outlook-2022-future-of-edtech-sector-digital-learning-in-2022-and-beyond-7699508/, viewed on 09.09.22.
Kovid, R. K., and Kumar, V. (Eds) (2022). *Cases on Emerging Markets Responses to the COVID-19 Pandemic*. Hershey, Pennsylvania, USA: IGI – Global Publications (ISBN13: 978-16-6843-504-5, DOI: 10.4018/978-1-6684-3504-5).
Kumar, V., and Ayodeji, O. G. (2021). Determinants of the Success of Online Retail in India. *International Journal of Business Information Systems (IJBIS), 37*(2), 246–262.
Kumar, V., and Bhardwaj, A. (2020). Role of Cloud Computing in School Education. In *Handbook of Research on Diverse Teaching Strategies for the Technology-Rich Classroom*. IGI Global, pp. 98–108 (ISBN 9781799802389).
Kumar, V., and Gupta, G. (Eds) (2021). *Strategic Management During a Pandemic*. Milton Park, Abingdon-on-Thames, Oxfordshire, England, USA: Routledge, Taylor & Francis Group (ISBN 9780367646479).
Kumar, V., and Malhotra, G. (Eds) (2021). *Stakeholder Strategies for Reducing the Impact of Global Health Crises*. USA: IGI – Global Publications (ISBN13: 978-17-9987-495-9, DOI: 10.4018/978-1-7998-7495-9).
Kumar, V., and Nanda, P. (2020). Social Media as a Tool in Higher Education: A Pedagogical Perspective. In *Handbook of Research on Diverse Teaching Strategies for the Technology-Rich Classroom*. IGI Global, pp. 239–253 (ISBN 9781799802389).
Kumar, V., and Rewari, M. (2022). A Responsible Approach to Higher Education Curriculum Design. *International Journal of Educational Reform (IJER)*, 31(4), 422–441.
Kumar, V., and Sharma, D. (2017). Cloud Computing as a Catalyst in STEM Education. *International Journal of Information and Communication Technology Education (IJICTE), 13*(2), 38–51.
Martin, A. (2020). How to optimize online learning in the age of coronavirus (COVID-19): A 5-point guide for educators. Retrieved from https://newsroom.unsw.edu.au/news/social-affairs/how-optimise-online-learning-age-coronavirus, viewed on 05.09.22.
Meraj, A. (2022, May 24). The Future of Edtech in India. Retrieved from https://www.highereducationdigest.com/the-future-of-edtech-in india/#:~:text=Future%20of%20Ed%2DTech%3A,in%20the%20next%2010%20years, viewed on 01.09.22.
Mukul, P. (2021). Boom in Ed-Tech gets bigger. Retrieved from https://indianexpress.com/article/business/boom-in-ed-tech-gets-bigger-mas-fundraises-soar-way-above-2-year-total-7575447/, viewed on 31.08.22.
Patnaik, A. (2022). The Indian edtech industry is taking India to the world, Mint, Aug 8. Retrieved from https://www.livemint.com/opinion/online-views/the-indian-edtech-industry-is-taking-india-to-the-world-11660148523819.html
Raghunathan, A. (2022). Retrieved from https://www.forbes.com/sites/anuraghunathan/2022/06/07/after-two-years-of-blockbuster-growth-edtech-giant-byjus-readies-for-new-normal/?sh=5f13f346748b, viewed on 11.09.22.
Reich, J. (2020). *Failure to Disrupt: Why Technology Alone Can't Transform Education*. Harvard University Press: Cambridge, MA and London, England (DOI: 10.4159/9780674249684).
Sharma, D., and Kumar, V. (2017). A Framework for Collaborative and Convenient Learning on Cloud Computing Platforms. *International Journal of Web-Based Learning and Teaching Technologies (IJWLTT)*, 12(2), 1–20.
Singh, J., and Kumar, V. (2021). End User Driven Approach for Regulatory Compliance in Public Cloud. *International Journal of Service Science Management, Engineering and Technology (IJSSMET)*, 12(2), 1–19.
Singh, J., and Kumar, V. (2022). Combating the Pandemic With ICT Based Learning Tools and Applications: A Case of Indian Higher Education. *International Journal of Virtual and Personal Learning Environments (IJVPLE) Platforms (IJVPLE)*, 12(1), 1–21.

Startup Talky (2022). Retrieved from https://startuptalky.com/byjus-learning-app-success-story/, viewed on 10.09.22.

Todorova, N., and Bjorn-Andersen, N. (2011). University Learning in Times of Crisis: The Role of IT. *Accounting Education*, *20*(6), 597–599. DOI: 10.1080/09639284.2011.632913.

Varindia (2021). Retrieved from https://varindia.com/news/byjus-to-take-over-language-learning-platform-hello-english, viewed on 08.09.22.

www.tracxn.com (2022). Retrieved from https://tracxn.com/d/acquisitions/acquisitionsbyBYJU'S, viewed on 05.09.22.

3 Flipped classrooms for engaged learning during the pandemic

Teachers' perspectives and challenges in a South African high school

Sivashnee Paragoo and Kershnee Sevnarayan

Introduction

Over the past three years, schools have been immediately impacted by the Coronavirus (Covid-19) pandemic's disruption of education (Kumar and Malhotra, 2021). The Covid-19 pandemic has caused an economic, social, political, and educational crisis that has brought to light several already-existing and well-known issues with education (such as the use of teacher-centred pedagogies, a lack of digital education strategies, and a lack of digital competence among teachers and learners) that have been made worse due to the pandemic (Singh and Kumar, 2022; Kovid and Kumar, 2022). The Organisation for Economic Co-operation and Development (OECD) (2021) states that by the end of March 2020, most countries had completely closed the educational institutions due to the Covid-19 crisis, and at the start of February 2021, many schools and educational institutions were still closed, limiting access of learners to their teachers and content knowledge (Kumar and Gupta, 2021).

With advances in e-learning technologies, new pedagogical models are being developed to bridge the divide between teachers and learners during the pandemic (Bhardwaj and Kumar, 2022). South African schools are under immense pressure to transform their teaching and learning in addition to supporting a progressively diverse learner cohort's transition from basic to higher education. This obligation calls for the implementation of transformative pedagogical approaches in the classroom (Kumar and Rewari, 2022). To deliver high-quality, inclusive education in online environments, innovative pedagogies, digital technologies, and methodologies have become crucial (Kumar and Nanda, 2020). The flipped classroom is an innovative pedagogy strategy that has drawn a lot of attention during the pandemic. A flipped classroom, which is also called "inverted classroom" by some scholars, is an alternative learner-centred pedagogical model that reverses the traditional classroom-teaching context (Gomez-Lanier, 2018; Karabatak and Polat, 2020). In other words, the lesson is viewed outside class hours while homework or interactive and learner-centred strategies are done during class hours (Sharma and Kumar, 2017). This pedagogical model allows

DOI: 10.4324/9781003491712-3

learners to be exposed to content outside of the classroom so that they can engage with their content intrinsically within the classroom. In the flipped classroom pedagogical model, learners are stimulated in the learning context by instructional strategies employed by the teacher. Teachers are regarded as facilitators who may assist learners' understandings.

After extensive literature reviews on research studies conducted on the flipped classroom as a pedagogical model for engaged learning, it was found that most studies conducted were in HEIs (Bishop and Verleger, 2013; O'Flaherty and Phillips, 2015) but to a lesser extent in high schools (Erbil and Kocabas, 2020; Unal et al., 2021; Wei et al., 2020; Winter, 2018). Interestingly, there is limited research done on flipped classrooms for engaged learning in South African schools. Researchers realize that there is a need to advance the knowledge gap pertaining to the practical side of this phenomenon that must be explored. Due to there being a plethora of studies on the flipped classroom conducted in HEIs, a limited body of research exists in high schools and very few on teachers' voices concerning the flipped classroom. Thus, this chapter fills this gap by exploring teachers' perspectives and challenges of flipping the classroom for engaged learning in a semi-rural high school in Durban, located in Kwa-Zulu Natal, South Africa. To achieve this purpose, the following research questions are presented:

RQ1: What are teachers' (facilitators') perspectives on flipping the classroom for engaged learning in a semi-rural high school?

RQ2: What challenges do teachers (facilitators) experience when flipping the classroom?

The rest of the chapter is organized as follows: related works on the flipped classroom are discussed, followed by the theoretical underpinning of the study – critical theory. The methodology is then presented, followed by a discussion of the findings. Lastly, recommendations emerging from this study are discussed.

Literature review and theoretical underpinning

The role of the teacher in a flipped classroom pedagogy

Globally, flipped learning is increasing in popularity in primary to secondary classrooms (Bergmann and Sams, 2012; Erbil and Kocabas, 2020; O'Flaherty and Phillips, 2015; Unal et al., 2021; Wei et al., 2020; Winter, 2018). The implication of a flipped classroom strategy is "a change in the role of students and teachers" (Thakare, 2018, p. 28). In the traditional classroom, teachers focus more on completing the curriculum rather than knowing whether learners can retrieve the knowledge taught (Lee and Martin, 2020). The flipped classroom, in contrast, supports collaborative learning and facilitator–learner interaction (Avery et al., 2018). In the realm of flipped classroom research in Science, Technology, Engineering and Mathematics education, most studies have reported a positive impact on student learning (Barba et al., 2016; Stohr, 2020). For Wei et al. (2020, p. 1462), "The flipped classroom emphasizes the leverage of online self-regulated learning and physical classroom interaction by adopting various pedagogies, such as, inquiry-based learning, project-based learning, problem-based learning and learning by doing among collaborative team members". Apart from projects and activities used to engage and motivate 88 sixth-grade Chinese students during class time, teacher–learner interaction has shown a positive impact on student learning through the flipped classroom approach. For the period of the in-class learning, the teacher had more time to interact with students in small groups or independently to guide students to a better understanding of the content and skills (Wei et al., 2020). Thus, teachers are facilitators and mediators in the teaching and learning process (Kumar and Sharma, 2021). Figure 3.1 depicts the roles of the facilitator and the learner when employing the flipped classroom pedagogy.

Figure 3.1 shows the pastoral, mediator, and facilitator role that they model in the flipped classroom approach (Defazio, 2018). Kelly (2020, p. 1) puts it best, "facilitating learning encompasses teaching learners to think critically and understand how the learning process works". To add to Kelly (2020), continuous support and supervision are critical roles of the facilitator in a flipped classroom pedagogy.

Towards a flipped classroom pedagogy for engaged learning

Based on data that was gathered from numerous journal articles, it was reported that the flipped classroom approach had a positive impact on K-12 learner achievement (Lo and Hew, 2017; Lee, 2018; Unal et al., 2021; Wei

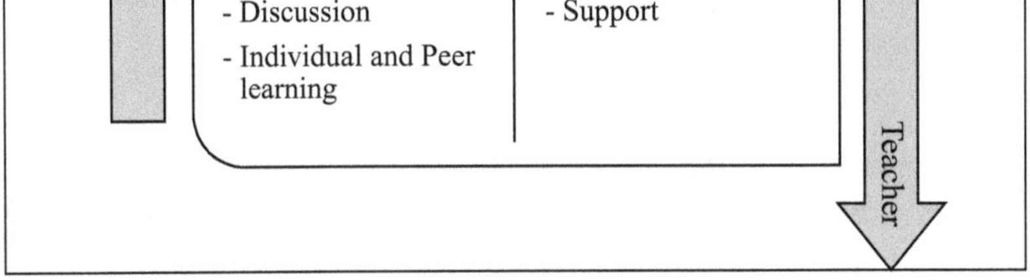

Figure 3.1 Teacher and learner relationship in a flipped classroom model.

et al., 2020; Winter, 2018). Winter (2018) conducted a research study on the flipped classroom model with his sixth-grade social studies class in a private school in Hawai'i. He states in his study that any type of online learning shows connection between performance and self-efficacy in learners. Motivation and engagement within learners had also shown an upsurge within technology-supported learning environments (Winter, 2018). The study also revealed how the flipped classroom method may not be optimal for all learners, especially learners who may not have internet access or a device at home. More schools are transitioning to implementing the "bring your own device" (BYOD) policy. This requires learners to use their own smartphones or other devices for learning during class time (Hackler, 2015; BYOD for Learning, 2017). It has been said that another method to bridge the gap of information and communications technology (ICT) in schools is through implementing a BYOD policy in schools (Adhikari et al., 2016). People opposing the BYOD policy claim that there is inequality and digital divide issues leads to the additional cost to learning (Kumar, 2014; BYOD for Learning, 2017). Parents or guardians of most learners cannot afford such devices; hence, the digital divide constructs and strengthens socio-economic inequalities amongst people. Another disadvantage is that such technological devices can become a distraction in the classroom (Wainwright, 2012).

Lee (2018) conducted a study on the flipped classroom approach in his middle school class in South Korea. From learners' interview responses on the flipped classroom pedagogy, a learner stated that when there is something he does not understand at home, he can replay the video to help him understand the subject content better. He stated that when he is watching the lecture videos, it feels like his facilitator is right there in front of him (Lee, 2018). Another learner said, "Before, I struggled to do my homework on my own, but now I can solve the problem by watching the video repeatedly" (Lee, 2018, p. 848).

The flipped network (Schmidt and Ralph, 2016) conducted a study of teachers incorporating the flipped classroom at the junior high and secondary school in the United States. The study found that 99% of facilitators who incorporated the flipped classroom will continue to use it. 67% reported improvements in learner performance, and 80% reported improvements in learner engagement. A few reasons these facilitators and authors are supporting that the flipped classroom works are that it enhances learning, encourages classroom discussion, offers personalized guidance for learners, builds up team-based skills, and increases engaged learning (Schmidt and Ralph, 2016). Learners will be more eager to work if they are engaged and interested. The quantitative results presented here are stimulating, but it would be interesting to understand facilitators' perspectives qualitatively in the discussion of findings section of this chapter. van Alten et al. (2019) concluded that even though a class applied flipped learning, and it might have had positive effects, it does not necessarily mean it is effective. This is because, in a sixth-grade mathematics class, in China, which switched to a flipped classroom, there was not a significant difference that resulted from the change. Although the facilitator noted increased engagement during collaborative activities in a flipped classroom in a middle school, the study found a minor difference in learners' conceptual understanding (Kirvan et al., 2015).

Literature shows that not all classes that are engaged in flipped learning are successful and satisfied. Abuhmaid (2020, p. 1007) maintains, "[Facilitators'] overall attitude toward [the] flipped learning model is positive since it improves learning and transforms the [facilitators'] role". To concur with Abuhmaid (2020), facilitators may be enthusiastic as the flipped classroom approach may open a path to exposure of a variety of sources for independent learning. However, creating instructional content to employ such a pedagogy is very much time-consuming for facilitators and requires them to be dedicated to implement such a model. Additionally, many facilitators are uncomfortable with the thought of creating video lessons or do not have the time to do so because of their busy lifestyles (Hunley, 2016). Additionally, facilitators are reluctant to implement the flipped classroom pedagogical model due to a lack of training and the failure to implement skills learned during training sessions. Yilmaz (2017) informs readers that learner motivation will increase if learners are trained and educated on the use of technological devices and sources, which is called "e-learning readiness". If learners do not have e-learning readiness, they may not feel motivated to work if they are unable to use the devices that are required of them to access the content.

Challenges experienced by teachers

During the epidemic, teachers instructing a chemistry course at three colleges of education in southern Ghana highlighted several obstacles and challenges while creating and utilizing the flipped classroom. According to Aidoo et al. (2022), access to the internet, digital tools, and technological know-how, according to educators, has an impact on their teaching, students' preparation, and class participation. Poor network connectivity in some neighbourhoods and residences made it challenging for students to access course materials (Bhardwaj and Kumar, 2024). In addition, "teacher educators found it challenging to communicate, interact, monitor students' online activities, and provide timely feedback due to large class sizes" (Aidoo et al., p. 11). Employing the flipped classroom approach for engaged learning can be overwhelming for facilitators since they are required to plan instructional activities (video, notes, podcasts, and problem-solving activities) to cater for all learning styles well in advance. This takes up a lot of time. Moreover, it can also be expensive since it requires a lot of data if facilitators were to upload videos or instructional content that is large. Schools should maintain a budget for maintaining the flipped approach. Software should be used to create a learning and teaching platform online. While some are paid software, Google Classroom is an example of a free application intended to help learners and teachers interconnect, collaborate, organize, and manage assignments (Bell, 2015). Phillips and Trainor (2014, p. 521) claim, "screen-capture software can be used to create the digital lectures, which can be accompanied by digital presentations". As much as computers have made the lives of teachers much easier, a lack of skill on the use of computer integration for engaged learning leads to a lack of self-confidence in their effort to incorporate computers into their classroom instruction.

For facilitators to be able to use such software in the learning context, they will have to familiarize themselves with it first. It is necessary for facilitators to be trained to transform a classroom into one that allows the involvement of learners that necessitates additional preparation as well as creativeness (Subramaniam and Muniandy, 2016). Whilst some facilitators may grasp the use of technology instantly, others may need to be trained to implement the flipped classroom for engaged learning.

Towards a critical theory for flipping the classroom

Critical theory (CT) was used as the theoretical framework to underpin this paper. Crossman (2019, p. 209) defines CT as "oriented toward[s] critiquing and changing society as a whole". Hence, the idea of this chapter is to determine faciliators' perspectives and challenges on flipping the classroom for engaged learning. In doing so, the following research questions are posed to direct the research in this chapter:

1 What are facilitators' perspectives on flipping the classroom for engaged learning?
2 What challenges do facilitators experience when flipping the classroom?

According to Crossman (2019, p. 2), CT "emerged out of the Marxist tradition and was developed by a group of sociologists at the University of Frankfurt in Germany who referred to themselves as The Frankfurt School". Thus, CT denoted "a school of academic thought which challenges dominant ways of explaining and exploring organizational phenomenon" (Harney, 2014, p. 2). CT analyses knowledge that is perceived as convincing, absolute, and beyond human interests. CT tries to disrupt such knowledge. In the place of this type of knowledge, CT seeks to generate new forms of knowledge that is shaped by social interests. CT, thus, seeks to "make problematic what is taken for granted in culture", and it does so in the interests of "social justice", especially in the interests of "those who are oppressed" (Nichols and Allen-Brown, 1996, p. 226). Accordingly, the main intention of CT is to elucidate and transform the situations that exist which dominate the powerless (Marcano, 2018). In support of Marcano's (2018) perspective, Asghar (2013, p. 3123) advocates, "critical theory challenges the status quo and strives for a balanced and democratic society". Hence, it is then clear that CT maintains its approach and is based on the conclusion that power amongst certain groups is an issue, and all groups should be liberated (Fuchs, 2017). CT is summarized as follows (Friesen, 2008, p. 3):

- Identifying ideas that are presented as convincing, final, obvious, or matter of fact in sources of knowledge;
- Analysing these ideas in the context provided in other more marginal knowledge forms or sources;
- Revealing through this scrutiny that behind dominant claims and ideas lay one or more politically charged and often contradictory ways of understanding the issue or phenomenon in question; and,
- Using this underlying conflict as the basis for developing alternative forms of understanding and point to concrete possibilities for action.

The idea of incorporating CT into the study is for the sole purpose of being critical of teachers' perspectives in flipping the classroom for engaged learning. By using CT as the foundation of the study, it would help to liberate the subordinate group, which may be the facilitators in this study.

Research methodology

Contextual focus in the study

The research context was one public high school located in Durban, Kwa-Zulu Natal, South Africa. A pseudonym was used to protect the identity of the school. Creswell (2014, p. 138) maintains that "researchers use aliases or pseudonyms for individuals and places, to protect the identities of participants". Hence, the school is referred to in the study as "Blossom High School". Through government support, the school is fully resourced. Blossom High School has a well-equipped media centre that is available to all learners. The media centre is equipped with computers that are connected to the internet. The school has a networked ICT lab used to teach Computer Applications Technology (CAT) and Information Technology (IT). The rationale for the choice of this school was due to the school being equipped with proper technological tools used for teaching and learning. This school was purposefully chosen as the demographics show that learners from various backgrounds attend the school, ranging from learners from previously disadvantaged families to learners from middle-class backgrounds. This school was an ideal choice for the study as the flipped classroom approach could be used within this diverse context with resources.

Research approach and design

This research is grounded in a qualitative approach as it is solely concerned about the views, opinions, and the challenges of the faciliators concerning flipping the classroom for engaged learning. Participatory Action Research (PAR) was selected to generate data of facilitators' perspectives of and challenges with the flipped classroom. Like CT, PAR promotes emancipation of powerless and marginalized groups (Datta et al., 2015). In PAR, an emphasis is based on collaborative and mutual associations among the participants and the researcher (Todd, 2016). Moreover, it has been proven from many studies (Benjamin-Thomas et al., 2018; Lake and Wendland, 2018; Mather-Pike, 2018; Machin-Mastromatteo, 2013; Pillay, 2018) that PAR is a prevailing approach for engaging with oppressed groups to enhance their own circumstances within society, and this is what this chapter intends to achieve. PAR creates a collaborative method of learning for which people try to change the situation in which they interrelate amid a collective society and raise critical awareness amongst individuals from all backgrounds (Balakrishnan, 2016). As a result, knowledge was generated by participants' shared efforts within the research process together with the researcher. By participants contributing towards the study, it demonstrated an awareness of their current situation so that they can be emancipated from the shackles of oppression which may exist.

Sampling and research instruments

Participants in PAR are of equal status to the researcher. The selection of participants is thus a significant factor in research. Random sampling was used and included the researchers and two female high school facilitators who volunteered to be part of the study. One facilitator was an ICT facilitator, and the other was a science facilitator. In support of this selection of participants, the purposive participant selection procedure enabled flexibility for the researcher to intentionally select those participants who are suitable for satisfying the purpose of the study which required the selection of a diverse group of individuals pertaining to the CAT subject (Palinkas et al., 2015). Since this is a PAR study, the researcher had to remain neutral in the data generation process. The researcher acted as a participant observer at the school; so participants did not feel powerless in the data generation process. According to Crossman (2019, p. 1), a participant observer "is when a sociologist becomes a part of the group, they are studying in order to collect data and understand a social problem". Hence, researchers cannot isolate themselves in the research context but allow themselves to become involved in the lives of those that are researched to gain a better understanding of how social influences affect different individuals and groups.

One-on-one interviews and particpant observations were conducted in 2020 with the two teachers to generate data for the two research questions in the study. Interviews and observations were conducted in a natural setting, in the classroom, to ensure the learners were comfortable when the data was generated. McGrath et al. (2019, p. 1002) maintain that qualitative interviews and observations "afford researchers opportunities to explore, in an in-depth manner, matters that are unique to the experiences of the interviewees".

Data analysis

Critical discourse analysis (CDA) was used for analysis of data generated within the study since the study fitted under the critical paradigm. Elsharkawy (2017, p. 3) describes CDA as "a field that is concerned with studying and analysing written and spoken texts to reveal the discursive sources of power, dominance, inequality and bias". Since the study intended on utilizing PAR for data generation, CDA may assist the researcher to analyse both written and spoken manuscripts in critically analysing the classroom for engaged learning. CDA further looks at how several groups may be misrepresented in numerous types of discourse (Sriwimon, 2017). According to Fairclough's model, CDA is viewed as three-dimensional. The first dimension is textual analysis, which includes what participants have said about flipping the classroom for engaged learning; the second is the processes which include how interaction is received, for example, by speaking, listening, or observing. The third dimension includes the context, which has led the participants to hold views that they may have regarding the use of the flipped class approach for engaged learning. CDA proved to be beneficial in the analysis of the study since it helped to uncover inequalities that existed. It is understood that CDA entails three important connections (Regmi, 2017).

Figure 3.2 illustrates how the language context, social context, and political context are linked in CDA. The function of CDA is to discover the connection between language, society, politics, and opinions. Furthermore, its purpose is to reveal the concealed and apparent social along with political standards and morals (Fatin et al., 2017).

Limitations and ethical considerations

Although this study was conducted at one public high school, it should be noted that the findings and conclusions cannot be generalized for all

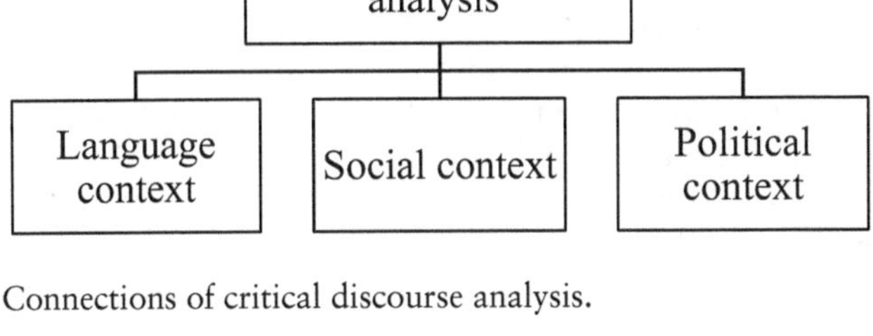

Figure 3.2 Connections of critical discourse analysis.

schools due to various circumstances. However, in schools where related challenges are experienced, under comparable circumstances, then the findings of this study could be related. Further research is needed to understand facilitators' perspectives and challenges on the flipped classroom for engaged learning in more than one school to get a broader understanding of the phenomenon.

Before conducting the study, ethical clearance was applied for and granted by the university's ethics committee (HSSREC/00000428/2019). The university policy stipulates that confidentiality and adherence to Covid-19 protocols be observed and adhered to before, during, and after the Covid-19 lockdown.

Discussion of findings

The facilitators' perspectives and challenges concerning the flipped classroom approach are discussed textually, discursively, and socially in this section. To answer the first research question on facilitators' perspectives on flipping the classroom for engaged learning, verbatim responses emerged from conversational one-on-one interviews with facilitators, who have been given pseudonyms, which are discussed in this section.

Facilitators' perspectives of the flipped classroom approach

On Mrs Moodley's understanding of the flipped classroom approach, she perceived that "teachers have to have necessary skills to record a lesson by means of audio or video, download content, and disseminate such multimedia. Not all teachers are daring enough to implement such an approach".

The textual analysis of discourse of "teachers have to have necessary skills . . ." implies that it is a necessity for teachers to possess technological skills. Moreover, such skills need to be effectively embedded in their teaching approach. A potential change is reflected in the statement, "Not all teachers are daring . . ." denotes that some teachers lack confidence in using technology as a resource to improve the teaching and learning process. A discursive analysis of discourse implies that there is a lack of confidence that facilitators have about integrating technology in their instructional approach. A sense of fear and uncertainty was received from the participant when the topic was discussed. It is, however, surprising that the teacher did not mention the sense of support in technology integration for teaching and learning. From a social analysis perspective, it can be determined that facilitators are powerless since many of them lack knowledge and skills to design instructional lessons that require engagement. Nevertheless, if facilitators lack education, then the quality of education delivered to learners becomes instantaneously poor. Teachers would not be able to empower learners if they themselves are not empowered with necessary skills. The phrase "Not all teachers are daring . . ." suggests that teachers lack the competency to modify their approach by frequently trusting that their current teaching strategies are functioning well. As a result, they are oblivious to the fact that they are disadvantaging learners since they fail to engage learners within the learning context. For Ms Khumalo:

> After recently discovering the new concept flipping the classroom, I realised that it could be an advantage to my learners since I personally feel that most learners will benefit tremendously. Every learner is unique, and some learners will not prefer to learn using the traditional method. We live in a modern era and learners want new ways to learn.

The expression "After recently discovering the new concept . . ." textually signifies that the flipped approach was unknown prior to data generation. Additionally, the utterance ". . . I personally feel that most learners will benefit tremendously" denotes that the teacher agrees with flipping the classroom for engaged learning. The phrase starting "Every learner is unique . . ." suggests that the way in which differentiation is recognized in terms of learners, teaching styles should also be differentiated according to such learning styles. Miss Khumalo's words discursively points to positivity towards the flipped approach in the phrase "I realised that it could be an advantage to my learners . . .". The utterance "Every learner is unique . . ." points to a realization in the participant's opinion of the importance of instilling a user-friendly approach for all. The use of the social word "We" in the phrase "We live in a modern era and learners want new ways to learn" establishes a realization that finding strategies to heighten the teaching and learning process should relate to the current trends of how knowledge is transferred. Incorporating various teaching methods within and out of the classroom creates a sense of resourcefulness. Thus, learners may find learning by this means interesting. Talbert (2019, p. 2) posits, "Flipped learning seems to affect students on a psychological level, making them more engaged, more motivated, and better able to self-regulate". The realization calls for equality in education and the shared ownership of the issue in addition to elucidations to implement a learning environment for all.

To answer the second research question on challenges that teachers experience in employing the flipped classroom, verbatim responses emerged from conversational one-on-one interviews with facilitators, who have been given pseudonyms, which are discussed in this section. Data also emerged from participant observation within the school context.

Facilitators' challenges of the flipped classroom

It is evident that numerous challenges pose a risk when employing the flipped classroom approach. The following challenges/sub-themes emerged from interviews with the two participants to answer the second research question in this chapter:

- Facilitators' inabilities to effectively engage learners in the classroom
- Facilitators' lack of knowledge and skills
- Lack of support from various stakeholders

Facilitators' inabilities to effectively engage learners in the classroom

Mrs Moodley uttered, "When we give learners tedious tasks, we find that most of them come to class not understanding anything or basically copying the answers from a fellow classmate". Textually, this is an indication of the lack of engagement amongst most learners in the classroom as lessons are tedious and monotonous, hence it does not challenge learners. Miss Khumalo said,

> Most of the time, it is always the teacher that has to deliver the content and the students have to sit and listen . . . learners were more responsive in reciprocating what was learnt through watching the videos in their own time.

This indicates regurgitation of knowledge and the latter indicates engagement amongst learners when a new teaching method and additional learning resources were used. Discursively, from what both participants noted, it can be understood that implementing the flipped classroom for engaged learning gives learners a sense of responsibility to go through the variety of content given to them in different platforms. More flexibility is given as they can internalize content in any context beside the school and at their own pace. Socially, it is assumed that the flipped classroom may give learners a feeling of responsibility to take charge of their own learning by allowing them to explore a variety of resources out of the classroom.

Another limitation discovered was due to class sizes. Mrs Moodley stressed, "As an ICT teacher, I would love to implement this approach, but our class sizes are maximum 48. It would be difficult to flip classes of this size". Textually, "our class sizes are maximum 48" signifies that classes are overcrowded. Teachers are reluctant to implement the flipped classroom for engaged learning since it would be "difficult to flip classes of this size". Hence, facilitators opt for traditional teaching approaches due to large class sizes. Discursively, besides being a resourced school, the flipped approach is more suitable for smaller groups since it allows for discussion during class time. Moreover, teachers should personalize lessons for learners based on their learning styles. This may be a lot of work for teachers. From a social analysis perspective, it can be assumed that class sizes in most schools cater for the traditional classroom setting. Interestingly, this may be one of the reasons why teaching approaches are more teacher-centred. Thus, regardless of teachers being oppressed, teachers conform to their oppression since it is seen as a norm in the South African education system.

From this theme, it can be construed from Blossom High School that facilitators cannot effectively engage learners in the classroom since they are hesitant to change their teaching methods to accommodate learners. This may be so since class sizes are fully capacitated. Hence, facilitators struggled to provide learners with individualized attention. During data generation, it was observed that facilitators maintained the traditional "sit down and listen" approach whilst they were the ones with more authority in the classroom. Miss Khumalo admitted that using the flipped classroom improved learner engagement as it allowed learners to explore instead of feeling restricted or limited in their learning.

Facilitators' lack of knowledge and skills

Employment of the flipped classroom approach may assist facilitators to be well acquainted with using technology for teaching and learning, that is creating and reusing instructional content (Joyner, 2021). While this may be the case in some schools, there are learners who come from disadvantaged backgrounds and who cannot afford such technology for the successful implementation of the flipped classroom approach. Hence, the flipped classroom may be considered a new pedagogical model in South Africa since a handful of schools are using this approach (Daniel, 2016). Mrs Moodley mentioned:

> We don't use the flipped approach. It is my first time using such an approach after you introduced me to it. Our teaching has always been standardised. We teach learners at school, and we give them homework in terms of what was discussed in class.

Miss Khumalo similarly expressed:

> I have tried it once in my classroom. I use the traditional approach. I prepare lesson plans only for the classroom and not out of the classroom. Learners are given homework to do out of the classroom. Honestly, this is a lot more work than I am used to. It was a fun exercise, but I don't think I can continue with it.

From a textual analysis perspective, both facilitators maintained that they do not use the flipped approach in their teaching but use the traditional approach. Mrs Moodley's refers to the traditional teaching style as the norm in their school by saying, "Our teaching has always been standardised". The phrase, "We don't use . . .", implies that many other facilitators in other schools are implementing a similar teaching strategy. For Miss Khumalo, "I prepare lesson plans only for the classroom. . ." implies that the traditional approach is currently used since teaching takes place only within the boundaries of the classroom. Furthermore, both facilitators revealed that they had never heard about the flipped classroom approach. It is comprehensible since the school does not centre on exposing learners to technology due to lack of funds. Socially, society perceives the traditional form of teaching and learning as standard since it is acceptable. Moreover, teachers themselves lack the knowledge and skills of technology-enabled learning. Teachers first need to be empowered so that they can do the same to learners.

From what was observed in class during data generation, it was evident that learners studied content at home. Miss Khumalo mentioned:

> I have noticed that the learners are more actively engaged in the learning process. I felt that when I did use this method in the classroom, learners were more responsive in reciprocating what was learnt through watching the videos in their own time. As I have mentioned previously, learners are yearning for new and creative techniques to spark an interest in the way that they receive and transfer knowledge.

Textually, "I have noticed . . ." indicates that the facilitator is expressing her opinions on the flipped approach. The expression ". . . the learners are more actively engaged. . ." demonstrates that Miss Khumalo sees reason for the flipped approach since learners were engaged. In the phrase, ". . . learners were more responsive in reciprocating . . ." Miss Khumalo acknowledged that engagement is enhanced when the flipped classroom approach was used. Discursively, the words, "I have noticed . . .", implies that Miss Khumalo acknowledges the effects of using a different approach other than the traditional approach. Thus, Miss Khumalo seemed positive about the flipped approach. She was optimistic about the flipped approach since she maintained that "learners were more responsive" as they watched videos pertaining to the lesson topic out of the school context. From a social analysis perspective, Miss Khumalo is conscious of the role that the attitudes of learners can play in the failure or success of the employment of the flipped classroom approach. When learners are active in the learning process, it gives the impression of engaged learning.

Mrs Moodley added, "I believe that for one to be engaged they have to find instruction interesting and challenging . . . learners were very happy when they were given so many resources instead of a traditional textbook". In the expression ". . . for one to be engaged they have to find instruction interesting . . ." the facilitator recognizes the need for instructional content that learners should find challenging. The statement, ". . . learners were very happy when they were given so many resources . . ." demonstrates the need and the effects of using a variety of teaching and learning resources. This statement reveals that Mrs Moodley is optimistic about the flipped classroom approach. It is evident that the facilitator acknowledged the importance of varying learning resources since learners were ecstatic about it. The facilitator was able to determine this by recognizing that learners were engaged in the lesson. Socially, by giving learners content to explore out of the classroom, they become curious and hungry for knowledge. Moreover, an assortment of resources stimulates the learning process. CT offers opportunities for the different perspectives of disadvantaged people of society. If instructional content is not challenging, learners are deprived of becoming critical thinkers.

From this theme, it can be presumed that facilitators lack the necessary skills to implement a change in their current standardized teaching approach to effectively implement the flipped classroom for engaged learning. This is indicative that there is no support coming in to assist facilitators. The white paper policy emphasizes the need to incorporate ICT in education for e-learning; however, not all schools are on par with this move (Vandeyar, 2015). This sequentially deprives not only the facilitators but the learners too.

Lack of support from various stakeholders

A stakeholder in terms of education is defined as someone who is interested or associated with the welfare and success of a school (Roundy, 2016). This may include entities directly or indirectly affected by the failure or success of an educational system. Data was generated from three stakeholders: learners, facilitators, and parents; however, this chapter focuses on the facilitators' perspectives and challenges. The current situation of Blossom High School indicated limited or no support from stakeholders in the school for flipping the classroom for engaged learning.

Mrs Moodley expressed

> Our school was given an ibox, tablets, and Wi-Fi from the Department of Education. I can say only maximum three teachers have used the ibox. The tablets have never been used and the Wi-Fi has never been loaded with data.

Textually, this indicates that some schools have resources but do not use it for its purpose. The statement ". . . I can say only maximum three teachers have used the ibox . . . tablets have never been used . . . Wi-Fi has never been loaded with data" is a strong suggestion that teachers are not willing to change their teaching approach since the tools given to the school have not been used. Mrs Moodley expresses the non-use of various resources. Discursively, a reason can be that minimal or no training was given to facilitators concerning the use of the tools. Moreover, for facilitators to create instructional content online, they need access to the internet. The school is forced to purchase data bundles for this to take effect since data bundles are expensive (Majola, 2021). According to South African Government (2019, p. 21), some of the responsibilities of the Department of Basic Education (DBE) with regard to teaching and learning resources in schools are to "focus on providing well designed print and digital content to teachers and learners; expanding access to and improving the use of ICT at schools; and providing teachers with essential tools and support". To counter this statement, it can be argued that this responsibility is not being fulfilled. The school has the necessary teaching resources, but most teachers are unskilled for the successful implementation of such resources.

The flipped classroom can be a success for engaged learning only if facilitators are confident with the skills they possess. Mrs Moodley articulated:

> There is no support from the DBE. Only a one-day workshop was given to teachers on the use of such technology in the classroom. Workshops should be a priority from the department. Our skills need to be updated. Teachers are hesitant to take on the initiative of using such tools in the class without proper supervision. Management also needs to be more supportive and encourage the DBE to hold workshops within the school.

The phrase "There is no support . . ." textually indicates that facilitators are not being assisted from the DBE, yet they are required to implement e-learning as per the white paper policy in their curriculum. The utterance "Workshops should be a priority from the department . . ." depicts the concern of training from teachers. The phrase "Teachers are hesitant . . ." reiterates the reason for facilitators to be trained to manipulate their teaching approach by incorporating technology in their lessons as a tool for engaged learning. The utterance "Management also needs to be more supportive . . ." shows that besides the DBE lending support, the management of the school is uncooperative in assisting teachers within the classroom to improve their teaching approach. According to Roland (2015, p. 3), from a discursive analyse perspective, "the nationwide survey of K-12 teachers revealed that while schools are putting more technology into classrooms, not enough is being done to ensure that teachers know how to integrate it into their lessons". It is for this reason that a series of workshops needs to be held to train teachers so that learners can benefit. From this discourse, it can be determined that a lack of skills is one of the reasons for facilitators resisting change. Engaged learning cannot be achieved if facilitators are unsuccessful in the classroom. Socially, facilitators have a profound effect on the learners they teach. According to Savides (2017, p. 7), "in 2016 KwaZulu Natal had 2,875 unqualified or under-qualified teachers last year, 57% of the total number of such teachers across the country". This indicates that such teachers pose in front of learners without the necessary knowledge and skills. Hence, this might be one of the reasons why learners are disengaged in their learning. Notwithstanding the fact that the DBE stresses the use of ICT in the classroom, however, many schools are not provided with such resources. Implementing the flipped classroom for engaged learning necessitates a great deal of training for facilitators and requires learners to have such technological resources at home. With support for internal and external stakeholders, facilitators might be willing to implement the flipped classroom approach.

Under this theme, it was comprehended that facilitators are given little to no training on resources given by the DBE, hence, facilitators are hesitant to incorporate such resources in their lessons without proper training. Besides support from the DBE, facilitators stressed that the School Management Team (SMT) encouraged them to change their methods but did not hold training sessions in this regard to lend support to teachers.

Conclusion and recommendations

The research undertaken revealed that collaboration, equal participation, and communication amongst all appropriate stakeholders at various levels may support flipping the classroom for engaged learning. The findings in this research indicated that facilitators were enthusiastic about the flipped classroom. Additionally, facilitators saw a positive difference in learner engagement when employing the approach. It is understood that facilitators in the study are keen to change their approach but are not assisted by stakeholders. They maintained that most of them in the school would choose not to employ the flipped classroom due to a lack of knowledge and skills. Additionally, there is a challenge of overpopulated classes. There is also a possibility that most learners may not have access to electronic content at home due to socio-economic factors and the negative effects of the Covid-19 pandemic. Facilitators are constrained to stand on their own and conform to the obligatory ICT changes relating to teaching and learning. It is for this reason that facilitators refuse to modify and adapt to the flipped classroom approach.

It is recommended that there should be support from the various stakeholders (learners, school governing body, parents, school management team, and Department of Basic Education) to ensure that the needs of facilitators are accommodated. VanDeWeghe (2009, p. 8) states, "the most engaging learning involves sufficient challenge at the right level of skill". For learners to be engaged, instructional activities ought to be set at the right level for them to challenge and motivate learners. Furthermore, activities should not be monotonous but incorporate various teaching and learning resources which should allow for exploration. To achieve successful implementation of the flipped classroom for engaged learning, learners should be involved throughout the creation and practice of instructional activities. For example, learners can be given evaluation sheets to rate their teachers and the way lessons are delivered. The significance of doing this is for facilitators to get an understanding of where learners are in the learning process. Moreover, it should be valued as constructive criticism whereby teachers can improve their existing teaching styles. This will help facilitators to design their lessons around the needs of learners. Parents should work closely with teachers and the school to ensure that learners are supervised at home. As facilitators pointed out during conversational interviews, there is minimal parental involvement. Hence, increasing parental involvement will address discipline and help learners to become more engaged in the learning context.

Professional development training in ICT for facilitators will help them to gain a stance on best practices to use ICT for engaged learning. The flipped classroom should not just be a bandwagon that all teachers jump on to use in their classrooms. It is vital that teachers approach the flipped classroom with care and knowledge. The implementation of such an approach can be made possible where there is teamwork and where teachers feel comfortable in their work environment.

References

Abuhmaid, A.M. (2020). Teachers' Perceptions on the Impact of Flipped Learning on Student Learning and Teacher's Role in Jordanian Schools. *Universal Journal of Educational Research, 8*(3), 1007–1016. doi:10.13189/ujer.2020.080335.

Adhikari, J., Mathrani, A., and Scogings, C. (2016). Bring Your Own Devices classroom: Exploring the Issue of Digital Divide in the Teaching and Learning Contexts. *Interactive Technology and Smart Education, 13*(4), 323–343.

Aidoo, B., Marey, A.M., Veli-Matti, V., Svava, P., and Berglind, G. (2022). Transforming Teaching with ICT Using the Flipped Classroom Approach: Dealing with COVID-19 Pandemic. *Education Sciences, 12*(6), 421. doi:10.3390/educsci12060421.

Asghar, J. (2013). Critical Paradigm: A Preamble for Novice Researchers. *Life Science Journal, 10*(4), 3121–3127.

Avery, K., Huggan, C., and Preston, J. (2018). The Flipped Classroom: High School Student Engagement Through 21st Century Learning. *In Education, 24*(1), 4–21.

Balakrishnan, V. (2016). Participatory Action Research in Culturally Complex Societies: Opportunities and Challenges. *Educational Action Research, 25*(2), 185–202. doi:10.1080/09650792.2016.1206480.

Barba, L. A., Kaw, A., and Le Doux, J. M. (2016). Guest Editorial: Flipped Classrooms in STEM. *Advances in Engineering Education, 5*(3), 1–6.

Bell, K. (2015). Teacher's Guide to Google Classroom. *Common Sense Education.* Retrieved from https://s3.amazonaws.com/scschoolfiles/546/teachers_guide_to_google_classroom.pdf

Benjamin, T., Corrado, A. M., McGrath, C., and Rudman, D. L. (2018). Working Towards the Promise of Participatory Action Research: Learning From Ageing Research Exemplars. *The International Journal of Qualitative Methods, 17*(1), 1–13.

Bergmann, J., and Sams, A. (2012). Before You Flip, Consider This. *Phi Delta Kappan, 94*(2), 25.

Bhardwaj, A., and Kumar, V. (2022). A Framework for Enhancing Privacy in Online Collaboration. *International Journal of Electronic Security and Digital Forensics (IJESDF), 14*(4), 413–432.

Bhardwaj, A., and Kumar, V. (2024). Challenges in Online Collaboration to Augment Industry 4.0. *International Journal of Technology, Policy and Management (IJTPM), 24*(1), 71–92.

Bishop, J., and Verleger, M. (2013). Testing the flipped classroom with model-eliciting activities and video lectures in a mid-level undergraduate engineering course. *IEEE Frontiers in Education Conference (FIE)*, pp. 161–163.

BYOD for Learning (2017). Retrieved from PDST Technology in Education website. Retrieved from https://www.pdsttechnologyineducation.ie/en/Technology/Advice-Sheets/Bring-your-own-Device-BYOD-for-Learning.pdf

Creswell, J. W. (2014). *Research Design: Qualitative, Quantitative and Mixed Methods Approaches* (4th ed.). Thousand Oaks, CA: Sage Publications.

Crossman, A. (2019, January 14). An Overview of Qualitative Research Methods. Retrieved from https://www.thoughtco.com/qualitative-research-methods-3026555

Daniel, B. (2016). Exploring the use of the Flipped Classroom as an Education Delivery Method. *IIESpace Repository*. Retrieved from http://iiespace.iie.ac.za/handle/11622/164

Datta, R., Khyang, N. U., Prue Khyang, H. K., Prue Kheyang, H. A., Ching Khyang, M., and Chapola, J. (2015). Participatory Action Research and Researcher's Responsibilities: An Experience with an Indigenous Community. *International Journal of Social Research Methodology, 18*(6), 581–599. doi:10.1080/13645579.2014.927492.

Defazio, J. (2018). Teaching Compassionate Care: Nurse Educators' Perspectives. Retrieved from https://scholarship.shu.edu/cgi/viewcontent.cgi?article=3590&context=dissertations

Elsharkawy, A. (2017). *What is Critical Discourse Analysis (CDA)?* Paper presented at the Second Literary Linguistics Conference, Johannes Gutenberg-Universität Mainz. Retrieved from https://www.researchgate.net/publication/311713796_What_is_Critical_Discourse_Analysis_CDA

Erbil, D.G., and Kocabas, A. (2020). Flipping the 4th Grade Social Studies Course in a Cooperative Way: Effects on Academic Achievement and Motivation. *Studies Educational Evaluation,* 66.

Fatin, N., Jabar, A., and Yunus, K. (2017). Critical Discourse Analysis (CDA) as an Approach to the Analysis of Language. *Man in India, 97*(16).

Friesen, N. (2008). Critical Theory: Ideology Critique and the Myths of E-Learning. *Ubiquity*, *1*(2). doi:10.1145/1403922.1386860.

Fuchs, C. (2017). *The International Encyclopaedia of Political Communication* (1st ed.). New York: John Wiley & Sons.

Gomez-Lanier, L. (2018). Building Collaboration in the Flipped Classroom: A Case Study. *International Journal for the Scholarship of Teaching and Learning, 12*(2), 1–11.

Hackler, R. J. (2015). An Analysis of a BYOD Program in a School District. *Technical Library*. Retrieved from http://scholarworks.gvsu.edu/cistechlib/225

Harney, B. (2014). Critical Theory. *Encyclopedia of Management, 1*(1), 1–4. doi:10.1002/9781118785317.weom110042

Hunley, R. (2016). *Teacher and Student Perceptions on High School Science Flipped Classrooms: Educational Breakthrough or Media Hype?* (Doctor of Education), East Tennessee State University. Retrieved from https://dc.etsu.edu/cgi/viewcontent.cgi?article=4383&context=etd

Joyner. (2021). *8 Benefits of a Flipped Classroom.* [Online]. Retrieved from https://www.viewsonic.com/library/education/8-benefits-of-a-flipped-classroom/

Karabatak, S., and Polat, H. (2020). The Effects of the Flipped Classroom Model Designed According to the ARCS Motivation Strategies on the Students' Motivation and Academic Achievement Levels. *Education and Information Technologies*, *25*(3), 1475–1495. doi:10.1007/s10639-019-09985-1.

Kelly, M. (2020, March 27). *How to Facilitate Learning and Critical Thinking.* Retrieved from https://www.thoughtco.com/how-to-facilitate-learning-8390

Kirvan, R., Rakes, C., and Zamora, R. (2015). Flipping an Algebra Classroom: Analyzing, Modeling, and Solving Systems of Linear Equations. *Computers in the Schools, 32*(3), 201–223.

Kovid, R. K., and Kumar V. (Eds) (2022). *Cases on Emerging Markets Responses to the COVID-19 Pandemic.* Hershey, Pennsylvania, USA: IGI – Global Publications (ISBN13: 978-16-6843-504-5).

Kumar, A. (2014). *Bring Your Own Device (BYOD) Advantages and Disadvantages.* Retrieved from the Windows Club website https://www.thewindowsclub.com/bring-your-own-device-byod

Kumar, V., and Gupta G. (Eds) (2021). *Strategic Management During a Pandemic.* USA: Routledge, Taylor and Francis Group (ISBN 9780367646479).

Kumar, V., and Malhotra, G. (Eds) (2021). *Stakeholder Strategies for Reducing the Impact of Global Health Crises.* USA: IGI – Global Publications (ISBN13: 978-17-9987-495-9, DOI: 10.4018/978-1-7998-7495-9).

Kumar, V., and Nanda, P. (2020). Social Media as a Tool in Higher Education: A Pedagogical Perspective. In *Handbook of Research on Diverse Teaching Strategies for the Technology-Rich Classroom.* IGI Global, pp. 239–253 (ISBN 9781799802389).

Kumar, V., and Rewari, M. (2022). A Responsible Approach to Higher Education Curriculum Design. *International Journal of Educational Reform (IJER), 31*(4), 422–441.

Kumar, V., and Sharma, D. (2021). E-Learning Theories, Components and Cloud Computing Based Learning Platforms. *International Journal of Web-Based Learning and Teaching Technologies, 16*(3), 1–16.

Lake, D., and Wendland, J. (2018). Practical, Epistemological, and Ethical Challenges of Participatory Action Research: A Cross-Disciplinary Review of the Literature. *Journal of Higher Education Outreach and Engagement, 22*(3), 11–42.

Lee, M. (2018). Flipped Classroom as an Alternative Future Class Model: Implications of South Korea's Social Experiment. *Educational Technology Research and Development, 66*(3), 837–857. doi:10.1007/s11423-018-9587-9.

Lee, Y., and Martin, K. I. (2020). The Flipped Classroom In ESL Teacher Education: An Example from CALL. *Education and Information Technologies, 25*(4), 605–2633. doi:10.1007/s10639-019-10082-6.

Lo, C. K., and Hew, K. (2017). A Critical Review of Flipped Classroom Challenges in K-12 Education: Possible Solutions and Recommendations for Future Research. *Research and Practice in Technology Enhanced Learning, 12*(4). doi:10.1186/s41039-016-0044-2.

Machin-Mastromatteo, J. (2013). *Participatory Action Research and Information Literacy: Revising an Old New Hope for Research and Practice.* Springer: Estonia.

Majola, G., (2021). *SA ranks 136 worldwide for the cost of mobile data.* [Online] Retrieved from https://www.iol.co.za/business-report/companies/sa-ranks-136-worldwide-for-the-cost-of-mobile-data-e2536315-ed01-4eab-a0f5-ec101398a0d4, accessed 18 April 2022.

Marcano, P. (2018). *Critical Theory and Social Media: Alternatives and the New Sensibility.* (Honors). University of Pennsylvania: USA (United States of America). Retrieved from https://repository.upenn.edu/cgi/viewcontent.cgi?article=1034&context=ppe_honors

Mather-Pike, C. E. (2018). *A Participatory Action Research Project to Improve School Readiness.* Dissertation, School of Education University of KwaZulu-Natal, Pietermaritzburg, pp. 1–164. https://researchspace.ukzn.ac.za/bitstreams/1157d267-b7ae-4ce2-ac13-1666a3b43a46/download

McGrath, C., Palmgren, P. J., and Liljedahl, M. (2019). Twelve Tips for Conducting Qualitative Research Interviews. *Medical Teacher, 41*(9), 1002–1006. doi:10.1080/0142159X.2018.1497149.

Nichols, R. G., and Allen-Brown, V. (1996). Critical Theory and Educational Technology. *Handbook of Research for Educational Communications and Technology, 1*, 226–252.

O'Flaherty, J., and Phillips, C. (2015). The Use of Flipped Classrooms in Higher Education: A Scoping Review. *Internet and Higher Education, 25*, 85–95.

OECD. (2021). *The State of Higher Education: One Year into the COVID-19 Pandemic.* OECD Publishing. Retrieved from https://doi.org/10.1787/83c41957-en

Palinkas, L. A., Horwitz, S. M., Green, C. A., Wisdom, J. P., Duan, N., and Hoagwood, K. (2015). Purposeful Sampling for Qualitative Data Collection and Analysis in Mixed Method Implementation Research. *Administration and Policy in Mental Health, 42*(5), 533–544. doi:10.1007/s10488-013-0528-y.

Phillips, C. R., and Trainor, J. E. (2014). *Millennial Students and the Flipped Classroom.* Paper presented at the ASBBS Annual Conference, Las Vegas.

Pillay, A. (2018). Enabling Agency Through Participatory Action Research in an Honours-Level Postgraduate Class in a School of Education. *South African Journal of Higher Education, 32*(6), 469–482. doi: 10.20853/32-6-2940.

Regmi, K. (2017). Critical Discourse Analysis: Exploring Its Philosophical underpinnings. *Method(e)s: African Review of Social Sciences Methodology*, 2. doi:10.1080/23754745.2017.1354555.

Roland, J. (2015, October 7). Empowering teachers to implement technology-driven educational programs. Retrieved from https://www.iste.org/explore/Innovator-solutions/Empowering-teachers-to-implement-technology-driven-educational-programs

Roundy, L. (2016, November 30). What Is a Stakeholder in Education? – Definition & Examples. Retrieved from https://study.com/academy/lesson/what-is-a-stakeholder-in-education-definition-examples.html

Savides, M. (2017, June 6). *South African schools have 5,139 teachers who are unqualified or under-qualified.* Retrieved from https://www.timeslive.co.za/news/south-africa/2017-06-06-south-african-schools-have-5139-teachers-who-are-unqualified-or-under-qualified/

Schmidt, S. M., and Ralph, D. L. (2016). The Flipped Classroom: A Twist on Teaching. *Contemporary Issues in Education Research (CIER)*, *9*(1), 1–6. doi:10.19030/cier.v9i1.9544.

Sharma, D., and Kumar, V. (2017). A Framework for Collaborative and Convenient Learning on Cloud Computing Platforms. *International Journal of Web-Based Learning and Teaching Technologies (IJWLTT)*, *12*(2), 1–20.

Singh, J., and Kumar, V. (2022). Combating the Pandemic with ICT Based Learning Tools and Applications: A Case of Indian Higher Education. *International Journal of Virtual and Personal Learning Environments (IJVPLE) Platforms (IJVPLE)*, *12*(1), 1–21.

South African Government. (2019). *Education.* Retrieved from https://www.gov.za/about-sa/education

Sriwimon, L. (2017). Applying Critical Discourse Analysis as a Conceptual Framework for Investigating Gender Stereotypes in Political Media Discourse. *Kasetsart Journal of Social Sciences*, *38*(2), 136–142.

Stohr, C., Demaziere, C., and Adawi, T. (2020). The Polarizing Effect of the Online Flipped Classroom. *Computers & Education*, 147.

Subramaniam, S. R., and Muniandy, B. (2016). Concept and Characteristics of Flipped Classroom. *International Journal of Emerging Trends in Science and Technology, 3*(10), 4668–4670. doi:10.18535/ijetst/v3i10.01.

Talbert, R. (2019, April 4). How does flipped learning affect student motivation? *Flipped Learning.* Retrieved from https://medium.com/@roberttalbert/how-does-flipped-learning-affect-student-motivation-328e877a4f53

Thakare, R. (2018, April 25). All About Flipped Classrooms and Why Teachers Should Adopt The Concept Now. *eLearning Industry.* Retrieved from https://elearningindustry.com/flipped-classrooms-why-teachers-adopt-concept-now

Todd, M. (2016, December 7). *Methods in Action: Participatory Action Research.* Retrieved from https://connection.sagepub.com/blog/sage-connection/2016/12/07/methods-in-action-participatory-action-research/

Unal, A., Unal, Z., and Bodur, Y. (2021). Using Flipped Classroom in Middle Schools: Teachers' Perceptions. *Journal of Research in Education*, 30(2), 90–112.

van Alten, D., Phielix, C., Janssen, J., and Kester, L. (2019). Effects of Flipping the Classroom on Learning Outcomes and Satisfaction: A Meta-Analysis. *Educational Research Review, 28*, 1–18.

VanDeWeghe, R. (2009). *Engaged Learning*. SAGE: United States of America.
Vandeyar, T. (2015). *Policy intermediaries and the reform of e-Education in South Africa*. Retrieved from https://repository.up.ac.za/bitstream/handle/2263/45369/Vandeyar_Policy_2015.pdf;jsessionid=2358D10D0E66756705EB980F8134DBC8?sequence=1, accessed 10 March 2022.
Wainwright, A. (2012, September 21). 20 Pros and Cons of implementing BYOD in schools. Retrieved from https://www.securedgenetworks.com/blog/20-pros-and-cons-of-implementing-byod-in-schools
Wei, X., Cheng, I., Chen, N., Yang, X., Liu, Y., Dong, Y., and Kinshuk. (2020). Effect of the Flipped Classroom on the Mathematics Performance of Middle School Students. *Educational Technology Research and Development*, *68*(3), 1461–1484. doi:10.1007/s11423-020-09752-x.
Winter, J. W. (2018). Performance and Motivation in a Middle School Flipped Learning Course. *TechTrends*, *62*(2), 176–183. doi:10.1007/s11528-017-0228-7.
Yilmaz, R. (2017). Exploring the Role of E-Learning Readiness on Student Satisfaction and Motivation in Flipped Classroom. *Computers in Human Behavior*, *70*, 251–260. doi:10.1016/j.chb.2016.12.085.

4 Challenges in conducting practical courses during Covid-19

Shafila Bansal, Santosh Bhukal, Shivangi Jain, and Parul

Introduction

Covid-19, a global public health emergency as declared by the World Health Organization, caused havoc in almost all areas of life, including the way we educate. Educating and training students became the most talked-of topic as the cases were surging day by day (Pokhrel and Chhetri, 2021; Kumar and Malhotra, 2021). When schools and other educational institutions were shut and nothing was coming to normalcy, teaching and training to the students were employed online that avoid face-to-face meetings. As a result, e-learning practice emerged as the most accessible means for education (Kumar and Gupta, 2021). This effort marked an abrupt shift in the lecture delivery method, from offline to online (Bhardwaj and Kumar, 2022). Educational environment comprehends the institution's infrastructure, teacher's behaviour, behaviour of fellow students, team work, and the methodology used for teaching, having a significant impact on the effectiveness of curriculum and educational outcomes (Kumar and Sharma, 2021). In online classes, learning and understanding reduced significantly for the subjects involving physical description and those which require a healthy discussion. This approach of learning works well for theoretical courses where delivering content may easily impart knowledge; however, for developing the practical skills, online mode has certain limitations. Learning through online mode denies the valuable hands-on experience to laboratory's complicated and expensive instruments and machines. So, during the pandemic, courses which required practical learning were among the most affected courses. E-learning forced the educators to impart practical knowledge *via* video demonstrations or verbal instructions that lack the physical performance of experiments by the students affecting their efficiency negatively to perform well, be it in labs, hospitals, or any practical demanding field. For instance, secondary chemistry teachers of Slovakia were using various online methods viz. descriptions writing assisted with photos, video-recordings, and live interactions to demonstrate the lab experiments, but the students still complained of missing physical experiments. Although some of them performed experiments at home, those experiments did not work as a satisfactory alternative for

DOI: 10.4324/9781003491712-4

lab experimentation at school. They did not find online experimentation as "cool" as lab experiments and also missed the live interaction with their teacher and classmates. Nevertheless, writing descriptions with photos was the most useful method for them for better understanding of virtual experiments (Babinčáková and Bernard, 2020). In Pace University, New York City, a comprehensive lab manual, Microsoft PowerPoint slides with voice-over recordings and YouTube videos links were used for demonstrating online practicals. Student participants were satisfied, particularly with the videos for illustration of lab practicals as they felt like they were performing the experiments themselves, though, a synchronous approach of delivering information where they could directly listen to their mentor was preferred (Mojica and Upmacis, 2022). Students of Portland State University in the United States struggled constantly to meet the skill-based learning in virtual classes (Hensen et al., 2020). Learners of the University of British Columbia Canada believed that e-learning cannot be compared favourably to a traditional lab experience, yet livestream methods were tremendously a better approach for a synchronous virtual laboratory (Petillion and Stephen McNeil, 2021). Due to the worldwide lockdown, some educational institutions had to shun their practical classes completely as their curriculum demanded practical knowledge with practice (Suart et al., 2021). As per report of May 27, 2020, research activities at the University of York, UK, were completely stopped. A similar situation was reported by the Indian Institute of Science, Bangalore on June 22, 2020 and Universidad de Cádiz/IMDEA Nanoscience, Spain on June 24, 2020 (Sandhu et al., 2021). In the United States, in March 2020, at Harvard University, research in arts and science was halted for at least 6–8 weeks. Similarly, in Tufts University, researchers were asked to immediately ramp down research in laboratories for at least two weeks. As per data collected by market research firm BioInformatics from Arlington County in the United States on April 2, 2020, 48% of academic and pharma/biotech labs (out of those responded to the survey) were completely closed for at least 2.5 weeks initially. Another 39% were operating with reduced capacity, and only 13% of labs were fully functioning (Samantha Black, n.d.). At Argonne National Laboratory, a US Department of Energy facility, during March 2020, 85% (approximately 3,000) of the workforce were teleworking, and only fewer than 100 were allowed to work on-site. However, during the first lockdown, a significant regional difference for accessing the labs was also reported, where labs in the United States, the UK, India, and Spain were not accessible in contrast to Singapore and Japan, where the researchers were allowed to access the labs within 1–2 months of the first lockdown (Sandhu et al., 2021). Hence, the hands-on practice of laboratory experiments was missed by most of the pupils during the lockdown period.

Though the educational institutions along with teachers and parents tried their best efforts to ensure continuous learning of students even during the tough time of pandemic, but digital, cultural, and structural gaps among learners posed a huge hurdle in attaining e-education (Bhardwaj and Kumar,

2023). Digital divide viz. disparate access to digital resources, different digital skills, and dissimilar digital tools uses have strong inferences in attaining e-learning. Even though, the usage of digital technologies is nearly universal in developed countries, however, social class is a strong determinant of digital inequalities (Kumar and Nanda, 2019). For example, during the lockdown period, in France approximately one out of five working-class families did not have individual access to the internet as compared to one out of 20 of rich families (Goudeau et al., 2021). Hence, those from working-class families are more vulnerable when education relies on comprehensive use of digital gadgets instead of on face-to-face learning.

Even if the digital divide would not be there, cultural divide viz. unequal academic knowledge along with skills and disparities in nature for self-studies affected their learning during the lockdown. Again, it was seen that pupils of upper middle-class families were better prepared for their continuation of education even during the pandemic, as they were more familiar with technology and skills required to attain virtual learning. In comparison to working-class families, students of upper-middle class were found to be more independent and autonomous, both traits are much valued in school culture and became even more important in lockdown (Goudeau et al., 2021).

Also, the unequal support from schools, structural divide, impacted the learners' e-education attaining capability. Literature shows that rather than providing additional support to the vulnerable students of underprivileged families, schools preferred to invest material and human resources in supporting those from the upper/middle class. In England, to illustrate, the upper/middle-class parents revealed taking benefits from online lectures and videoconferencing with the mentors more regularly than those of the working class (Andrew et al., 2020a). Furthermore, active support from schools like private tutoring and frequent chatting with the educator was also reported by richest households (64%) than the poorest (47%) (Goudeau et al., 2021).

Along with the students, teachers also faced problems in conducting virtual lectures – theoretical as well as practical. Even though they were familiar with the technology operations for enhanced learning, yet were not ready for such utter shift. Academicians of all streams – schools, colleges, polytechnics, and even of kindergarten – were suddenly expected to teach online effectively. The teaching quality of those from science, research, and information technology background was tremendously affected as they were not able to use science laboratory facilities and computer lab for demonstrating the practical work. Also, teachers hailing from different cultures were having tough time during the pandemic, as in most cultures, women are primarily responsible for caregiving and household chores (Atkinson and Hall, 2009). So, for women teachers, working from home was more challenging due to a lack of support with their own children's care and elder care along with daily maintenance responsibilities like cooking and cleaning (Wallengren-Lynch et al., 2021).

There are plenty of in-depth things people are unaware about this new method of teaching. This chapter gives an account of cumulative information of challenges faced by the educators and learners of each sector and group in holding up practical classes in different resource-strained situations. It also gives an insight about best practices taken up worldwide by the governments and institutions to cope up with those challenges.

Major common challenges

Unequal access to digital resources

The Covid-19 pandemic brings a great transition in education system where e-learning is promoted to a greater extent. However, everyone has not been able to adapt to this change due to a substantial inequality in the access to technology in various regions addressing a new crisis to education system. During the lockdown, the problem of lack of technology and educational materials in the absence of physical classes was faced by many countries. Higher educational institutions, colleges, and universities had fairly adopted and managed with the uninvited situation. Unfortunately, schools (primary and secondary), particularly in central and eastern Europe were not equipped with required software, hardware, and skilled staff for holding online classes as they never believed e-learning as a valuable alternative to physical classes (Babinčáková and Bernard, 2020). In some regions, where parents were unable to provide educational support to their children had almost no means of doing so. Although learning crisis existed before Covid-19, currently, education is in a deep and increasingly divisive crisis. In 2020 in the UK, for example, 20% of schoolchildren availing free meals were not having access to a computer as compared to 7% of other children (Green, 2020). In 2021, in the United States, 41% of working-class families did not have a laptop/desktop computer, and 43% were not having a broadband in comparison to 8% and 7% of upper-/middle-class households respectively (Emily A. Vogels, 2021). A comparable digital gap was apparent among lower- and higher-income nations (McBurnie et al., 2020). In India in 2018, for instance, only 10.7% of families owned a digital device (Ahmed and Siddique, 2020), while in Pakistan in 2020, 68.4% teachers of higher education did not own a laptop, and 26.31% did not have access to the internet. Also, just having a desktop and connection to the internet were not suffice in ensuring e-learning, as most of the study materials sent by the mentors needed to be printed, and thereby an access to a printer was also required. Moreover, learners from families having one shared computer faced tough time in acquiring online education in comparison to those where each member had their own desktop. Additionally, during the lockdown period, the availability of a suitable learning place was more likely assured by upper-/middle-class families to their children than their working-class counterparts (Goudeau et al., 2021). As per reports, in the Netherlands, learners from working-class households had less space to study than upper/middle-class children (Bol, 2020). In the UK, a survey of around 4,000 participants showed that more than 50% of primary school children of the poorest families did not have their own study space than rich families (Andrew et al., 2020b). Hence the school closures had huge repercussions for the continuity of education of students because of such disparities. In Bangladesh, for instance, the time spent on education during lockdown reduced by 80%. A similar trend was noticed in Kenya and Burkina Faso with 22% and 50% children engaging in e-learning, respectively. Also, in Ghana, 26–32% of children spent no time at all on education during the pandemic period (Goudeau et al., 2021).

Technical issues

The internet has made it possible for everyone to connect with far-flung distant areas. However, one of the major issues with online learning during the lockdown was the dearth of efficient and stable internet connections. For many students as well as teachers, just logging in for a class itself was a big challenge, as the usual available internet connection was with low bandwidth (Ferri et al., 2020; Seun et al., 2020). In traditional classes, the textbooks are probably the main source of information to both instructors and students. But online teaching is different, where the basic tools used by teachers while conducting theoretical as well as practical sessions were photos/pictures of experiments with a description or recorded videoclips. The virtual education has made the role of a teacher more complex and hence increased the workload, as they have to gather, formulate, and present the information through the internet (Adedoyin and Soykan, 2020; Adnan, 2020). Teachers of Slovakia used photos with description and video recordings to explain lab experiments with their students (Babinčáková and Bernard, 2020). Mentors of Pace University, New York City, shared lab manuals, Microsoft PowerPoint slides with voice-over recordings, and YouTube videos links with students for the demonstration of general chemistry laboratory course online (Mojica and Upmacis, 2022). To demonstrate organic chemistry lectures, pre-recorded laboratory video lectures were shared with students by the teachers of University of British Columbia, Canada (Petillion and Stephen McNeil, 2021). However, technology and time constraints enabled them to pick one of the various techniques that they consider the most appropriate for each experiment without considering the level of understanding of the students. Furthermore, the slow or poor internet connection was a major trouble for the learners to download high-quality videos and somewhere even pictures.

Uninterrupted power supply was another problem that played havoc with the online education in many regions. In developing countries, power outages are very common that interrupt the online education severely even if one is having high internet bandwidth. Many countries were facing a lack of computers- and mobile phones-related services also.

Challenges faced by students

No hands-on practice for practical courses

The Covid-19 pandemic led students to a situation where they were clueless about their return to universities to start with lab experiments (Singh and Kumar, 2022). Initially, they were happily spending time at homes, but after a specific time, when everything came to a standstill and they were not able to hold lab experiments, mentors and students became anxious.

Physical labs are essential for training students of particularly science and engineering streams with necessary skills for real-world problem resolving, and such studies cannot be replaced by remote learning completely. Many study courses are designed with an objective of imparting theoretical and practical knowledge to the learners. The practical aspects are specifically developed to emphasize experiments, to observe the synthesizing conditions, and to transmit the lifelong skills of lab practices. During the pandemic, the virtual mode of education was quickly adopted by educational institutions; however, this approach does not provide complete guidance for developing practical laboratory skills even though it offers content and oversees some processes.

A working laboratory environment often involves the use of many kinds of expensive and complicated instruments. Nevertheless, operating under the e-learning mode prevents students from gaining valuable hands-on experience and appreciating what it means to immerse oneself in such environment. During the pandemic, the mentees were worried about the completion of degrees without completing hands-on experiments (Li et al., 2021). Experimental work that could be easily performed with the existing chemical and instrumental facilities was less affected, however, those where reagents or specimens were required to be purchased became difficult due to restricted logistics. Also, the major problem was encountered by practical courses demanding the use of equipment facility not owned by personal labs which required the students to go to other places or laboratories to perform experiments that was majorly disrupted because of restricted personnel movement.

Biology students lost strains of various microorganisms or insects they were working on before the pandemic owing to worldwide lockdown (Li et al., 2021). Reordering the same was laborious because of transportation control.

Hence, this transition from face-to-face learning to e-learning proved to be more challenging for science courses as compared to non-science fields due to involvement of experimental work. Practical courses encountered significant challenges as the time devoted to practical classes was reduced resulting in less experimental proficiency among students. According to a survey conducted on students in Slovakia, 46% of the learners complained of missing lab experiments in e-learning (Babinčáková and Bernard, 2020). However, teachers made efforts in designing experiments in such a way that they could be easily performed at home with the available material; still students were not satisfied with this mode of experimentation.

PhD students were not able to conduct their ongoing experiments virtually. Many of the partially completed experiments remained pending because of halt in their further analysis. For instance, a student working on nanoparticles required to conduct the full characterization of the synthesized nanoparticles which includes the involvement of sophisticated instruments like scanning electronic microscope, transmisson elctron microscope, x-ray diffraction. Lack of advance instruments at one's home has adversely impact the progress of research during pandemic. As result, many of them were forced to apply for extension of their PhD for 1–2 years, which further will affect their career in future.

Students of dental education also faced the issues of personal contact with the people as their curriculum demands physical interactions and clinical skill training. Although e-learning served as an alternative method of teaching during tough times of the pandemic, many students in School of Dentistry, National Taiwan University believed that face-to-face education in physical classrooms with hands-on practical classes is mandatory for effective learning (Yu-Fong Chang et al., 2021).

During the pandemic, medical students lost the access to practical material including pro-sections, pathology specimens, models, skeletons, and to dissection laboratories. Due to which there were limited or less hands-on experience opportunities for them in pre-clinical years which compelled them to struggle later in the clinical years. In medical practice, clinical experience where students have to assist in surgeries along with other medical procedures and physical interaction with the patients is extremely important. But the pandemic disrupted those practices, which affected the acquaintance and behaviour of future doctors severely and hence, the quality of healthcare. A medical university in Ireland tried to mitigate the risks of losing experimental proficiency by providing recorded video lectures to their pharmacy students, but those video lectures cannot replace traditional experiments (Strawbridge et al., 2021). A study conducted by Mahdy (Mahdy, 2020) involving 1,392 participants from 92 countries revealed a severe impact on academic performance of most of the participants (96.7%) of different subjects, particularly students from medical and dental backgrounds and radiology, as these courses include practical sessions. Learners of veterinary science also faced profound problems while attending online sessions as clinical settings and personal contact with the animals were lacking in e-learning. So conducting practical courses is a major challenge in online education in medical science as well.

Chemistry students also encountered obstacles to grasp virtual lab-related activities. The main pedagogical constraint was for those who carried out experiments at homes without the supervision of lab instructors. They were not able to perform experiments with enough accuracy to obtain the meaningful data and devoid of requisite lab techniques and skills as traditional lab environment cannot be imitated at homes.

Engineering schooling is among other challenging areas that entail an amalgamation of theoretical teaching with coordinated lab instructions. A survey conducted by Ghannam (Ghasem and Ghannam, 2021) on UAEU chemical engineering students shows the intense difficulties met by them to accomplish their graduation projects during the pandemic period. As project work demanded the requisite teamwork, technical discussions with academic guides, coordinators, and colleagues which they had to coordinate virtually were a strenuous task for them as compared to the face-to-face approach.

Above all, when partial opening of universities was declared, learners experienced serious issues as they had to resume the ongoing research projects. Educational institutions were expected to prepare by restricted movements, intense cleaning, supply of PPE kits, installation of protective shielding, dispensing stations, and maintenance of minimum two-metres social distances while performing experiments in labs. Students coming for research were to undergo daily electronic sign-in and health check-up procedures to avoid the spread of Covid-19, and if anyone was suspected he/she had to quarantine for a specific period, then that was another challenge for them.

Challenges for teachers

Designing online practical sessions

The Covid-19 pandemic forced the educators to shift from physical classes to online. For science subjects like chemistry, physics, and biology, experiments play a marvellous role in learning. A science teacher was comparatively in a difficult situation, as he also had to design science practical for online point of view along with the preparation of theoretical lectures (Babinčáková and Bernard, 2020). They were challenged to organize live-video lectures while performing experiments to impart complete knowledge of experiments to the students, which was difficult especially for a non-technical person. Not every teacher at each level of education was prepared for this situation, still several of them tried to switch to online classes. However, many of the journals, search engines, and platforms provided free access of their e-resources to help the educators during the trying time along with holding of myriad of webinars to support them.

Science cannot be educated by just readings and discussions but through the integration of minds-on and hands-on experience. Creating virtual classrooms in a way that maintains e-learning momentum considering the factor that students and educators cannot interact physically was a huge challenge for teachers, especially for those who were not familiar with the technology.

Universal Testing Machine (UTM) is one of the important experimental hardware in mechanics of solids (Achuthan et al., 2021). However, the mechanics teachers were challenged to design UTM experiments in remote labs for smooth conduct of virtual practical and for better understanding of learners. A report presented by Wisanti (Wisanti et al., 2021) on teachers of Indonesia shows the difficulties faced by them for implementation of practical work and concept explanation. The study reveals that the problem of concept explanation was overcome by them easily. But conducting practical class virtually remained a main issue for them till the schools were closed resulting which, most of them chose to flip practical work with another task, and only few teachers of them actually used online platforms to implement the practical work.

A data of chemistry teachers collected by Shidiq et al. (2021) discloses that educators tried numerous technology platforms for imparting learning among students. Some of them attempted to alternate the physical lab activities with lab-work multimedia, but physical laboratory experience cannot be replaced by multimedia and could not provide the requisite skills to the students during the lockdown. Since everybody was clueless about how long the pandemic will last, so to continue learning, chemistry teachers were too greatly burdened to design chemistry lab work experiments virtually as learning chemistry is indispensable from lab work activities. For improved knowledge of chemical's micro representation, students have to engage in lab work experiments, which was unfortunately hampered by the worldwide lockdown.

For engineering educators also, creating an artificial e-lab environment to deliver almost all basic tools to the students was a major challenge as experiments are the integral part of engineering for learning the fundamental concepts. So the mentors from various courses encountered the hindrance of holding online lab experiments. They were also challenged to have an innovative thinking and to use the up-to-date material.

Time constraints

Time constraint was another aspect in managing practical classes online. The experiments which need a record of observations for periodic and longer durations in the experimental atmospheric conditions were greatly absent in virtual labs. If anyhow the practical was being performed online by teachers, the technical glitch took humungous time to settle. This is the reason that many educators preferred to skip those time-demanding experiments. Many of them tried to take observations before commencing the class and showed the final result of experiments to the students, but that did not help as students could not witnesses the actual experiment. Courses needing 24×7 surveillance by guides were significantly affected as teachers couldn't manage to keep an eye on everyone at once. This ultimately affected the quality of education worldwide, where the students in future would be less experienced and less keen to perform their work on ground level.

Best practices to take up the challenges

Owing to the spread of the Covid-19 virus, face-to-face academic activities were completely suspended worldwide, implementing alternative ways of teaching (Kovid and Kumar, 2022). Then, online approach of teaching and learning became popular, and many educational institutions implemented it almost successfully. Theory classes were easily conducted online, but the challenge was to operate the laboratory classes online (Kumar and Malhotra, 2021). While operating online, one would not be able to have hands-on exposure to complicated instruments and machines and appreciate the delicate nature of being absorbed in lab environment. Therefore, to achieve learning outcomes whilst maintaining a high-quality educational experience, a critical approach to design online lab-based practical experiments is important (Kumar and Rewari, 2022). For developing lab experiments, to have a feel of real experiments, it is important to incorporate photographs and data of real equipment, showing best results of real experiments and connecting to real industrial world (Endean, 2012).

Virtual labs (VL), remote control labs (RL), and video-based labs are best alternative choices for e-learning (Zhai et al., 2012). VL is a laboratory operated using computer software with real laboratory look-like equipment (Sulistiowati et al., 2013). It can be used to replace those traditional laboratory experiments which are expensive and unsafe. VL is characterized by safe, easy operation and availability, low cost, high efficiency, and ease of sharing resources. Through VL, there is privilege of repeating the experiments again and again for getting more accuracy and precision to deeply understand the concept (Usman et al., 2021).

RL can also be used for performing online experiments. RL is an experiment that is physically away from students but can be operated and controlled remotely via the internet. However, RL is comparatively new and needs more advanced expensive equipment, so that it is not easy to apply in learning globally, especially in developing nations.

Video-based laboratories, which give a step-by-step overview of real experiments so that students can visualize the whole procedure through a video, were commonly used by most of the institutions during the Covid-19 pandemic. For instance, at ECUST Shanghai, approximately 160 online experiments of science, engineering, computer were already designed back in 2012 for delivering online education (Endean, 2012).

Among the possible online methods for holding experimental classes, VL is an ideal option that can overcome hurdles in accessing laboratories by replacing traditional labs (Usman et al., 2021). It has the ability to strengthen the creativity, critical thinking, problem-solving skills, conceptual understanding, perceptual interest, and motivation (Padilla, 1986). The importance of such laboratories became more evident during worldwide lockdown, as many educational institution shifted to online and used VL to impart necessary skills in students for their future employment in industry and academia

(Vasiliadou, 2020; X. Zhai, 2021). Studies have shown that, in India, the usage of virtual labs had increased from 1.35 million to 49.6 million during the Covid-19 pandemic. Also, earlier it was used for computer domain only, but during the pandemic its use was obvious in almost all the domains (Choppella and Pillutla, 2021). Hence, in general, VL has been accepted as a viable substitute of traditional labs in inculcating practical skills in students, particularly of STEM (Science, Technology, Engineering and Maths) courses (Achuthan et al., 2020; Gamage et al., 2020; Stegman, 2021).

In India, The Ministry of Human Resource Department, Government of India, has started VLs under the scheme "National Mission on Education Through ICT". The main objective of this scheme is to facilitate the academic institutions a remote access to operate lab experiments at different levels. These VLs include video lecturers, animations, and online resources related to the experiments. The Amrita University, India, is also providing approximately 211 VL experiments in biotechnology (*Virtual Labs Project Launched by MHRD under NMEICT – DigitalLEARNING Magazine – Elets Digital Learning*, n.d.). Other Indian educational institutions viz. The International Institute of Information Technology – Hyderabad, Indian Institutes of Technologies, College of Engineering, Pune, NITK, and Dayalbagh University are also participating in developing VLs experiments related to STEM courses. Not only for students, but trainings on VLs for faculty were also been initiated at various levels (Kapilan et al., 2021). In the country, virtual labs like OLabs were designed for high school students consisting of more than 173 science labs, and approximately 10,000 mentors across the country have been trained (Chandrashekhar et al., 2020). OLabs allow the users to repeat the experiments and are completely free. The advent of lockdown has increased the total number of users for OLabs by 93.92% between April–December 2019 and April–December 2020 (Pantina et al., 2018).

In Open University of Sri Lanka, a "virtual chemistry lab space" (VCLS) was created to facilitate learning in lockdown among undergraduate students, where 70% of learners believed that VCLS was helpful while 82% of the students indicated their good use in future as well (Wijenayaka and Iqbal, 2021). To convey the requisite lab skills related to the science courses to high school students, The University of Toronto integrated short campus visits and Labster-enabled VLs (Callaghan et al., 2021).

VL can be the future

VL can be used as a replacement of traditional lab in future as well. VL enables autonomous, interactive, and collaborative learning of experiments. Further, these labs overcome the need of space for conducting traditional experimental work (Gamage et al., 2020; G. Zhai et al., 2012). Another remote lab "Virtual Instrument Systems In Reality" can also be a good choice for delivering practical knowledge (Odeh et al., 2015). It comprises a web interface, measurement server, equipment server, and switching matrix. The web interface allows one to do same activities as if he/she is in real lab. The measurement server acts the role of virtual instructor which controls the commands passing from the web interface to equipment server to prevent hazardous circuit designs and subsequently the instruments. The commands from the measurement server are passed to the equipment server which are further executed on real instruments. The switching matrix performs the connections between components and instruments that the user has carried out in web interface.

The major drawback of these online labs is the lack of real hands-on experience of techniques and equipment. Further, the mentees are not able to attain the experience of analysing and interpreting uncharacteristic or incorrect data. Also, it is very important to have prior right knowledge and access to technology to operate the VLs before entering the learning stage. In Rio de Janeiro, for example, an attempt to online chemistry classes was affected due to lack of required technology like mobile phones, computers, laptops, among learners of lower socio-economic strata, inadequate training to the faculty handling the abrupt shift in platform and pedagogy, and the limitations of the platform itself (Soares et al., 2020).

Conclusion

The conversion of physical classes to distance learning was challenging for all the courses, particularly the subjects involving practical sessions. Experimental observations and evidences are the base to answers of most of the questions in STEM courses. Hands-on experience is one of the situational factors often considered as the awakening point for the interest and motivation of the students to study science, and it can enhance students' scientific knowledge. But, worldwide complete lockdown owing to the spread of the Covid-19 pandemic forced teachers to conduct experiments online to continue the learnings of students. While holding online classes, many serious issues were faced by both students and teachers. Unequal access of digital resources and technical issues were among the mutual problems confronted by both mentors and mentees in succeeding e-learning. Students were particularly affected by the lack of hands-on practices of experiments and among all, students of STEM courses were greatly challenged. Instructors met the hurdles related to designing of virtual experiments and performing the time-consuming experiments online. Online methods such as virtual labs, remote control labs, and video-based labs were developed at various levels to conduct practical classes. However, virtual labs were the most popular substitute of traditional laboratories for most educational institutions worldwide. Further studies have shown that mentees have indicated VLs as replacement of traditional labs in future; however, these are associated with the limitation of lack of hands-on experience of laboratory techniques and equipment.

References

Achuthan, K., Nedungadi, P., Kolil, V. K., Diwakar, S., and Raman, R. (2020). Innovation Adoption and Diffusion of Virtual Laboratories. *International Journal of Online and Biomedical Engineering*, *16*(9), 4–25. doi:10.3991/ijoe.v16i09.11685.

Achuthan, K., Raghavan, D., Shankar, B., Francis, S. P., and Kolil, V. K. (2021). Impact of Remote Experimentation, Interactivity and Platform Effectiveness on Laboratory Learning Outcomes. *International Journal of Educational Technology in Higher Education*, *18*(1). doi: 10.1186/s41239-021-00272-z.

Adedoyin, O. B., and Soykan, E. (2020). Covid-19 Pandemic and Online Learning: The Challenges and Opportunities. *Interactive Learning Environments*, 1–13. doi: 10.1080/10494820.2020.1813180.

Adnan, M. (2020). Online Learning Amid the COVID-19 Pandemic: Students Perspectives. *Journal of Pedagogical Sociology and Psychology*, *1*(2), 45–51. doi:10.33902/jpsp.2020261309.

Ahmed, S., and Siddique, M. Z. (2020). Disparity in access to quality education and the digital divide. In *Ideas for India*, pp. 1–9. Retrieved from https://www.ideasforindia.in/topics/human-development/disparity-in-access-to-quality-education-and-the-digital-divide.html

Andrew, A., Cattan, S., Costa Dias, M., Farquharson, C., Kraftman, L., Krutikova, S., Phimister, A., and Sevilla, A. (2020a). Inequalities in Children's Experiences of Home Learning During the COVID-19 Lockdown in England*. *Fiscal Studies*, *41*(3), 653–683. doi:10.1111/1475-5890.12240.

Andrew, A., Cattan, S., Costa Dias, M., Farquharson, C., Kraftman, L., Krutikova, S., Phimister, A., and Sevilla, A. (2020b). Inequalities in Children's Experiences of Home Learning During the COVID-19 Lockdown in England*. *Fiscal Studies*, 41(3), 653–683. doi:10.1111/1475-5890.12240.

Atkinson, C., and Hall, L. (2009). The Role of Gender in Varying Forms of Flexible Working. *Gender, Work and Organization*, *16*(6), 650–666. doi:10.1111/j.1468-0432.2009.00456.x.

Babinčáková, M., and Bernard, P. (2020). Online Experimentation During Covid-19 Secondary School Closures: Teaching Methods and Student Perceptions. *Journal of Chemical Education*, *97*(9), 3295–3300. doi:10.1021/acs.jchemed.0c00748.

Bhardwaj, A., and Kumar, V. (2022). A Framework for Enhancing Privacy in Online Collaboration. *International Journal of Electronic Security and Digital Forensics (IJESDF)*, *14*(4), 413–432.

Bhardwaj, A., and Kumar, V. (2023). Social Media as an Enabler to Combat Misinformation, In *Pandemics in the Age of Social Media: Information and Misinformation in Developing Nations*. Routledge: New York (USA), pp. 1–15.

Bol, T. (2020). Inequality in homeschooling during the Corona crisis in the Netherlands. First results from the LISS Panel. *SocArXiv Papers*, 1–21.

Callaghan, N. I., Khaira, S., Ouyang, A., Cadavid, J. L., Chang, H. H., Co, I. L., Diep, P., Ivanov, N., Li, G., Li, N. T., Tran-Nguyen, N., Smith, C., Davenport Huyer, L., and Kilkenny, D. M. (2021). Discovery: Virtual Implementation of Inquiry-Based Remote Learning for Secondary STEM Students During the COVID-19 Pandemic. *Biomedical Engineering Education*, *1*(1), 87–94. doi:10.1007/s43683-020-00014-z.

Chandrashekhar, P., Prabhakaran, M., Gutjahr, G., Raman, R., and Nedungadi, P. (2020). Teacher Perception of OLabs Pedagogy. *Advances in Intelligent Systems and Computing, 1027*, 419–426. doi:10.1007/978-981-32-9343-4_33.

Choppella, V., and Pillutla, R. S. (2021). *The Impact of Virtual Labs during the Pandemic Period*. Retrieved from file:///D:/Book chapter covid/Chapters with M.Sc.-Students/References/shivangi/India.mhtml

Endean, M. (2012). Online practical work for science and engineering students – a collaborative scoping activity between the UK Open University and East China University of Science and Technology Contact: Mark Endean Findings. August.

Ferri, F., Grifoni, P., and Guzzo, T. (2020). Online Learning and Emergency Remote Teaching: Opportunities and Challenges in Emergency Situations. *Societies*, *10*(4), 1–18. doi:10.3390/soc10040086.

Gamage, K. A. A., Wijesuriya, D. I., Ekanayake, S. Y., Rennie, A. E. W., Lambert, C. G., and Gunawardhana, N. (2020). Online Delivery of Teaching and Laboratory Practices: Continuity of University Programmes During COVID-19 Pandemic. *Education Sciences*, *10*(10), 1–9. doi:10.3390/educsci10100291.

Ghasem, N., and Ghannam, M. (2021). Challenges, Benefits & Drawbacks of Chemical Engineering On-Line Teaching During Covid-19 Pandemic. *Education for Chemical Engineers*, *36*, 107–114. doi:10.1016/j.ece.2021.04.002.

Goudeau, S., Sanrey, C., Stanczak, A., Manstead, A., and Darnon, C. (2021). Why Lockdown and Distance Learning During the COVID-19 Pandemic Are Likely to Increase the Social Class Achievement Gap. *Nature Human Behaviour*, *5*(10), 1273–1281. doi:10.1038/s41562-021-01212-7.

Green, F. (2020). *Schoolwork in lockdown: new evidence on the epidemic of educational poverty*. London: Professor of Work and Education Economics, UCL Institute of Education. Executive Summary, pp. 1–20.

Hensen, C., Glinowiecka-Cox, G., and Barbera, J. (2020). Assessing Differences Between Three Virtual General Chemistry Experiments and Similar Hands-On Experiments. *Journal of Chemical Education*, *97*(3), 616–625. doi:10.1021/acs.jchemed.9b00748.

Kapilan, N., Vidhya, P., and Gao, X. Z. (2021). Virtual Laboratory: A Boon to the Mechanical Engineering Education During Covid-19 Pandemic. *Higher Education for the Future*, *8*(1), 31–46. doi:10.1177/2347631120970757.

Kovid, R. K., and Kumar, V. (Eds) (2022). *Cases on Emerging Markets Responses to the COVID-19 Pandemic*. Hershey, Pennsylvania, USA: IGI – Global Publications (ISBN13: 978-16-6843-504-5, doi: 10.4018/978-1-6684-3504-5).

Kumar, V., and Gupta, G. (Eds) (2021). *Strategic Management During a Pandemic*. London: Routledge, Taylor & Francis Group: USA (ISBN 9780367646479).

Kumar, V., and Malhotra, G. (Eds) (2021). *Stakeholder Strategies for Reducing the Impact of Global Health Crises*. Hershey, Pennsylvania, USA: IGI – Global Publications (ISBN13: 978-17-9987-495-9, DOI: 10.4018/978-1-7998-7495-9).

Kumar, V., and Nanda, P. (2019). Social Media in Higher Education: A Framework for Continuous Engagement. *International Journal of Information and Communication Technology Education (IJICTE)*, *15*(1), 109–120.

Kumar, V., and Rewari, M. (2022). A Responsible Approach to Higher Education Curriculum Design. *International Journal of Educational Reform (IJER)*, *31*(4), 422–441.

Kumar, V., and Sharma, D. (2021). E-Learning Theories, Components and Cloud Computing Based Learning Platforms. *International Journal of Web-Based Learning and Teaching Technologies*, *16*(3), 1–16.

Li, H., Zhang, D., Liang, B., Zhong, L., Cao, Y., and Shen, J. (2021). Challenges for Graduate Students' Mentors During COVID-19 Pandemic. *Biochemistry and Molecular Biology Education*, *49*(6), 841–842. doi:10.1002/bmb.21568.

Mahdy, M. A. A. (2020). The Impact of COVID-19 Pandemic on the Academic Performance of Veterinary Medical Students. *Frontiers in Veterinary Science*, 7(October), 1–8. doi:10.3389/fvets.2020.594261.

McBurnie, C., Adam, T., and Kaye, T. (2020). Is There Learning Continuity During the Covid-19 Pandemic? A Synthesis of the Emerging Evidence. *Journal of Learning for Development*, 7(3), 485–493.

Mojica, E. R. E., and Upmacis, R. K. (2022). Challenges Encountered and Students' Reactions to Practices Utilized in a General Chemistry Laboratory Course During the COVID-19 Pandemic. *Journal of Chemical Education*, *99*(2), 1053–1059. doi:10.1021/acs.jchemed.1c00838.

Odeh, S., Alves, J., Alves, G. R., Gustavsson, I., Anabtawi, M., Arafeh, L., Jazi, M., and Arekat, M. R. (2015). A Two-Stage Assessment of the Remote Engineering Lab VISIR at Al-Quds University in Palestine. *Revista Iberoamericana de Tecnologias Del Aprendizaje*, *10*(3), 175–185. doi:10.1109/RITA.2015.2452752.

Padilla, M. J. (1986). *ERIC – ED266961 – The Science Process Skills* (p. 3).

Pantina, C., Prabhakaran, M., Gutjahr, G., Raman, R., and Nedungadi, P. (2018). Effectiveness of online labs teacher training workshop. In *Proceedings – IEEE 18th International Conference on Advanced Learning Technologies, ICALT 2018* (pp. 249–251). doi:10.1109/ICALT.2018.00064.

Petillion, R. J., and Stephen McNeil, W. (2021). Student Satisfaction With Synchronous Online Organic Chemistry Laboratories: Prerecorded Video vs Livestream. *Journal of Chemical Education*, *98*(9), 2861–2869.

Pokhrel, S., and Chhetri, R. (2021). A Literature Review on Impact of COVID-19 Pandemic on Teaching and Learning. *Higher Education for the Future*, *8*(1), 133–141. doi:10.1177/2347631120983481.

Samantha Black. (n.d.). *COVID-19 shuts down research labs as concern grows among scientists*. Retrieved from https://www.scienceboard.net/index.aspx?sec=sup&sub=bioproc&pag=dis&itemId=623&origin=b368f82e457cacefe9b8735dd62e8395

Sandhu, A., Hany, R., Hirohata, A., Hishita, S., Kimlicka, K., Naito, M., and Nishimura, C. (2021). Global Snapshot of the Effects of the COVID-19 Pandemic on the Research Activities of Materials Scientists Between Spring and Autumn 2020. *Science and Technology of Advanced Materials*, *22*(1), 173–184. doi:10.1080/14686996.2021.1894756.

Seun, G., Bunmi, S., and Yetunde, A. (2020). *Since January 2020 Elsevier has created a COVID-19 resource centre with free information in English and Mandarin on the novel coronavirus COVID-19. The COVID-19 resource centre is hosted on Elsevier Connect, the company's public news and information. (January)*.

Shidiq, A. S., Permanasari, A., Hernani, and Hendayana, S. (2021). Chemistry Teacher Responses to Learning in the COVID-19 Outbreak: Challenges and Opportunities to Create Innovative Lab-Work Activities. *Journal of Physics: Conference Series*, *1806*(1). doi:10.1088/1742-6596/1806/1/012195.

Singh, J., and Kumar, V. (2022). Combating the Pandemic with ICT Based Learning Tools and Applications: A Case of Indian Higher Education. *International Journal of Virtual and Personal Learning Environments (IJVPLE) Platforms (IJVPLE)*, *12*(1), 1–21.

Soares, R., De Mello, M. C. S., Da Silva, C. M., MacHado, W., and Arbilla, G. (2020). Online Chemistry Education Challenges for Rio De Janeiro Students During the Covid-19 Pandemic. *Journal of Chemical Education*, *97*(9), 3396–3399. doi:10.1021/acs.jchemed.0c00775.

Stegman, M. A. (2021). Comment on Zacharia et al., A Review of Data About Effectiveness of Guidance in Computer Supported, Inquiry Based Learning Laboratories and Simulations. *Educational Technology Research and Development*, *69*(1), 259–262. doi:10.1007/s11423-020-09927-6.

Strawbridge, J., Hayden, J. C., Robson, T., Flood, M., Cullinan, S., Lynch, M., Morgan, A. T., O'Brien, F., Reynolds, R., Kerrigan, S. W., Cavalleri, G., Kirby, B. P., Tighe, O., Maher, A., and Barlow, J. W. (2022). Educating Pharmacy Students Through a Pandemic: Reflecting on Our COVID-19 Experience. *Research in Social & Administrative Pharmacy: RSAP*, *18*(7), 3204–3209. https://doi.org/10.1016/j.sapharm.2021.08.007

Suart, C., Suart, T. N., Graham, K., and Truant, R. (2021). When the Labs Closed: Graduate Students' and Postdoctoral Fellows' Experiences of Disrupted Research During the Covid-19 Pandemic. *Facets*, *6*, 966–997. doi:10.1139/facets-2020-0077.

Sulistiowati, N., Yuanita, L., and Wasis. (2013). Perbedaan Penggunaan Laboratorium Real Dan Laboratorium Virtual Pada Keterampilan Proses Dan Hasil. *Pendidikan Sains Pascasarjana Universitas Negeri Surabaya*, *2*(2), 191–197.

Usman, M., Suyanta, and Huda, K. (2021). Virtual lab as distance learning media to enhance student's science process skill during the COVID-19 pandemic. *Journal of Physics: Conference Series*, *1882*(1). doi:10.1088/1742-6596/1882/1/012126.

Vasiliadou, R. (2020). Virtual laboratories during coronavirus (COVID-19) pandemic. *Biochemistry and Molecular Biology Education*, *48*(5), 482–483. doi:10.1002/bmb.21407.

Virtual Labs Project Launched by MHRD under NMEICT – digitalLEARNING Magazine – Elets Digital Learning. (n.d.).

Vogels, E. A. (2021). Lower-income Americans still less likely to have home broadband, smartphone | Pew Research Center. In *Pew Research Center*. Retreived from https://www.pewresearch.org/fact-tank/2021/06/22/digital-divide-persists-even-as-americans-with-lower-incomes-make-gains-in-tech-adoption/

Wallengren-Lynch, M., Dominelli, L., and Cuadra, C. (2021). Working and learning from home during COVID-19: International experiences among social work educators and students. *International Social Work*. doi:10.1177/00208728211051412.

Wijenayaka, L. A., and Iqbal, S. S. (2021). Going virtual with practical chemistry amidst the COVID-19 pandemic lockdown: significance, constraints and implications for future. *Asian Association of Open Universities Journal*, *16*(3), 255–270. doi:10.1108/AAOUJ-09-2021-0102.

Wisanti, Ambawati, R., Putri, E. K., Rahayu, D. A., and Khaleyla, F. (2021). Science online learning during the covid-19 pandemic: Difficulties and challenges. *Journal of Physics: Conference Series*, *1747*(1). doi:10.1088/1742-6596/1747/1/012007.

Yu-Fong Chang, J., Wang, L. H., Lin, T. C., Cheng, F. C., and Chiang, C. P. (2021). Comparison of learning effectiveness between physical classroom and online learning for dental education during the COVID-19 pandemic. *Journal of Dental Sciences*, *16*(4), 1281–1289. doi:10.1016/j.jds.2021.07.016.

Zhai, G., Wang, Y., and Liu, L. (2012). Design of Electrical Online Laboratory and E-learning. *IERI Procedia*, *2*, 325–330. doi:10.1016/j.ieri.2012.06.096.

Zhai, X. (2021). Advancing automatic guidance in virtual science inquiry: from ease of use to personalization. *Educational Technology Research and Development*, *69*(1), 255–258. doi:10.1007/s11423-020-09917-8.

5 Determining students' behavioural intention towards online learning using EdTech apps applying the UTAUT model

A case study of school students during the Covid-19 pandemic

Sangeeta Gupta, Ritu Bajaj, Bhaskar Das, Jaspreet Kaur, and Nitika Kapoor

Introduction

As per the World Bank, (2020), the level of "Learning Poverty", measured by identifying 10-year-old children who are not proficient in reading, stands at 55% in India. To strengthen learning and improve education standards around the world, information and communication technology (ICT) in education systems or "EdTech" is being extensively used (The World Bank Group, 2020). Given that the number of internet users in India is at its highest ever, second highest in Asia, with penetration at 54.2%, a large number of web-based learning platforms have sprung up (Kumar and Nanda, 2024). Advancements in information technology have made it possible to deliver learning in multiple formats addressing different learning needs. Various e-learning platforms address a wide variety of educational needs and learning styles (Esichaikul and Bechter, 2010). A range of platforms and formats let students supplement their existing studies and allow them to do courses that might not be available at school or college (Delgado et al., 2015). This has become even more important during the Covid-19 period 2020–2021, as during this time most of the students have not been exposed to the physical classrooms.

As learning becomes more and more student-centric as the learners are getting to choose their preferred medium of study that includes video, audio, face-to-face, peer learning, discussion forums, case study analysis, and application-based methods (FICCI, 2021). This is making flexi education in blended or hybrid mode combining online with face-to-face instruction more desirable at many higher education institutions (Sunand Chen, 2016). During the Covid-19 period, the high growth observed by the key providers of supplement education affirms that blended education is being recognized in India (Suneja and Bagai, 2021). Online teaching and learning include students and

DOI: 10.4324/9781003491712-5

teachers interacting virtually through different types of software and using interactive platforms to supplement learning. The size online learning market in India in 2021 is estimated at US$1.96 billion with five major sectors playing an important role, namely the higher education, primary and secondary supplemental education, reskilling and online certifications, test preparation, languages, and casual learning. A CAGR of 44% is expected in the EdTech segment of market in India (KPMG, 2017). Several important players with interactive learning platforms exist in the Indian market such as Khan Academy and Byju's (Mukherjee et al., 2020; Morrison and Disalvo, 2014). Many developing countries such as Indonesia and Thailand are investing in e-learning courses to improve the learning quality (Al-Adwan et al., 2018; Kim and Park, 2018). Some of these platforms focus on curating content that is aligned with school curriculum, instead of developing new content which is significantly time-consuming (the World Bank, 2020).

It is, however, argued that despite investing in education technology, online learning is not gaining popularity in developing countries. This is due to lack of infrastructure, low adoption rates of technology, and insufficient information sharing (Kim and Park, 2018; Bhardwaj and Kumar, 2023). In spite of the merits of online learning such as higher access, more offerings, enhanced quality, reduced cost and better cost-efficiency of education, the key challenges of student retention and high retention remain (Perna et al., 2014). As the online learning using interactive platforms is advancing, there is also a growing concern among learners who feel isolated and demotivated due to little guidance (Phirangee, 2016). It is also noted that self-management is crucial for students in online education, unlike traditional classroom education (Zhu and Bonk, 2019). Thus, there is a need of a research study in this area and to understand the parameters of technology adaptation which could lead to an increase in the acceptance of the online learning apps in India. A key area of academic research focus has been awareness of these platforms among target segments and conditions facilitating adoption of online learning. With an upsurge of EdTech companies in India, this area of study becomes even more relevant.

One of the theoretical models used in many past literatures to examine the problem of users on online platforms is the UTAUT model. The UTAUT model is a widely used tool for application- and test-based researches in the fields of M-learning (Chao, 2019), online platforms like interactive boards (Šumak and Šorgo, 2016; Šumak et al., 2017), technology innovation in communication (Khalilzadeh et al., 2017), enterprise resource planning (ERP) software use and acceptance by industry (Chauhan and Jaiswal, 2016), and online healthcare services (Hoque and Sorwar, 2017), for making decisions related to technology adoption and usage. UTAUT was also applied in a study to understand the experience of novice users in a Somali university (Omar et al., 2015) and to study the usage of Moodle, an e-learning system in Jordan (Abbad, 2021). The UTAUT model explains barely 26% of changes in behavioural intention (Altalhi, 2020). But the literature is scarce in application of UTAUT model for educational technology companies (EdTech) specializing in secondary and higher secondary education in India. This implies the importance to understand the key constructs/elements impacting the usage of EdTech technology to promote secondary and higher secondary education and to successfully adopt online learning. Further, this study is novel as it makes a prediction of behaviour intention of students on the basis of two new constructs, namely playfulness and learning self-management. These constructs play a very vital role when it comes to students studying on their own without a face-to-face class in the schools for the past 1.5 years. These constructs become even more important when it comes to a country like India where there is a huge segment below the poverty line who cannot afford buying devices at home for their children for such self-managed classes. Moreover, this study is unique in analysing the UTAUT model for the impact of observed heterogeneity among the gender groups in the sample. Thus, the study of the moderating impact of gender on these new constructs added to the conceptual model make this study novel. Thus, the research questions of the study can be listed as follows RQ1: what are the major factors which can influence the students of India while using the EdTech applications for online learning? RQ2: how can factors of self-management of learning and perceived playfulness have an influence on the behaviour intention of use of such EdTech applications?

The outline of this chapter is as follows. The first section (Introduction) of this study introduces the reader to the UTAUT model, the various constructs of the theory, and its relevance to the present study in online learning acceptance among Indian school students, college students, and working professionals. The second section (Literature review) reviews past research literature on the online learning acceptance in Indian context and attempts to establish the need gap of the present study. The third section (Research methodology) explains the tools and methods applied in the study while the fourth section (Data and analysis) brings an overview of the findings. The fifth section (Result and discussion) summarizes the outcome of the current study. The final section (Conclusion) draws the conclusion of the research study while the section References gives the references used in this research.

Literature review

Theoretical model

United Theory of Acceptance and Use of Technology (UTAUT), presented by Venkatesh et al. (2012), is extensively employed in technology adoption and diffusion research as a theoretical lens by researchers conducting empirical studies of user intention and behaviour since 2003. "United Theory of Acceptance and Use of Technology (UTAUT)" integrates elements of eight eminent constructs including performance expectancy (PE), effort expectancy (EE), social influence (SI), and facilitating conditions (FC) and the model outperformed the others significantly towards determining the user behaviour intention (BI) as well as use and acceptance of technology. For this fact, the UTAUT model had been cited in more than 5,000 research papers in the context of internet technologies, web-based information providers, healthcare services, and mobile technology amongst others. Many UTAUT studies were conducted to test the acceptance and use of technology in sectors related to banking services by government (Williams et al., 2015). Research studies in the past have examined the model constructs with moderators such as the gender, ease of use, and education of the user. The same has been very successfully applied to user groups including school students, working professionals, and academicians.

In the context of online learning too, the model has been used in mobile online learning and factors impacting content developers to enhance user experience when it comes to online learning (Pal and Vanijja, 2020). Further literature identifies acceptance of online learning in rural areas in India which include ease-of-use technologies, training, standard operating procedures, and features like gamification that could positively impact the acceptance of the platform (Pai and Alathur, 2019). In the Indian context, EdTech apps have been seen as an exciting and mentally stimulating platform (Pattansheti et al., 2016). Research on online learning acceptance in Indian context are a plenty related to various life stages of schooling, college and higher education, and working professionals; however, the examination of the impact of EdTech platform on the early life stages of school students is still limited.

Frequently used constructs of the UTAUT model in the research include "social influence (SI)", "performance expectancy" (PE), and "effort expectancy" (EE) which have been inculcated in this study. Past studies have not considered the influence of self-management of learning (SL) and perceived playfulness (PP) on voluntariness to engage in the e-learning apps (Smith et al., 2003). Further, the moderation of gender with these new variables has not been seen in the past literature. This study covers this gap.

Hypothesis framework

The development of the hypothesis materialized from the literature review of the study and is detailed hereon.

Performance-expectancy (PE): The term could be explained as a degree or level to which a learner believes the usage of online learning will help them to gain personal satisfaction, social interaction, personal accomplishment, and improve his performance (Venkatesh et al. 2003). At the same time, behaviour intention (BI) infers readiness to act, intent to use, or/and intention of adopting a behaviour based on expectation and needs towards a particular thing with positive relation to satisfaction (Keng et al., 2007). In the context of the present research study, PE could refer to the degree to which a student feels that an EdTech app will increase his performance when it comes to academic studies and skills. The findings of a study by Raza et al.

(2021) on Covid fear among students on social isolation show a positive link of performance expectancy (PE) on behavioral intention of use of learning management system (EdTech apps). With an adjustment in performance expectancy in the EdTech context, online learning will be a great experience for school students as learners could be enabled to instantly accomplish the learning activities and thus uplift their education skills even in a self-learning mode of education prevalent in the Covid-19 year 2020–2021. Based on the UTAUT model, Venkatesh et al. (2012) found that performance expectancy is directly related to the online learner's behavioural intention for its usage. Li et al. (2018) showed that performance expectancy could positively impact the behaviour intention of a learner towards the use of an online learning (EdTech) platform. Performance expectancy could also enhance the intention to use a product as was evident in the findings of Šumak and Šorgo (2016). Thus, the hypothesis derived from the earlier can be presented as follows:

H1: Performance expectancy positively impacts the behaviour intention to use EdTech apps during the pandemic.

Effort Expectancy (EE)

As per Venkatesh et al. (2003), UTAUT model EE is the extent of ease associated with the usage of the online platform by the user or student. In context of the present research study, EE is the learner's belief that EdTech apps will help in an effective and easy method for knowledge and skill development for the student. The internet consumption intention among students is a result of the adequate levels of performance and effort expectancy (Martín and Herrero, 2012). Effort expectancy could be a contributing factor for the individuals' objectives and thus becomes a crucial vital element of behavioural intention to use EdTech apps. The acceptance of the EdTech apps in the home study environment could depend on the ease and user-friendliness of the app. Dulle and Minishi-Majanja (2011) and Venkatesh et al. (2012) have also concluded that effort expectancy and behavioural intention have a significant relation. According to Hoque and Sorwar (2017); Khalilzadeh et al. (2017); and Šumak et al. (2017), effort expectancy is a straight determinant of BI. The findings of a study by Raza et al. (2021) on Covid fear among students on social isolation show a positive link of effort expectancy (EE) on behavioral intention (BI) of use of learning management system (EdTech apps). From this review, the following hypothesis can be constructed.

H2: Effort expectancy positively influences the behaviour intention for usage of EdTech apps during the pandemic.

Social influence: Social influence is the extent to which an individual perceives social factors and interaction to be important for usage of online learning, UTAUT model (Venkatesh et al., 2003). In the present study setting, the social influence implies that of the social groups like friends and family to encourage the use of EdTech apps (Colombo et al., 2015; Suki and Suki, 2017). Social influence could enhance the active involvement and adoption of online learning. It has been seen that students tend to communicate with others to discuss their technology acceptance (Thongsri, 2018). Social influence of the peers could also significantly affect the attitude towards the behavioural intentions to use technologies (Cheung and Vogel, 2013; Falloon and Khoo, 2014), which is a critical component of acceptance of online learning. Venkatesh et al. (2012) also explains that there is a positively active relationship between factors of social influence and behavioural intention to use (of online learning). Research have concluded that the students' intention towards acceptance of EdTech apps in online learning is due to significant factors such as social influence (Salloum et al., 2021). The findings of a study by Raza et al. (2021) on Covid fear among students on social isolation show a positive link of social influence (SI) on behavioral intention of use of learning management system (EdTech). The hypothesis derived can be detailed as follows.

H3: Social influence positively influences the behaviour intention to use EdTech apps during pandemic

Perceived playfulness (PP): The term implies the pleasure and interest of users participating in the system. In the context of the study, perceived playfulness can imply a state of mindful pleasure of the students during the use of the EdTech apps. In case the students are actively enthusiastic to engage in learning a subject/topic or have a strong belief in their preparedness to successful completion of a course/module, then it applies that there will be an increase in their participation intention. As per Mittal et al. (2022), playfulness is a prime factor which determines a user's intention for use (BI) in user-created content services. Wang et al. (2021) presented the outcome of a research study which showed perceived playfulness has a positive impact on participation intention of students during the pandemic crisis of Covid-19. Lin et al. (2021) in their study of behavioural model of students' smartphone usage verified that the students experienced perceived playfulness while using the smartphone which was interesting and easy. Perceived playfulness aims to have a wilful influence on student's usage intention (Balkaya and Akkucuk, 2021). The hypothesis derived is as follows.

H4: Perceived playfulness definitively influences the behaviour intention towards usage of EdTech apps during pandemic.

Self-management of learning: The term can be explained as the scope of discipline to engage in self-learning by a student (Xiao et al., 2019). In the context of this research study, self-efficacy relates to the self-discipline related to the school students when they are using the EdTech apps for studies especially in the Covid-19 time where the curriculum has been completed online without physical interaction with the teachers in the school. During the Covid-19 pandemic a research study by Sangsawang (2020) on multimedia app (EdTech) use by students showed high satisfaction towards self-managed learning. Self-management has been considered to be one of the key predictors of learning outcomes (Bellhäuser, 2016). Studies have shown that students having a high level of self-regulated learning skills would be most likely to have a better learning performance as compared to those who possess lower levels of self-regulated learning skills (Kizilcec et al., 2017; Broadbent, 2017). Students with higher self-management skills will have a positive attitude towards using the EdTech apps for enhancement of academic outcome. Thus, the following can be hypothesized.

H5: Self-management of learning definitively influences the behaviour intention towards usage of EdTech apps during pandemic.

Research methodology

Scope of study

This research study has been conducted with the students of mid-school and high schools in India. The data was mostly received from students studying in public schools of India. The permission to collect data from the students was obtained from their parents. Students from Indian schools were chosen for the study as they are the target segment of the EdTech apps companies. Further, these students have not experienced face-to-face classes with their teachers during Covid-19 time due to the lockdown scenario in India (from March 2020 till 2021).

Data collection and sample

The research tool used is an online questionnaire due to the lockdown scenario in India (in and after March 2020 till 2021 during the time of this study). The online survey has been conducted with a probability random sampling method. The questionnaire was adapted from items of the authors of various constructs of the proposed model. The measurement scale of all questionnaire items was set on Likert-7 scale where 1 implies strongly disagree and 7 indicates strongly agree.

The study sample was conducted on students. During the process of data collection, students were informed about the purpose of the study. Any student who hadn't used an EdTech app for studying post March 2020 was not included in this study. Participation in the research study was based on voluntariness and anonymous.

The questionnaires were reviewed by a set of two experts in the online learning domain. The questionnaire used adapted scales which were also modified as per the suggestions of the experts to judge the five antecedents to behavioural intention of EdTech apps in the UTAUT model. The review was performed to check the form, layout, sequence difficulty, length of the questionnaires, and completion time for the research.

The questionnaires were converted into a Google form and the link was sent to 1,100 middle and high school students who were taking online classes and enrolled in EdTech apps for a period of one year. The data was downloaded from Google Forms as an Excel sheet. The data was collected through the online link which was active throughout the month of August 2021.

The response rate in the student sample was 50% (545 received out of 1,100 questionnaires). After data cleaning, a total number of 521 questionnaires were used for the study. The sample consisted of an equal number of students for both genders. The demographics of the same have been detailed in Table 5.1.

Measures

Standard scales were used for measurement of all the constructs. Performance expectancy was tested with a four-item questionnaire on a Likert scale of 7 with questions including "Using the EdTech apps enables me to accomplish tasks more quickly" Venkatesh et al. (2003). The effort expectancy has been measured on a Likert scale of 7 with a four-item questionnaire by author

Table 5.1 Demographic Characteristics of the Sample

School Data			
	Age Group	6–14 Years	15–20Years
Gender	Boys	113	74
	Girls	116	218
	Total	**229**	**292**
Type of School	Private	51	37
	Government	109	210
	Aided	19	34
	Others	50	11
	Total	**229**	**292**
Exam Board	ICSE	52	60
	CBSE	81	68
	State	52	105
	Others	44	59
	Total	**229**	**292**

Venkatesh et al. (2003) like "It would be easy for me to become skilful using the EdTech apps". The four items of the social influence construct were taken from Venkatesh et al. (2003) and judged on 7-point Likert and included items like "People whose opinions I value would like me to use EdTech Apps". Perceived playfulness consisted of five items adapted from Wang and Wang and it was evaluated on Likert scale of 7. Behavioural intention with three-item questionnaires authored by Venkatesh et al. (2003), including "I intend to use EdTech apps in the next <n> days" was tested on 7-point Likert.

Data and analysis

A total of 545 responses were received, and 521 responses were considered for analysis after data sanitization. The same were taken for the final PLS-SEM analysis. The analysis method used was the Partial Least Square Structural Equational Modelling (PLS-SEM) where data was analysed on the Smart PLS Software 3.3.2 version. PLS-SEM had been chosen as a method of analysis as this was the most preferred method for analysis suggested by past researchers for a multivariate analysis which was the case in our study (Ringle et al., 2015). The method is also suited for the exploratory research where formative scales are used (Hair et al., 2017). PLS-SEM can be suitably used for non-parametric data when applying the SEM technique (Hair et al., 2018). The first step of analysis was developing the measurement model. The outer loadings of the various items of the scale were calculated with the average variance extracted (AVE) for examining the convergent validity in the data for the study. Further as per Hair et al. (2017), the measures of discriminant validity were also calculated. The same had been analysed with the help of cross loading and Fornell-Larcker criterion. Discriminant validity was further checked by the Heterotrait-Monotrait method (Henseler et al., 2015). Next, the structural model was made, and the path coefficients and the coefficient of determination (R2) were measured.

Lastly, the common method bias was examined by Harman's single factor analysis. For the sake of analysis, all the statements were loaded into a single factor. The results proved that no single factor explains a total of 47.9% variance in data. This was less than the threshold limit which was taken to be 50%. Thus, it was concluded that there is no common method bias in the current study (Babin et al., 2016).

Results and discussion

Measurement model assessments

The internal and convergent reliability had to be examined for the Outer model specifications. The internal reliability was examined with the use of Cronbach's alpha. Also, the composite reliability (CR) and rho A were calculated. The same were found to be above the threshold limit of 0.70

Table 5.2 Internal Reliability and Convergent Validity Results

Construct	*Items*	*Loadings*	*Cronbach's Alpha*	*rhoA*	*CR*	*AVE*
BI	BIintendS	0.956	0.948	0.949	0.967	0.906
	BIplanS	0.947				
	BIpredictS	0.953				
EE	EEOLclearunderstandS	0.865	0.881	0.883	0.918	0.737
	EEOLeasyoperateS	0.830				
	EEOLeasyunderstandS	0.865				
	EEOLeasyuseS	0.873				
PE	PEOLaccomplishS	0.905	0.897	0.902	0.929	0.766
	PEOLgradeS	0.815				
	PEOLproductivityS	0.896				
	PEOLusefulS	0.881				
PP	PPenjoyS	0.865	0.871	0.880	0.912	0.723
	PPexploreS	0.868				
	PPstimulateS	0.902				
	PPtimeS	0.760				
SI	SIbehaviourS	0.885	0.822	0.829	0.895	0.740
	SIseniorS	0.785				
	SIthinkS	0.906				
SL	SLhomeworkS	0.853	0.834	0.855	0.886	0.661
	SLinitiativeS	0.823				
	SLmanagetimeS	0.777				
	SLselfdirectS	0.798				

(Ali et al., 2018). Thus, it was concluded that there was a presence of internal reliability in the data set. The average variance extracted (AVE) was calculated, and it was seen that all the constructs in the proposed conceptual model did report an AVE value above 0.5 which was taken as a threshold value (Hair et al., 2019). The results of the internal reliability and convergent validity are shown in Table 5.2. The next step was to examine the discriminant validity. This was examined by the Fornell and Larcker's Criterion (1981). The formula used for the same was the under root of AVEs, which was found to be higher than their inter-item correlation values. The results of the discriminant validity shown in Table 5.3 show that each construct did show a discriminate validity. The discriminant validity was further checked with the Heterotrait-Monotrait ratio of correlations (HTMT). The value of the HTMT among the constructs was found to be less than 1. Also, the ratio of correlations was acceptable. The maximum ratio of 0.85 was also acceptable (Voorhees et al., 2016). The value of EE and PE construct was found to be above 0.85 but less than 0.9, thus the confidence intervals for HTMT were found to be within the given limits. Thus, we inferred through this that the constructs are unique and vary from one another. These results are shown in Table 5.4.

Table 5.3 Discriminant Validity Results

	BI	*EE*	*PE*	*PP*	*SL*	*SI*
BI	**0.952**					
EE	0.703	**0.858**				
PE	0.709	0.781	**0.875**			
PP	0.739	0.730	0.728	**0.850**		
SL	0.494	0.482	0.400	0.471	**0.813**	
SI	0.532	0.598	0.573	0.599	0.456	**0.860**

Table 5.4 Discriminant Validity Results According to HTMT Criterion

	BI	*EE*	*PE*	*PP*	*SL*	*SI*
BI						
EE	0.768					
PE	0.767	0.878				
PP	0.810	0.829	0.822			
SL	0.531	0.554	0.446	0.537		
SI	0.602	0.703	0.673	0.710	0.546	

Structural model assessments

Structural model is an examination which can speak about the relationship among constructs and also assess their predictive relevance (Hair et al., 2017). The process of Bootstrapping was used to compute the p-values for the hypotheses with recommended 5,000 bootstraps without changing sign (Hair et al., 2020). Next the values of Tolerance and Variance Inflation Factor (VIF) were computed. It was seen that the VIF values were below 3.33 (Diamantopoulos, 2008). The inner VIFs values for the constructs were reported to be as follows: EE (3.2070, PE (3.021), PP (2.694), SL (1.413), and SI (1.800) on BI. These values were less than the threshold limit; thus we concluded that there is no collinearity in the data set (Hair et al., 2017). The significance values of the path coefficients were not calculated, and the same varied from –1 to +1. These values were a result of the bootstrapping process where 5,000 subsamples were used in the PLS algorithm for analysis. The outer weights of all constructs were computed and were found to be significant at 99% level of significance. The values of the same were not equal to zero (Muller et al., 2018). Figure 5.1 shows the results of the structural model evaluations. In social sciences, an R^2 value of 0.20 or above can be seen to be high (Rasoolimanesh et al., 2017). The coefficient of determination (R^2) for the endogenous construct like behavioural intention (BI) which was 63.8% was found to be highly significant. The standardized root mean square residual (SRMR) is a global fit indices that has been examined for

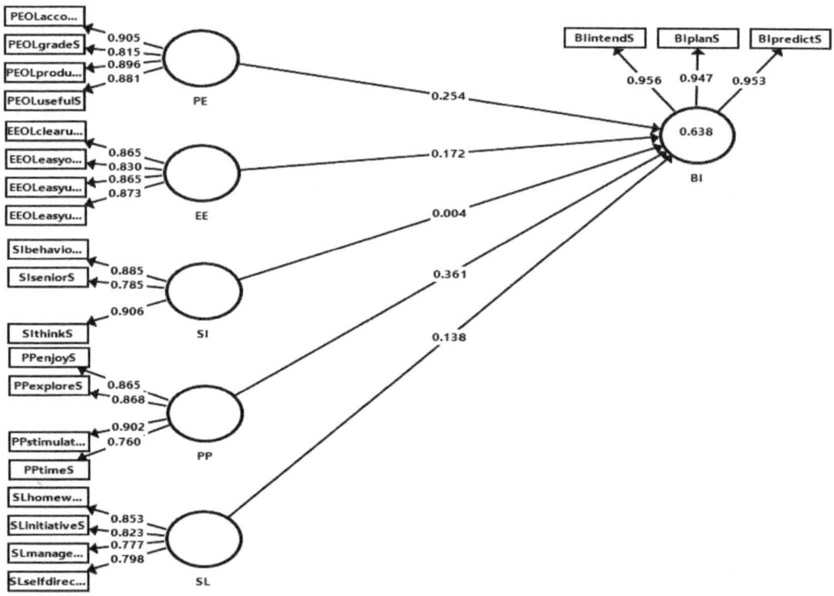

Figure 5.1 Structural model of the complete model.

goodness of fit for the model (Hair et al., 2020). The SRMR value stood at 0.056, which was below the threshold value of 0.08. Thus, we concluded that the proposed conceptual model had good explanatory power. Table 5.5 summarizes the structural model assessment and hypotheses testing results.

Table 5.5 and Figure 5.1 show that PP was the most prominent construct. The same was significantly and positively impacting BI (β=.361, p value<.00). Thus, this value supported H3. The beta coefficient value of PE with BI was also significant (β=.254, p value<.00), thus supporting the H2. EE and SL also showed a positive and significant impact on BI with β=.172, p value<.05; β=.138, p value<.00, thus supporting H1 and H4. SI was the only construct which showed an insignificant impact on BI.

Further, the effect size (f^2) and predictive importance and relevance (Q^2) of the present model were tested. As per Cohen (1988), the values of 0.02 (small effects), 0.15 (moderate effects), and 0.35 (large effects) were taken as benchmark for inferences. The study shows that SI (f^2=.00) showed no effect on BI but EE (f^2=0.026), PE (f^2=0.059), PP (f^2=0.134), and SL (f^2=0.037) have weak effect size on BI. However, PP (f^2=0.137) was found to be the most important composite that could explain the dependent construct. The predictive importance was analysed with the help of Stone-Geisser's Q^2criterion, the value of the same was found to be 0.570 for BI which shows a highly predictive importance and a high relevance of the model (Geisser, 1975). The value

Table 5.5 Hypothesis Testing

Hypothesis	*Path Relationship*	*Std. Beta*	*Sample Mean (M)*	*t-value*	*CI 2.5%*	*CI 97.5%*	*Decision*
H1	PE→BI	0.254	0.253	3.333**	0.106	0.403	Supported
H2	EE→BI	0.172	0.173	2.473*	0.038	0.310	Supported
H3	SI→BI	0.004	0.003	0.100	−0.076	0.085	Not Supported
H4	PP→BI	0.361	0.360	6.295**	0.246	0.474	Supported
H5	SL→BI	0.138	0.140	3.322**	0.062	0.225	Supported

Notes: (*p<0.05 and **p<0.00).

above 0.02 was seen to have a satisfactory predictive power for the model (Richter et al., 2016). Thus, it was concluded that the independent constructs were crucial and relevant in the conceptual model of the study. These results could be generalized in different contexts in future.

Conclusion

Globally, the Covid-19 pandemic brought a transactional change of knowledge sharing and learning from face-to-face to online or virtual learning. Many EdTech companies entered the market, and they capitalized this opportunity as huge investments in hardware, software, and training began to create online models of education. This study started with the identification of factors of behavioural intent of students to adapt EdTech application. The UTAUT model is being used in this chapter, as it is the well-recognized model to judge adoption of technology (Reyes-Mercado, 2022). Researchers consider three main constructs of this model, namely performance expectancy, effort expectancy, and social influence. Further two more factors, perceived playfulness and self-management of learning, were identified which were less studied particularly in e-learning and Indian scenario. To confirm these five factors are antecedents of behavioural intention of students, reliability and validity of all the constructs were conducted. All constructs were found to be reliable as their Cronbach's alpha, Composite Reliability (CR), and rho A values were above 0.7. Further, all constructs have convergent validity with an AVE above 0.5 and discriminate with each other as the value of the HTMT among the constructs were found to be less than 1. It was found that all constructs have positive and significant impact on BI of students to adopt EdTech application for learning, except social influence (0.004) although its impact is positive but insignificant. Playfulness (0.361) has the highest impact on BI which shows how student enjoys this method of learning and impact their BI for EdTech applications. Playfulness is a prime factor which determines intention for use (BI). During Covid-19 moving to online education and adoption of EdTech by teachers required new pedagogical skills and knowledge, where teachers were self-motivated and performed self-managed learning to make EdTech as a tool for playfulness among students. The results have shown that the prevailing UTAUT model along with the new constructs of self-managed learning and playfulness form a new extended and comprehensive framework for the model. These findings are novel and pave a way forward for students' online learning for global educational opportunities and the future of EdTech companies.

References

Abbad, M. M. M. (2021). Using the UTAUT model to understand students' usage of e-learning systems in developing countries. *Education and Information Technologies, 26*, 7205–7224.

Al-Adwan, A. S., Al-Madadha, A., and Zvirzdinaite, Z. (2018). Modeling students' readiness to adopt Mobile learning in higher education: An empirical study. *International Review of Research in Open and Distributed Learning, 19*(1).

Ali, F., Rasoolimanesh, S. M., Sarstedt, M., Ringle, C. M., and Ryu, K. (2018). An assessment of the use of partial least squares structural equation modeling (PLS-SEM) in hospitality research. *International Journal of Contemporary Hospitality Management, 30*(1), 514–538.

Altalhi, M. (2020). Toward a model for acceptance of MOOCs in higher education: the modified UTAUT model for Saudi Arabia. *Education and Information Technologies, 26*(2), 1589–1605.

Babin, B. J., Griffin, M., and Hair Jr, J. F. (2016). Heresies and sacred cows in scholarly marketing publications. *Journal of Business Research, 69*(8), 3133–3138.

Balkaya, S., and Akkucuk, U. (2021). Adoption and Use of Learning Management Systems in Education: The Role of Playfulness and Self-Management. *Sustainability, 13*(3), 1127.

Bellhäuser, H., Lösch, T., Winter, C., and Schmitz, B. (2016), Applying a web-based training to foster self-regulated learning – Effects of an intervention for large numbers of participants. *The Internet and Higher Education, 31*, 87–100.

Bhardwaj, A., and Kumar, V. (2023). Social Media as an Enabler to Combat Misinformation. In *Pandemics in the Age of Social Media: Information and Misinformation in Developing Nations*. Routledge: New York (USA), pp. 1–15.

Broadbent, J. (2017). Comparing online and blended learner's self-regulated learning strategies and academic performance. *The Internet and Higher Education, 33*, 24–32.

Chauhan, S., and Jaiswal, M. (2016). Determinants of acceptance of ERP software training in business schools: empirical investigation using UTAUT model. *The International Journal of Management Education, 14*(3), 248–262.

Chao, C. (2019). Factors Determining the Behavioral Intention to Use Mobile Learning: An Application and Extension of the UTAUT Model. Advanced Learning. *Frontiers in Psychology, 10*.

Cheung, R., and Vogel, D. (2013). Predicting user acceptance of collaborative technologies: An extension of the technology acceptance model for e-learning. *Computers & Education, 63*, 160–175.

Cohen, J. (1988). *Statistical Power Analysis for the Behavioral Sciences* (Second ed.). Lawrence Erlbaum Associates Publishers: New Jersey.

Colombo, M. G., Franzoni, C., and Rossi–Lamastra, C. (2015). Internal social capital and the attraction of early contributions in crowdfunding. *Entrepreneurship Theory and Practice, 39*(1), 75–100.

Delgado, A. J., Wardlow, L., McKnight, K., and O'Malley, K. (2015). Educational Technology: A Review of the Integration, Resources, and Effectiveness of

Technology in K-12 Classrooms. *Journal of Information Technology Education: Research*, *14*, 397–416.

Diamantopoulos, A. (2008). Formative indicators: Introduction to the special issue. *Journal of Business Research*, *61*(12), 1201– 1202.

Esichaikul, V., and Bechter, C. (2010). Catering for Different Learning Styles in e-Learning. In Spector, J. M., Ifenthaler, D., Isaías, P., Kinshuk, and Sampson, D. (Eds), *Learning and Instruction in the Digital Age*. New York: Springer, pp. 361–374.

Falloon, G., and Khoo, E. (2014). Exploring young students' talk in iPad-supported collaborative learning environments. *Computers & Education*, *77*, 13–28.

FICCI. (2021). Post show report 2021, Proceedings of 16th FICCI Higher Education Summit2021. Retrieved from https://ficci.in/events/25391/ISP/HES_Post_Show_Report.pdf

Fornell, C. G., and Larcker, D. F. (1981). Evaluating Structural Equation Models with Unobservable Variables and Measurement Error. *Journal of Marketing Research*, *18*(1), 39–50.

Geisser, S. (1975). A Predictive Approach to the Random Effects Model. *Biometrika*, *61*(1), 101–107.

Hair, J. F., Howard, M. C., and Nitzl, C. (2020). Assessing measurement model quality in PLS-SEM using confirmatory composite analysis. *Journal of Business Research*, *109*, 101–110.

Hair, J. F., Hult, G. T. M., Ringle, C., and Sarstedt, M. (2017). *A Primer on Partial Least Squares Structural Equation Modeling (PLS-SEM)* (2nd ed.). Sage: Los Angeles, California.

Hair J. F., Sarstedt, M., and Ringle, C. M. (2019). Rethinking Some of the Rethinking of Partial Least Squares. *European Journal of Marketing*, *53*(4).

Hair, J. F., Sarstedt, M., Ringle, C. M., and Gudergan, S. P. (2018). *Advanced Issues in Partial Least Squares Structural Equation Modeling*. SAGE: Los Angeles, CA.

Henseler, J., Ringle, C. M., and Sarstedt, M. (2015). A New Criterion for Assessing Discriminant Validity in Variance-based Structural Equation Modeling. *Journal of the Academy of Marketing Science*, *43*(1), 115–135

Hoque, R., and Sorwar, G. (2017). Understanding Factors Influencing the Adoption of mHealth by the Elderly: An Extension of the UTAUT Model. *International Journal of Medical Informatics*, *101*, 75–84.

Keng, C. J., Huang, T. L., Zheng, L. J., and Hsu, M. K. (2007). Modeling Service Encounters and Customer Experiential Value in Retailing: An Empirical Investigation of Shopping Mall Customers in Taiwan. *International Journal of Service Industry Management*, *18*(4), 349–367.

Khalilzadeh, J., Ozturk, A. B., and Bilgihan, A. (2017). Security-related factors in extended UTAUT model for NFC based mobile payment in the restaurant industry. *Computers in Human Behaviour*, *70*, 460–474.

Kim, B., and Park, M. J. (2018). Effect of personal factors to use ICTs on e-learning adoption: Comparison between learner and instructor in developing countries. *Information Technology for Development*, *24*(4), 706–732.

Kizilcec, R. F., Pérez-Sanagustín, M., and Maldonado, J. J. (2017). Self-regulated learning strategies predict learner behavior goal attainment in massive open online courses. *Computers & Education*, *104*, 18– 33.

KPMG. (2021). Online Education in India: 2021, KPMG, India. Retrieved from https://assets.kpmg/content/dam/kpmg/in/pdf/2017/05/Online-Education-in-India-2021.pdf

Kumar, V., and Nanda, P. (2024). Social Media and Micro-Lessons: A New Paradigm of Online Learning. In *Optimizing Education Through Micro-Lessons: Engaging and Adaptive Learning Strategies*. Hershey, Pennsylvania: IGI Global, pp. 157–172.

Li, B., Wang, X., and Tan, S. C. (2018). What makes MOOC users persist in completing MOOCs? A perspective from network externalities and human factors. *Computers in Human Behavior*, *85*, 385–395.

Lin, C.-W., Lin, Y.-S., Liao, C.-C., and Chen, C.-C. (2021). Utilizing Technology Acceptance Model for Influences of Smartphone Addiction on Behavioural Intention. *Mathematical Problems in Engineering, 2021*, Article ID 5592187, 7. https://doi.org/10.1155/2021/5592187

Martín, H. S., and Herrero, A. (2012). Influence of the User's Psychological Factors on the Online Purchase Intention in Rural Tourism: Integrating Innovativeness to the UTAUT Framework. *Tourism Management*, *33*(2).

Mittal, S., Kumar, V., and Seppi, J. (2022). Targeting Mobile Gamers Community for Marketing Campaigns. *Journal of Content, Community & Communication (JCC)*, *16*(2), 106–117.

Morrison, B. B., and DiSalvo, B. (2014). Khan Academy Gamifies Computer Science. SIGCSE'14 – Proceedings of the 45th ACM Technical Symposium on Computer Science Education 2014. New York: Association for Computing Machinery, pp. 39–44.

Mukherjee, S., and P.S. (2020). Byju's the Learning App: An Investigative Study on the Transformation from Traditional Learning to Technology Based Personalized Learning. *International Journal of Scientific & Technology Research*, *9*(3).

Muller, T., Schuberth, F., and Henseler, J. (2018). PLS path modeling – A confirmatory approach to study tourism technology and tourist behavior. *Journal of Hospitality and Tourism Technology*, *9*(3), 249– 266.

Omar, M., Vrieler, T., et al. (2015). E-learning Opens Door to the Global Community: Novice Users' Experiences of E-learning in a Somali University. *MERLOT Journal of Online Learning and Teaching*, *11*(2).

Pai, R. R., and Alathur, S. (2019). Predicting Mobile Health Technology Acceptance by the Indian Rural Community. *International Journal of Electronic Government Research*, *15*(4), 37–62.

Pal, D., and Vanijja, V. (2020). Perceived usability evaluation of Microsoft teams as an online learning platform during COVID-19 using system usability scale and technology acceptance model in India. *Children and Youth Services Review*, *119*, 105523.

Pattansheti, M., Kamble, S. S., Dhume, S. M., and Raut, R. D. (2016). Measurement and validation of an integrated technology readiness acceptance and planned behaviour model for Indian mobile banking industry. *International Journal of Business Information Systems*, *22*(3).

Perna, L. W., Ruby, A., Boruch, R. F., Wang, N., Scull, J., Ahmad, S., and Evans, C. (2014). Moving through MOOCs: Understanding the progression of users in massive open online courses. *Educational Researcher*, *43*(9), 421–432.

Phirangee, K. (2016). Students' Perceptions of Learner-Learner Interactions that Weaken a Sense of Community in an Online Learning Environment. *Online Learning*, *20*(4), 14.

Rasoolimanesh, S. M., Jaafar, M., Kock, N., and Ahmad, A. G. (2017). The effects of community factors on residents' perceptions toward world heritage site inscription and sustainable tourism development. *Journal of Sustainable Tourism*, *25*(2), 198–216.

Raza, S. A., Qazi, W., Khan, K. A., and Salam, J. (2021). Social isolation and acceptance of the learning management system (LMS) in the time of COVID-19 pandemic: an expansion of the UTAUT model. *Journal of Educational Computing Research*, *59*(2), 183–208.

Reyes-Mercado, P., Barajas-Portas, K., Kasuma, J., Almonacid-Duran, M., and Zamacona, G. (2022). Adoption of digital learning environments during the COVID-19 pandemic: merging technology readiness index and UTAUT model. *Journal of International Education in Business*. *16*. doi:10.1108/JIEB-10–2021–0097.

Richter, N. F., Cepeda, G., Roldán, J. L., and Ringle, C. M. (2016). European management research using partial least squares structural equation modeling (PLS-SEM) Editorial. *European Management Journal*, *34*(6), 589–597.

Ringle, C. M., Wende, S., and Becker, J. M. (2015). SmartPLS 3. Bönningstedt: SmartPLS. Retrieved from https://www.smartpls.com

Salloum, S. A., Mahdi, N., Alahbabi, N., Habes, M., Aburayya, A., and Akour, I. (2021). Predicting the Intention to Use Social Media Sites: A Hybrid SEM – Machine Learning Approach. In Hassanien, A. E., Chang, K. C., Mincong, T. (Eds), *Advanced Machine Learning Technologies and Applications. AMLTA 2021. Advances in Intelligent Systems and Computing*. Springer: Cham, p. 1339.

Sangsawang, T. (2020). An instructional design for online learning in vocational education according to a self-regulated learning framework for problem solving during the COVID-19 crisis. *Indonesian Journal of Science and Technology*, 283–198.

Smith, P. J., Murphy, K. L., and Mahoney, S. E. (2003). Towards identifying factors underlying readiness for online learning: an exploratory study. *Distance Education*, *24*(1), 57–67.

Suki, N. M., and Suki, N. M. (2017). Determining students' behavioural intention to use animation and storytelling applying the UTAUT model: The moderating roles of gender and experience level. *The International Journal of Management Education*, *15*(3), 528–538.

Šumak, B., Pušnik, M., Herièko, M., and Šorgo, A. (2017). Differences between prospective, existing, and former users of interactive whiteboards on external factors affecting their adoption, usage and abandonment. *Computers in Human Behavior*, *72*, 733–756.

Šumak, B., and Šorgo, A. (2016). The acceptance and use of interactive whiteboards among teachers: differences in UTAUT determinants between pre-and post-adopters. *Computers in Human Behavior*, *64*, 602–620.

Sun, A., and Chen, X. (2016). Online education and its effective practice: A research review. *Journal of Information Technology Education: Research*, *15*, 157–190.

Suneja, V., and Bagai, S. (2021). *Examining the Impact of COVID-19 Pandemic on Online Education: Reviewing the Indian Schooling System Based on the Perspective of Major Indian E-tutoring Platforms. Vision*. MDI Sage. doi:10.1177/09722629211029011

The World Bank. (2020). Digital technologies in education. The World Bank Group. Retrieved from https://www.worldbank.org/en/topic/edutech

Thongsri, N., Shen, L., Bao, Y., and Alharbi, I. M. (2018). Integrating UTAUT and UGT to explain behavioral intention to use M-learning. *Journal of Systems and Information Technology*, *20*(3), 278–297.

Venkatesh, V., Morris, M. G., Davis, G. B., and Davis, F.D. (2003). User acceptance of information technology: Toward a unified view. *MIS Quarterly*, 425–478.

Venkatesh, V., Thong, J. Y. L., and Xu, X. (2012). Consumer acceptance and use of information technology: extending the unified theory of acceptance and use of technology. *MIS Quarterly*, *36*(1), 157–178.

Voorhees, C. M., Brady, M. K., Calantone, R., et al. (2016). Discriminant Validity Testing in Marketing: An Analysis, Causes for Concern, and Proposed Remedies. *Journal of the Academy of Marketing Science*, *44*(1), 119–134.

Wang, S., Tlili, A., Zhu, L., and Yang, J. (2021). Do playfulness and university support facilitate the adoption of online education in a crisis? COVID-19 as a case study based on the technology acceptance model. *Sustainability*, *13*(16), 9104.

Williams, M. D., Rana, N. P., and Dwivedi, Y. K. (2015). The unified theory of acceptance and use of technology (UTAUT): a literature review. *Journal of Enterprise Information Management*, *28*(3), 443–488.

Xiao, S., Yao, K., and Wang, T. (2019). *The Relationships of Self-Regulated Learning and Academic Achievement in University Students*. SHS Web of Conferences. 60. 01003. EDP Sciences (2019 [online]). https://doi.org/10.1051/shsconf/20196001003

Zhu, M., and Bonk, C. J. (2019). Designing MOOCs to facilitate participant self-directed learning: An analysis of instructor perspectives and practices. *International Journal of Self-Directed Learning*, *16*(2).

6 Constraints and impediments to the conduct of extracurricular activities in engineering education during the pandemic – an industrial engineering insight

G.V.S.S. Sharma, M. Srinivasa Rao, V. Rambabu, G. Sasikumar, Sujana Chamarty, and C.L.V.R.S.V. Prasad

Introduction

In the global pandemic clutches, imparting education is a real big challenge (Kumar and Malhotra, 2021). In such a situation, the online medium of instruction emerged as the preferred mode of pedagogy (Grodotzki et al., 2021; Ahmed and Opoku, 2022). Engineering learning requires understanding of the practical experimentation aspect of the subject (Kumar and Sharma, 2017). In such a scenario, the digital twin concept (Rassudov and Korunets, 2020) plays an important role, wherein a balance is struck between online delivery and performing experiments through virtual simulators. Virtual laboratory (Kapilan et al., 2021) emerged as the saviour for imparting practical knowledge to students during Covid-19 pandemic. On the other hand, a research carried out in the University of Sharjah (Mushtaha et al., 2022) revealed that students preferred a blended mode of learning rather than solely depending on either virtual or face-to-face mode of learning. In a developing nation like India, the Covid-19 pandemic acted as an accelerator for implementing many new useful schemes and policies by Government of India promoting open and distant learning (ODL) (Singh and Kumar, 2022).

The prime aspect of engineering education during pandemic is to be humane (Nebrida and Bangud, 2022). Students are in extreme stress both physically and mentally due to continuous exposure to online learning gadgets like smartphones and laptops (Kovid and Kumar, 2022). Faculty must be patient with their students and help them in the mastery of their subjects (Sharaievska et al., 2022). Apart from learning the core engineering subject, the positive coping and emotional well-being of the students through strength-based parenting plays a vital role (Allen et al., 2022). Overcoming the psychological stress is very important to overcome the unusual behaviour, lack of confidence, and improper sleeping patterns during the pandemic

DOI: 10.4324/9781003491712-6

(Akram et al., 2022). Helping others through outreach programmes could generate a sense of satisfaction and belongingness which act as stress-busters (Hermanstyne et al., 2022). Adaptive learning and flipped learning (Clark et al., 2022) offer yet another advantage during the pandemic times. Another study examined the students' perception of online learning and concluded that male students did not much favour the online learning experience, whereas the female students were much positive to the shift to online mode of learning during the pandemic (Warfvinge et al., 2022).

With the onset of the pandemic, student participation in extracurricular activities showed a steep decline due to restrictions like social lockdown (Ilari et al., 2022; Bhardwaj and Kumar, 2023). Art activities like painting and music sustained the pandemic (Ng et al., 2022). Research suggested that music students coped up better and managed better with their workload stress during the trying times of the Covid-19 pandemic (Jääskeläinen et al., 2022). A gamified approach towards the extracurricular activities helped retain interest and boosted the creativity and confidence among the students (Shoaib, 2022). In today's information technology revolution, the facet of extracurricular activities has been broadened to include the online component of the domain apart from traditional offline activities (Ng, 2021). Students' expertise in effective usage of the online social media platforms is the new gauge for assessing success in life (Kumar and Nanda, 2020). The online component of the extracurricular activities constitutes a major part of today's holistic development of the student (Heymann et al., 2022). Extracurricular activities not only help improve students' personality but also help them in their academic achievement (Balaguer et al., 2020). Traditionally, industrial engineering is the interface between engineering and management. Concepts of industrial engineering on the other hand are applied for the betterment of education quality (Köksal and Eğitman, 1998). The concepts of industrial engineering are widely applied into service sectors for proposing improvements in the capability of the processes (Sharma et al., 2021b). The Ishikawa (cause-and-effect) diagram (Prasad et al., 2021) and the FMEA (Sharma et al., 2022) are two such powerful industrial engineering tools which are adopted in this work for proposing improvement in the process of conduct of extracurricular activities in engineering education.

Research objectives

Extracurricular activities constitute a vital part of the overall personality development of the student. Through EC activity, the student interacts with the peers, learns to present his conduct in the public which is very important and is not taught in the regular technical classroom sessions. EC activities also help the student to learn management skills and develop social responsibility through the concept of giving back to the society. The pandemic times have witnessed a tough time where the operations and functions are stalled in every walk of life including the education sector, ranging from primary schools to graduate institutions. Engineering pedagogy is no exception and was hit hard because of the Covid-19 pandemic (Kumar and Gupta, 2021). The instructions primarily went online and extracurricular activities were given least priority and appeared nowhere in the scene. Thus, there exists a need to address the conduct of extracurricular activities under such difficult times. The objective of this research is to propose a structured and scientific approach for achieving improvement in the process of conduct of EC activities in an engineering education environment with reference to the pandemic times.

Ishikawa (cause-and-effect) diagram

The Ishikawa (cause-and-effect) diagram is the industrial engineering tool used for enlisting the potential causes responsible for the common end effect (Sharma et al., 2018). Here the end effect is considered as "overcoming constraints and impediments in the conduct of extra-curricular activities". Figure 6.1 portrays the Ishikawa (cause-and-effect) diagram in the context of extracurricular activities in engineering education.

The Ishikawa diagram is branched into four sub-categories, namely nature of activity, students and faculty, safety and timing, and finance and resources.

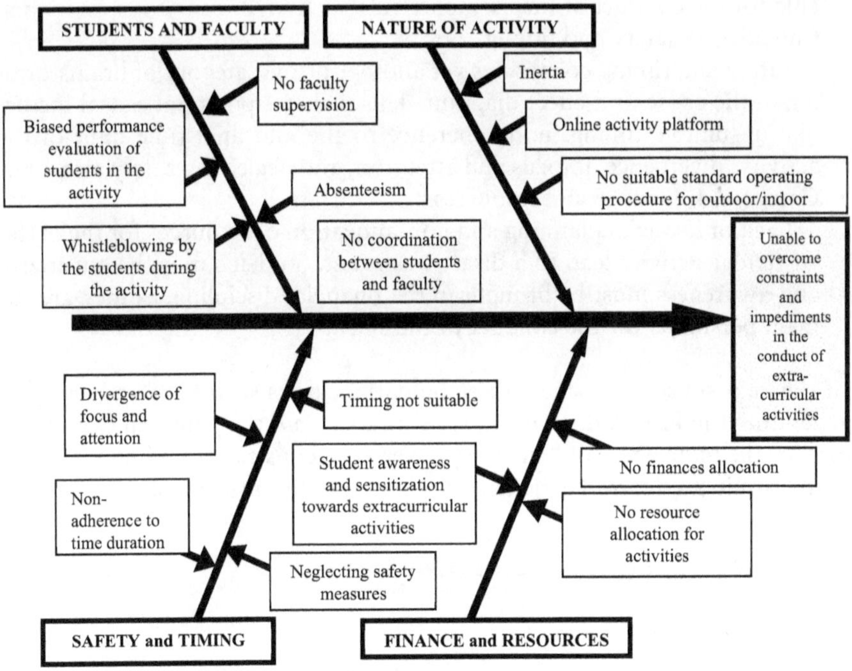

Figure 6.1 Ishikawa (cause-and-effect) diagram.

Potential causes are brainstormed and enlisted under each of these four subcategories as follows:

- **Category 1: Nature of Activity**
  The nature of the activity determines whether the activity can be done indoors or outdoors and whether the activity can be performed offline physically within/outside the premises of the institute or can be performed online through a well-streamed internet connection. The type and nature of activity also determine the inertia of the students to come forward and participate in the extracurricular activity. For example, if the activity involves a group discussion, then the "inertia of rest" exists till the first participant opens up the discussion. Once the discussion starts, then there shall be uninterrupted seamless participation of the candidates. Also, there must be a Standard Operating Procedure, predefined before the start of the activity depending on the nature and type of activity.
- **Category 2: Students and faculty**
  This category comprises the main section which accounts for causes like whistleblowing by the students during the conduct of the activity, general absenteeism, lack of coordination between faculty and students, no faculty supervision during the conduct of the event, and biased performance evaluation of the students in the activity. Thus, this category accounts for the potential causes involving both the faculty and the students accountable for the conduct of the extracurricular activity.
- **Category 3: Safety and timing**
  Safety and timing constitutes yet another prime category of brainstorming in the cause-and-effect diagram. This includes potential causal factors like unsuitable timing, non-adherence to the allocated time limit of the activity, divergence of focus and attention, and neglecting safety measures.
- **Category 4: Finance and resources**
  Lack of financial planning and non-allocation of resources for the extracurricular activity lead to a disastrous event. Students must be sensitized, and awareness must be brought in the financial discipline, as they are the main personnel for the conduct of the show.

At the next subsequent stage, these potential causes shall be found useful in generating the FMEA document. Thus, in this way, the potential causal factors for the main effect of "Unable to overcome constraints and impediments in the conduct of extra-curricular activities" are brainstormed.

Failure modes and effects analysis (FMEA)

Introduction to FMEA

FMEA is an industrial engineering tool for structured brainstorming and witnessing improvements in any organization. It is a group activity wherein members across the cross-functional team come together for a common goal of defined improvement within the firm. There are different kinds of FMEA pertaining to the field of application. They are, the design FMEA (DFMEA), the process FMEA (PFMEA), the maintenance FMEA, and the service FMEA. The DFMEA is for analysing the system under designing process which failed to meet the design criteria. The PFMEA is for analysing the manufacturing process initiated before the feasibility stage and prior to tooling for production. The maintenance FMEA is used for the diagnosis of a problem or prior to any new equipment purchase, as the potential failure modes regarding the maintenance process are brainstormed. The service FMEA is an extension of the process FMEA into the service sectors like banking, finance, health, hospitality, and education to name a few.

First, the process of FMEA starts with the identification of the function or the scope of the design product or manufacturing process or maintenance system or service domain depending on the type of FMEA being performed. Disintegrate the scope into separate sub-systems comprising individual parts, sub-assemblies, and process sub-steps and identify the functions of each of the disintegrated components. For each component, extrapolate on how the failure of the component may occur. This forms the failure mode or the manner in which the failure may occur. For each failure mode, recognize the effects on the immediate customer/assemblies, as well as on the end customer. Give a severity ranking to this effect on the scale of 1 to 10, where 1 being the least severe effect and 10 being the most severe effect hampering the system severely with the loss of life or property or irreversible damage to the system as a whole.

Next to this, for each identified failure mode brainstorm the potential causes for that failure mode. For doing so, the Ishikawa diagram may be useful. One such diagram is shown in Figure 6.1. The more diversified and varied is the experience and knowledge of the cross-functional team members, the more is the range of diversity of the identification of the potential causal factors. After identifying the causes, allocate the occurrence rating for each potential cause. Occurrence rating is the probability of failure occurring because of that particular cause in a scale of 1 to 10, where 1 refers to extremely unlikely occurrence and 10 depicts the unavoidable occurrence rating. After allocating the occurrence rating, for each cause, identify the process controls. The process controls refer to the tests, procedures, or standards which are now in place to prevent the failure from reaching the customer by preventing the cause not to occur. The controls implemented must be proactive or before the failure rather than being reactive or after the failure. For each of the control, allocate the detection ranking on the scale of 1 to 10, where 1 means that the control is absolute to detect the problem, and 10 means that the control certainly does not detect the problem or in other words, the control does not exist.

The next stage is to determine the RPN (Risk Priority Number). This is obtained by multiplying the ranking numbers allotted for the severity, occurrence, and detection scales. Recognize the corrective actions to be taken for the elimination of the causal factors. Higher the RPN, early preference must be given for taking the corrective action. Thus, prioritization for corrective actions must be in the descending order of the RPN. After taking the corrective measures, the new severity, occurrence, and detection rankings must be given. These new rankings must be lower than those of previous rankings before implementation of the corrective actions. Thus, in this way, FMEA is a powerful tool for maintaining the quality and reliability standards.

FMEA application to the research objective

FMEA is an industrial engineering tool for prioritizing the corrective actions to be taken based on the RPN generated from the severity, occurrence, and detection ratings (Sharma et al., 2021a). Failure modes and effects analysis is predominantly used in design and manufacturing sectors (G. Sharma and Rao, 2014). The same has been innovatively used for targeting improvement in the educational use (Kenchakkanavar and Joshi, 2010). Table 6.1 depicts the FMEA document for the conduct of EC activities.

In the FMEA document, first, the process for which the improvement is to be realized is clearly defined. Next to this, the potential failure modes are identified. Failure modes describe the manner in which the failure may occur. Here, there are two potential failure modes identified, as, "unable to overcome the constraints and impediments" and "partially able to overcome the constraints and impediments" during the conduct of extracurricular activities. After this, the potential effects of the failure modes are identified and given a severity ranking on the scale of 1 to 10, where 1 is least severe and 10 is most severe. The potential causes for the identified failure modes are listed, and the occurrence ranking is given similar to that of the severity ranking on a scale of 1 to 10 with 1 being the least occurrence and 10 being catered to the most occurrence. Subsequent to this, detection ranking is allocated for the controls present to detect the causes. 1 being easy to detect and 10 being the most difficult to detect. Finally, the risk priority number (RPN) is generated by multiplying the rankings given to severity (Sev.), occurrence (Occ.), and detection (Det.). This RPN prioritizes the action to be taken for overcoming constraints and impediments in the conduct of extracurricular activities.

From Figure 6.1, it is noticed that the highest RPN number obtained is 392, pertaining to the cause that of "Inertia of the students to participate". Hence, the first corrective action to be taken is that of eliminating this causal factor. In many cases of EC activity, it is observed that most of the students initially hesitate to come out of their comfort zone and possess a lot of inertia to take part in the activity. In such times, it is the duty of the faculty to break the ice and make the students at ease, so that they actively and willingly take part in the activity and benefit out of it. Thus, FMEA concepts of design and manufacturing sectors can be applied to the educational service sector for proposing improvements in the identified educational process.

Table 6.1 Failure Modes and Effects Analysis (FMEA) for the Conduct of EC Activities

Process	*Potential Failure Modes*	*Potential Effects*	*Sev.*	*Potential causes*	*Occ.*	*Current controls*	*Det.*	*RPN*
Constraints and impediments in the conduct of extracurricular activities	Unable to overcome the constraints and impediments	No conduct of extracurricular activities	10	Clash of EC activity with regular class-timings	2	Usage of software tool for timetable to avoid clashes	1	20
				No allocation of finance and resources	3	Creating of a separate header for finance and resources within the institute's system	3	90
				Students absent for the EC activity	5	Embedding EC activity within the regular timetable after the class hours	1	50
				Non-availability of proper safety and medical aid at the EC activity site	2	First aid for disposal at the in-house dispensary	2	40
				Students unaware of the importance of EC activities	2	Conducting sensitization programme for the students	3	60
				Whistleblowing by the students leading to insecurity among the staff	8	Prior notice to the staff via circular to be lenient and give space to the students to enjoy the EC activity	3	240
	Partially able to overcome the constraints and impediments	Ineffective conduct of extracurricular activities	8	Process and method not distinguished for outdoor and indoor EC activities	5	A clear rule book to be designed for EC activities	6	240

(*Continued*)

Table 6.1 (Continued)

Process	*Potential Failure Modes*	*Potential Effects*	*Sev.*	*Potential causes*	*Occ.*	*Current controls*	*Det.*	*RPN*
				No faculty supervision during the EC activity	5	Allocate responsibility to faculty within their individual timetables	2	80
				Gender suitability not taken into consideration	3	EC activity design to incorporate the gender suitability	3	72
				Peer interaction missing in online platform during the conduct of EC activity	4	Prior notice to the staff via circular to be lenient and give space to the students to interact in the EC activity	3	96
				Improper coordination between students and faculty	4	Advanced planning of the EC activity	4	128
				Inertia of students to participate	7	Faculty and students to make the participants at ease	7	392
				Non-adherence to time duration	5	Fixed in timetable	4	160
				Divergence of focus and attention from the EC activity	4	Faculty supervision	4	128
				The participating jury is not from the domain of that particular EC activity	3	Suitable selection of the jury for the EC activity	3	72

Constraints and impediments

The following are the key issues which delve into the constraints and impediments aspects during the conduct of extracurricular activities in engineering education.

- **Timings** – The conduct of extracurricular activities is not possible in regular classwork hours. Hence, it is advisable to plan the extracurricular activity in a day with devoid of any classwork. This prevents any interruption in the regular lecture sessions and allows the students to participate in the activities with full freedom without the fear of missing the classwork. Preferably, the EC activities may be planned in the weekends of Fridays and Saturdays of the week instead of during the weekdays. This demarcates and distinguishes the EC activities from the regular work timings thereby catering the necessary time and attention towards the extracurricular activities. During the pandemic situation, an interrupted time-slot pattern with a regular break of 15 minutes may be allocated during the conduct of the EC activity. This gives the participants with time to sanitize themselves at these regular interval time slots. In this way, the timing of the EC activity must be carefully planned in the interests of the student participants.
- **Finance and resources** – A separate header for finance and resources needs to be created at the institute level of functioning to take care of the expenses incurred during the conduct of the EC activities (Kumar and Rewari, 2022). This is very much required to keep an account of the cash flow involved in the revenue generation as well as the money spent during the defined time period of the academic year. During the pandemic situation, the revenue generation has dwindled across all the sectors including the education sector. Thus, to prevent undue expenses and generate revenue through the EC activities, a separate bank account may be opened to keep track of the finances involved. Certain EC activity competitions, like cooking, painting, embroidery, and so on, require investment in the raw materials which incurs expenses. Other EC activities like singing and dancing hardly require any monetary input. Thus, depending on the type of the activity the resource allocation needs to be done wisely.
- **Process and method** – Depending on the nature of the activity, the process and method for carrying out the extracurricular activity vary. Whether the activity is an indoor or outdoor, the approach differs. During the pandemic situation, in an indoor activity, care has to be taken for proper ventilation, lighting, arrangement of the related equipment within the arena. Also, an indoor event calls for proper acoustic design to avoid any sound echoes. The outdoor events call for a different process and method. In an outdoor event, the pandemic protocol must be followed. Prior intimation to the police and other administrative personnel must be done regarding the conduct of the activity, and permissions must be taken prior to the activity to avoid confusion and chaos.

- **Supervision** – Faculty supervision is needed for maintaining the discipline and decorum within the EC activity hours. For high emotional quotient competitive activities like a cricket match or a wrestling match, there requires a strict supervision from security view point. It is a natural tendency of the youngster students to cheer and make noise during an activity. If this is in a controlled pattern, then there is no problem. But in case the noise exceeds the regular decibel levels, then comes the role of supervision and proctored conduct of the students into picture. Moreover, during the pandemic time, it becomes imperative to allocate supervisors for the extracurricular event to prevent any unforeseen incidents.
- **Gender suitability** – Gender suitability is one such aspect which must be taken into prime consideration for conducting extracurricular activities. Care must be taken, and the activity must be so designed that it leverages advantage for both the genders and brings in a win-win situation for both of them. Activities involving physical strength and energy burnout may be allocated to boys and those involving soft-skills, aesthetics may be catered to both the student genders.
- **Absenteeism** – Absenteeism is a common problem as students may take the extracurricular activity in a lighter vein. Prior sensitization regarding the seriousness of the activity must be carried out. Value addition and recognition through distribution of certificates for the winners as well as for the participants shall motivate the student participants and create a positive vibe during the extracurricular activity. The extracurricular activity must be scheduled in the regular weekly timetable during the weekends to bring in seriousness with the student group. Another method of curtailing absenteeism is to allocate credits to the extracurricular activities within the semester course work, which shall inculcate seriousness in the student towards the EC activities and bring down absenteeism.
- **Blended mode of conduct** – During the pandemic situation, the conduct of extracurricular activities is not possible physically in the premises of the institute of learning. Because of the Covid-19 pandemic, all the activities may not be carried out in physical presence and may require to be switched over to online platform. Activities suitable for online platform may be either carried out completely online or given a blended mode of approach. Activities which can be suited for a blended mode are like debate, extempore, paper, or poster presentation which do not require either any materialistic inputs or processing of any kind of materials like model making or cooking competitions and so on.
- **Safety and first-aid** – Extracurricular activities, like cycling race, running race, go-karting, and so on, require the adherence to proper safety measures. Medical aid must be readily available within the reach for any unseen medical emergencies. During the pandemic situation, face masks and gloves must be distributed as a part of the protocol for the conduct of the extracurricular activity. Hand sanitizers must be installed at every nook and corner of the arena. Temperature-sensing devices must be used

to sense any abnormal rise in body temperature of the participants as well as administration personnel. Thus, first-aid and safety must always be placed at the utmost priority.

- **Coordination** – The students as well as faculty coordinators must work as a team in synchronization with each other. With the advent of smartphones and socializing applications, the exchange of information has become easily accessible. This aspect must be leveraged for achieving better coordination between all the stakeholders of the EC activity. Prior intimation through online circular, structured distribution, and delegation of the responsibilities among the student as well as staff coordinators shall spring up an excellent performance during the activity. This is the era of a postdigital world wherein there is an abundant of information at the disposal of the students. Information exchange has become easy at the fingertips of the stakeholders. Thus, coordination through mutual information exchange is the order of the day for putting up any successful activity.
- **Inertia** – Along with learning, one of the main mottos of extracurricular activities is enjoyment and stress relief. Active student participation is to be promoted and students to come out of their clutches of inertia and shyness so that they may give their 100% efforts. Not all students have same capabilities. Some are extraordinarily good, some are average, and some are below average. The aim of extracurricular event is to encourage the below average and the average to come out of their comfort zone and put up an excellent performance by overcoming their inertia, so that the left-skewed bell curve shall be right skewed reflecting the enhanced performance of the below-par students also.
- **Awareness** – Students to be sensitized regarding the importance of extracurricular activities on leadership and personality development. In many institutes, the students lack the awareness of extracurricular activities, and they are limited to only academics within the four walls of the lecture hall. This hampers the all-round development of the student and makes them limited to academics only. They then lack the soft skills which are very essential for achieving success in the professional life after the college life. Extracurricular activities form an excellent platform for honing of soft skills which enable holistic development of the student. Thus, it is very important to bring in awareness about extracurricular activities and their importance in the regular curriculum.
- **Adherence to time duration** – The proposed activity is to be completed within the allocated time duration. It must neither exceed the time limit nor be completed before the stipulated time. Adherence to the time duration develops time management skills within the student. For example, during a debate competition, talking less than the time limit reflects lack of content, knowledge, and confidence within the subject and talking more than the time limit reflects mismanagement of the time by undue prolonging of the given task. Hence, adherence to the time duration marks an important role in the extracurricular activity.

- **Focus** – Divergence of focus and loss of attention are to be avoided during the activity hours. Participation in the extracurricular activities must be done wholeheartedly with full zeal and enthusiasm. The focus must be completely set on the activity and undertaking the activity in true sense with conviction. This boosts the confidence and enables the student to solve real-life problems with ease and achieve greater heights in life.
- **Insecurity** – Whistleblowing by students may create insecurity among the staff who are not involved in the activity. So confidence of the staff who are not involved in the activity is to be taken into consideration. This may be done by disseminating information regarding the activity through a proper academic circular well in advance. At the same time, the whistleblowing by the students must be controlled and not be fuelled up.
- **Result of the activity** – Eminent personnel who have expertise in the activity are to be selected as judges for evaluating the performance of the participants in the activity. This is mandatory for generating honest and bias less judgement of the EC activity. Incapable or unsuitable jury members may lead to incorrect decision for the performance of the activity, and this make take a wrong direction of losing faith in the activity by the students. Thus, it must be ensured that the result of the activity is true, honest, and unbiased.

These key issues provide a meaningful insight into the constraints and impediments faced during the planning as well as execution process of the conduct for extracurricular activities within the engineering education domain. It is reiterated here that the whole world is gripped within the pandemic of Covid-19. Physical presence of the student as well as faculty is uncertain during the pandemic due to the social lockdown imposed. Continuous house arrest during the pandemic has also led to emotional imbalance and other psychological problems. This has hampered the complete education system of the whole world. But there is a ray of hope in these tough times. The world has switched over to the online mode of pedagogy to combat with the restrictions posed by the pandemic. All possibilities are explored for the conduct of EC activities in the online mode. The concept similar to that of open-book examination can be adopted in the conduct of EC activities where the content of the activity is disclosed beforehand, and the participants are given prior time for preparation and presentation of the content through online mode. Also, group activities like online group discussions and extempore can be conducted where the students get an opportunity to showcase their skills and vent out the mental stress, even during the pandemic situation. It is stressed that participation in EC activities plays a prominent role in character building, personality development, motivation, and self-regulated development of the pupil (Feraco et al., 2022) and must be given equal weightage with that of knowledge acquisition for all-inclusive development of the student.

Conclusion

At the outset, extracurricular activities play an important role in the students' holistic growth. Overall development of the student is the call of the day. Apart from academics, the student must excel in all walks of life for preparing to face the hurdles posed by the life. This can be accomplished through extracurricular activities outside the realm of academics. Extracurricular activities call for application of techniques for the event planning, conduct, management, and optimization which can be adopted from the domain of industrial engineering. Principles of industrial engineering are truly flexible and can be camouflaged for application into any technical, managerial, financial, business, educational, or any other contemporary field. An attempt to leverage this truly remarkable characteristic of the industrial engineering in the trying times of pandemic has been tried out in this piece of work. This work documents one such improvement methodology proposal through the industrial engineering principles of Ishikawa (cause-and-effect) diagram and failure modes and effects analysis (FMEA). The process of addressing constraints and impediments faced in the conduct of extracurricular activities in an engineering education environment within the limelight of pandemic situation has been considered as the central theme of this work. Brainstorming is carried out for enlisting the potential causal factors for the consequence of inability to overcome constraints and impediments in the conduct of extracurricular activities. A service FMEA helped in systematically charting out the effects, causes, and controls for the potential failure modes of the process in consideration. Thus, FMEA helped in detecting out the loopholes in the educational process under consideration. Proposal and prioritization of the corrective actions required for the elimination of these potential causal factors are carried out through the industrial engineering and quality assurance technique of failure modes and effects analysis. Finally, it is concluded that the concepts of industrial engineering can be applied for proposing improvement in the service sector of education and for the smooth conduct of extracurricular activities in engineering education in the trying times of pandemic, which humanity is facing in the present era.

References

Ahmed, V., and Opoku, A. (2022). Technology supported learning and pedagogy in times of crisis: the case of COVID-19 pandemic. *Education and Information Technologies*, 27(1), 365–405.

Akram, H., Bhutto, M. H., and Chughtai, M. S. (2022). An analysis of business students' stressors and their coping strategies in the post-pandemic era. *Decision*, 1–14.

Allen, K. A., Waters, L., Arslan, G., and Prentice, M. (2022). Strength-based parenting and stress-related growth in adolescents: Exploring the role of positive reappraisal, school belonging, and emotional processing during the pandemic. *Journal of Adolescence*, 94(2), 176–190.

Balaguer, Á., Benítez, E., Albertos, A., and Lara, S. (2020). Not everything helps the same for everyone: relevance of extracurricular activities for academic achievement. *Humanities and Social Sciences Communications*, *7*(1), 1–8.

Bhardwaj, A., and Kumar, V. (2023). Social Media as an Enabler to Combat Misinformation. In *Pandemics in the Age of Social Media: Information and Misinformation in Developing Nations*. Routledge: New York (USA), pp. 1–15.

Clark, R. M., Kaw, A. K., and Braga Gomes, R. (2022). Adaptive learning: Helpful to the flipped classroom in the online environment of COVID? *Computer Applications in Engineering Education*, *30*(2), 517–531.

Feraco, T., Resnati, D., Fregonese, D., Spoto, A., and Meneghetti, C. (2022). An integrated model of school students' academic achievement and life satisfaction. Linking soft skills, extracurricular activities, self-regulated learning, motivation, and emotions. *European Journal of Psychology of Education*, 1–22.

Grodotzki, J., Upadhya, S., and Tekkaya, A. E. (2021). Engineering education amid a global pandemic. *Advances in Industrial and Manufacturing Engineering*, *3*, 100058.

Hermanstyne, T. O., Johnson, L., Wylie, K. M., and Skeath, J. B. (2022). Helping others enhances graduate student wellness and mental health. *Nature Biotechnology*, *40*(4), 618–619.

Heymann, P., Bastiaens, E., Jansen, A., van Rosmalen, P., and Beausaert, S. (2022). A Conceptual Model of Students' Reflective Practice for the Development of Employability Competences, Supported by an Online Learning Platform. *Education+Training*, *64*(3), 380–397. https://doi.org/10.1108/ET-05-2021-0161.

Ilari, B., Cho, E., Li, J., and Bautista, A. (2022). Perceptions of Parenting, Parent-Child Activities and Children's Extracurricular Activities in Times of COVID-19. *Journal of Child and Family Studies*, *31*(2), 409–420.

Jääskeläinen, T., López-Íñiguez, G., and Phillips, M. (2022). Music Students' Experienced Workload in Higher Education: A Systematic Review and Recommendations for Good Practice. *Musicae Scientiae*, 10298649221093976.

Kapilan, N., Vidhya, P., and Gao, X. Z. (2021). Virtual Laboratory: A Boon to the Mechanical Engineering Education During Covid-19 Pandemic. *Higher Education for the Future*, *8*(1), 31–46.

Kenchakkanavar, V. D., and Joshi, A. K. (2010). Failure mode and effect analysis: A tool to enhance quality in engineering education. *International Journal of Engineering*, *4*(1), 52–59.

Köksal, G., and Eğitman, A. (1998). Planning and design of industrial engineering education quality. *Computers & Industrial Engineering*, *35*(3–4), 639–642.

Kovid, R. K., and Kumar, V. (Eds) (2022). *Cases on Emerging Markets Responses to the COVID-19 Pandemic*. IGI – Global Publications: USA (ISBN13: 978-16-6843-504-5, DOI: 10.4018/978-1-6684-3504-5).

Kumar, V., and Malhotra, G. (Eds) (2021). *Stakeholder Strategies for Reducing the Impact of Global Health Crises*. IGI – Global Publications: USA (ISBN13: 978-17-9987-495-9, DOI: 10.4018/978-1-7998-7495-9).

Kumar, V., and Nanda, P. (2020). Social Media as a Tool in Higher Education: A Pedagogical Perspective. In *Handbook of Research on Diverse Teaching Strategies for the Technology-Rich Classroom*. IGI Global, pp. 239–253.

Kumar, V., and Gupta G. (Eds) (2021). *Strategic Management During a Pandemic*. Routledge, Taylor & Francis Group: USA (ISBN 9780367646479).

Kumar, V., and Rewari, M. (2022). A Responsible Approach to Higher Education Curriculum Design. *International Journal of Educational Reform (IJER)*, *31*(4), 422–441.

Kumar, V., and Sharma, D. (2017). Cloud computing as a catalyst in STEM education. *International Journal of Information and Communication Technology Education (IJICTE)*, *13*(2), 38–51.

Mushtaha, E., Dabous, S. A., Alsyouf, I., Ahmed, A., and Abdraboh, N. R. (2022). The challenges and opportunities of online learning and teaching at engineering and theoretical colleges during the pandemic. *Ain Shams Engineering Journal*, *13*(6), 101770.

Nebrida, J., and Bangud, A. (2022). Challenges in Hybrid Teaching Amidst Pandemic: The Proposed Model. *Journal of Engineering Research and Reports*, 2(9), 51–64.

Ng, D. T. K., Ng, E. H. L., and Chu, S. K. W. (2022). Engaging students in creative music making with musical instrument application in an online flipped classroom. *Education and Information Technologies*, 27(1), 45–64.

Ng, T. K. (2021). New interpretation of extracurricular activities via social networking sites: A case study of artificial intelligence learning at a secondary school in Hong Kong. *Journal of Education and Training Studies*, 9(1), 49–60.

Prasad, C. L. V. R. S. V., Sharma, G. V. S. S., and Pavani, P. N. L. (2021). Capability Resurrection of DC Sputtering Machine: A Case Study. *International Journal of Surface Engineering and Interdisciplinary Materials Science (IJSEIMS)*, 9(1), 60–76.

Rassudov, L., and Korunets, A. (2020). COVID-19 pandemic challenges for engineering education. Paper presented at the 2020 XI International Conference on Electrical Power Drive Systems (ICEPDS).

Sharaievska, I., McAnirlin, O., Browning, M. H. E. M., Larson, L. R., Mullenbach, L., Rigolon, A., D'Antonio, A., Cloutier, S., Thomsen, J., Metcalf, E. C., and Reigner, N. (2022). "Messy Transitions": Students' Perspectives on the Impacts of the COVID-19 Pandemic on Higher Education. *Higher Education*, 1–18.

Sharma, G. V. S. S., and Rao, P. S. (2014). A DMAIC approach for process capability improvement an engine crankshaft manufacturing process. *Journal of Industrial Engineering International*, *10*(2), 1–11.

Sharma, G. V. S. S., Rao, P. S., and Babu, B. S. (2018). Process capability improvement through DMAIC for aluminum alloy wheel machining. *Journal of Industrial Engineering International*, *14*(2), 213–226.

Sharma, G. V. S. S., Vara Prasad, C. L. V. R. S., and Rambabu, V. (2021a). Online Machine Drawing Pedagogy – A Knowledge Management Perspective Through Maker Education in the COVID-19 Pandemic Era. *Knowledge and Process Management, 22*(9), 51–64.

Sharma, G. V. S. S., Vara Prasad, C. L. V. R. S. V., and Srinivasa Rao, M. (2021b). Industrial engineering into healthcare–A comprehensive review. *International Journal of Healthcare Management*, *14*(4), 1288–1302.

Sharma, G. V. S. S., Vara Prasad, C. L. V. R. S., and Santa Rao, K. (2022). Post-COVID-19 era: An Enabler for the Implementation of Blended Learning in Compliance With the NEP 2020. *International Journal of Educational Reform*, 10567879221112059.

Shoaib, A. M. (2022). Activating a Directed Motivational Current Through a Gamified Extracurricular Activity in Higher Education: A Pilot Study. Paper presented at the UICELL Conference Proceeding.

Singh, J., and Kumar, V. (2022). Combating the Pandemic with ICT Based Learning tools and applications: A case of Indian Higher Education. *International Journal of Virtual and Personal Learning Environments (IJVPLE) Platforms (IJVPLE)*, 12(1), 1–21.

Warfvinge, P., Löfgreen, J., Andersson, K., Roxå, T., and Åkerman, C. (2022). The rapid transition from campus to online teaching–how are students' perception of learning experiences affected? *European Journal of Engineering Education*, 47(2), 211–229.

7 E-learning

An attribute to physical, psychological, and mental distress among students

Shafila Bansal, Simranjot Kaur, Ayushi Pathak, Priya Saharan, and Santosh Bhukal

Introduction

Covid-19 is a highly transmissible respiratory disease affecting people of all ages and from all walks of life worldwide (Kumar and Gupta, 2021). However, for developing countries this pandemic was a disaster with public health implications. The virus transmission affected all the fields including the educational sector. Owing to the Covid-19 spread, university closures resulted in the introduction of novel educational approach that ensured students' continuous study. The pandemic provoked drastic changes in students' lifestyle including changes in their physical activities, sedentary behavior, eating habits, mental health, and psychological behavior. Education sector was severely influenced negatively because of enduring pandemic situation and grueling actions like lockdown and staying-at-home instructions.

During the pandemic, students' mental health became a critical issue, where this vulnerable community has come into spotlight (Kovid and Kumar, 2022). The teenagers have become more clingier, attention seeker, and dependent on their parents because of the long-term change in their routine (Marques et al., 2021). This type of illnesses hinders their academic achievements, affects their motivation, attentiveness, and social networks (Bhardwaj and Kumar, 2023). Before lockdown, education was mostly relied on face-to-face physical engagement with the teachers and friend circle. But the global pandemic and lockdown protocols significantly affected millions of students across the world as their schools and educational institutions were shut (Singh and Kumar, 2022). As of March 2020, a closure of educational institutions in 150 countries affected the learning of 1,379,344,914 students or over 80% of the world's student learners (McCarthy, 2020; Sahu, 2020). As per reports of April 2020, more than 157 crore students of 191 nations were severely impacted owing to closure of educational institutions due to coronavirus (Kritika, 2020). Particularly, for schools, from March 2020 to March 2021, education of more than 168 million schoolchildren was affected. Also, another analysis on school closures report shows a staggering effect on 98 million schoolchildren of 14 countries, two-thirds of whom belong to

DOI: 10.4324/9781003491712-7

Latin America and the Caribbean, including Panama, Bangladesh, El Salvador, and Bolivia (UNICEF, 2021). In countries like India, due to a complete lockdown in 2020, 1.5 million schools remained shut affecting 247 million pupils of elementary and secondary schools (Hopkins, n.d.). A report on colleges in the United States revealed that a minimum of 1,102 colleges and universities were closed because of the fear of spread of the deadly Covid-19 in March 2020, which further impacted learning of over 14 million students (*How Coronavirus Changed College for over 14 Million Students*, n.d.).

Although most of the institutions had accepted the new normal situations and shifted the education from offline to online mode completely, a lack of technological infrastructure remained a great barrier for the students in acquiring e-learning (Bhardwaj and Kumar, 2022). During the lockdown period, it was easy for the educators to give online assignments along with stern deadlines, but this practice exacerbated students' nervousness (Kumar and Malhotra, 2021). To attend online classes many students operated cell phones for 6–8 hours a day at a stretch on a daily basis which added uncontrollable stress and other health issues among them (Balasopoulou et al., 2017; *Manage Screen Time in the Age of Online Learning – Oxford Learning*, n.d.; *Online Classes, Increased Screen Time Leading to Eye Conditions in Kids_ Doctors*, n.d.; Rajanbir Singh, 2020). Studies have reported emergence of health problems like burning sensation in eyes, dry eye syndromes, itchy eyes, blurry vision, neck and back pain, ear-related issues because of enhanced screen time among students (*How Too Much Screen Time Affects Kids' Eyes: Tips to Prevent Eye Strain | Children's Hospital of Philadelphia*, n.d.; *Online Classes, Increased Screen Time Leading to Eye Conditions in Kids_ Doctors*, n.d.; *Online Classes: Students Complain of Eye and Ear Problems – The Hindu*, n.d.; Torsheim et al., 2010).

In schools, students not only learn a structured academic syllabus but also develop social, emotional, and communication skills, sports, behavior in public places, friendship circles, etc. (Kumar and Nanda, 2020). So, a regular schooling is necessary for the holistic well-being of the students (*Wave of Online Learning & Its Impact on Holistic Development of Children*, n.d.). However, the pandemic situation has worsened the sedentary behavior of students as they had to spend more time on the internet for acquiring education. Lack of physical activities is a well-known factor to contribute in serious illnesses such as high blood pressure, diabetes, obesity, and cardiovascular diseases and is responsible for lowering the psychological and physical strength.

A complete lockdown and e-learning have also affected the confidence of mentees, their exam-attempting skills, along with memory sharpness greatly, which is expected to worsen in future. The online classes and exams affected the students in such a way that there is a fear among them regarding offline exams. Now, when educational institutions have reopened, social anxiety, that is a hesitation for going to school and re-establishing relations with their mentors and peers, can be witnessed among them (*COVID-19 Pandemic_*

Reopening of Schools Causing Anxiety Among Kids_ Here's How You Can Help Them, n.d.; *School Not so Easy after Two Years – The Hindu*, n.d.; *Social Anxiety in the New Normal_ Not Everyone Is Ready to Go Back to Campus – Telegraph India*, n.d.). Numerous studies have been conducted worldwide in the past two years to study the feedback of students regarding online classes that give a mixed data where in some countries like India and Georgia, students are receptive toward online learning and find this mode of education more comfortable and flexible, whereas in countries like the Philippines and Pakistan, students feel e-learning as a non-motivated way of learning (Bast, 2021; *Students Are More Comfortable with Self-Learning via Online*, n.d.).

Hence, the spread of Covid-19 has affected the student learners in a significant way and this chapter accounts for the physical, psychological, and mental impacts of online learning on students.

Impacts of e-learning among students

As per reports of UNESCO, the Covid-19 pandemic has disrupted the study of more than one billion learners in 129 nations (Mali and Lim, 2021). Worldwide, many academic institutions turned to emergency remote teaching using online platforms for providing continuous learning to the students, which increased students' concern about their studies. The practice of online education affected the mentees in one or another way, where they did not feel motivated, and their energy was not getting channelized in a right way, which eventually made them mentally, physically, as well as psychologically sick.

Psychological and mental health impacts

Worldwide, the pandemic affected people's lives with an uncertainty and concern about what may come next. The Covid-19 stress had severely affected the mental health of students irrespective of their age. This stress includes anxiety, future of their education, fear about their career, and so on. During the lockdown, a long-term closure of schools interrupted the routine of students, whereby they are now lacking in fresh ideas about academic and extracurricular activities. A significant change in overall behavior and well-being can be seen among them as they were not allowed to go out to meet their friends, to play, and to participate in school events physically during this period. The restriction in their physical activities may have a long-term negative impact on their general psychological well-being (Singh et al., 2020). Anxiety, depression, lethargy, poor social interaction, weakened or damaged immune system, and loss of appetite are among common repercussions of psychological stress in children. Psychological discomfort is worsened by online learning glitches and the worry of losing an academic year. Various case studies have revealed that students are hit hard psychologically during and after the Covid-19 pandemic. According to a study conducted on undergraduate students of Jordanian universities (Maqableh and Alia, 2021), 80% of the participants experienced psychological troubles during the lockdown. Also, students had to deal with a variety of learning-related concerns, including mental health, time management, loneliness, and finding a work–life balance. According to a survey conducted in Shaanxi Province of China (Jiao et al., 2020), clinginess, inattention, impatience, and fear of asking about the epidemic are among the most common psychological and behavioral disorders among children and adolescents aged 3 to 18. The main psychological conditions evaluated were relatives' health, sleeplessness including nightmares, poor eating, physical uneasiness, agitation, distraction, and separation troubles.

Lack of socialization

Studies have shown that a lack of physical interaction with peers and teachers made the students anxious during the pandemic period as socialization is imperative for overall academic development (UNESCO IESALC, 2020). Online classes are devoid of social interaction, this social isolation and the lack of connection with other friends and teachers increased the feelings of social anxiety and academic stress (Zurlo et al., 2020) among students which negatively impacted their mental and psychological health. Face-to-face interactions help in building friendship which provides a sense of security and self-esteem to students and eventually helps in relieving mental stress. A regular peer-to-peer interaction is directly linked to better self-efficacy and less academic stress resulting in better mental health among students (Procentese et al., 2020). Researchers have shown the importance of student interactions in the teaching and learning process where peer-to-peer interaction enables better learning. Most people have a fundamental motivation to interact socially (Baumeister and Leary, 1995), but worldwide lockdown minimized face-to-face interactions which affected friendships. Studying with friends has always been claimed to improve the well-being of students along with the academic success, but it requires physical proximity and regular meetings (Boda et al., 2020; Stadtfeld et al., 2019). Online mode indeed enhanced the virtual collaboration, but for fostering social ties, personal meetings are important (Boda et al., 2020; Doreian and Conti, 2012). E-learning does not provide opportunities to meet and learn from fellow classmates physically, and poor learning adds up to mental stress. Hence, in virtual learning, learners feel isolated, unmotivated, and discouraged. This may lead to mental and pomological stress (Elmer et al., 2020).

Socioeconomic disparity

Socioeconomic status is another predictor of stress and anxiety among students. Throughout the pandemic, a digital disparity was seen where the students had unequal learning opportunities because of financial difficulties of their families (Meier and Hoppe, 2020). During this period when most of the educational institutions were shut and learners were using online platforms like Google Classroom, Zoom, WhatsApp, and YouTube for attaining e-learning, there were many of them who were not able to access important devices like mobile phone, computers, laptops, or tablets for attending online classes. Poverty and psychological stress are strongly related (Jiang, 2020), where digital dividend and dearth of access to modern technology by students from impoverished families result in high mental and psychological impacts (Nayar and Kumar, 2018). As per reports by the Teacher Task Force, an international alliance coordinated by UNESCO, 50% of the total student learners, that is 826 million, did not have computer access at their household during the pandemic and 43%, that is 706 million, were not having internet available at their home (O'Hagan, 2020). The lack of access to online classes forced them to draw a comparison with upper-class fellow mates which further added to the mental and psychological distress. This type of situation was very much common in developing countries like India and Bangladesh, where almost a large percentage of the population live below the poverty line.

Fear of academic loss

During this difficult time, everything was uncertain – when schools or universities will open for offline classes, how examinations would happen, in offline or in online mode, whether the students will be promoted to the next class or not – all these worries were making the mentees nervous about their academics. As the pandemic had delayed the previous and current academic sessions, so to complete the syllabi, teachers had to share online reading material including audio/video lectures that further added burden to students for listening to them on time for better learning. The fear of lagging behind of syllabus and loss of academic year was among other aspects that enhanced student's psychological anxiety. The uncertain pandemic did not allow the academicians and administrations to declare the results on time.

Lack of IT knowledge

All learners are not equal in a single online classroom from different views (Lata and Gupta, 2021). Many of them coped up effortlessly to e-learning, however some were not able to acquire this knowledge prominently, as the procedure of learning depends on availability of resources and access to learning tools. Students lacking in IT knowledge suffered from multiple stressors (Crooks et al., 2020). The burden of online classes was one of the contributing aspects to students' stress levels, as they were expected to use online platforms ceaselessly that they have just learned to use. This problem was aggravated among school students in comparison to university learners as the latter are more familiar with digital gadgets. Furthermore, as the education had suddenly shifted from offline to online mode, most of the instructors continued to use and share the same curriculum and learning methods that were originally designed for face-to-face learning, which did not sit well with students and hence exposed to a great deal of stress and anxiety.

Uncertainty of future

The pandemic-driven closure of educational institutions had affected the learning of students significantly. According to the reports, worldwide lockdown had left the K-12 students on an average 5 months behind in mathematics and 4 months behind in reading by the end of the session (Dorn et al., 2021). The lockdown has not only affected the internal assessments of students but also delayed the examinations for main public qualifications like General Certificate of Secondary Educations, which was the only grim possibility in that tough time. Several state-level board exams, university-level exams and entrance exams, and recruitment exams had been postponed/rescheduled (Pokhrel and Chhetri, 2021) leading to a feeling of uncertainty about future among students. Also, the traditional academic calendars of various schools/colleges/universities were heavily interrupted, where the working days of educational institutions were minimized (Abidjan and Côte d'Ivoire, 2021). However, some universities have made up the loss of shortened academic year by following a 6-day working week instead of five days resulting in unnecessary pressure on learners (*New Academic Year Postponed by up to Three Months*, n.d.). This uncertainty of academic calendars triggered future career anxiety among students (Mahmud et al., 2021). Fewer job opportunities and less internship facilities by universities, fear of not getting admissions in higher classes and appropriate jobs in future contributed to depression and stress. Now, after spending almost two years at home, graduates are mentally as well as psychologically depressed about launching their careers as they are lacking in skills of getting suitable jobs (Chowdhury et al., 2022).

Lack of concentration

During online classes, environmental factors at home like noise, lighting, and temperature had a substantial impact on students' academic performance (Realyvásquez-Vargas et al., 2020). These issues are directly related to hitches in focusing and concentrating while e-learning (Amir et al., 2020). Worldwide lockdown had forbidden the students from visiting libraries or reading halls where they were obligated to study and learn; however, noise and distractions were major challenges for them while learning from home. Mentees with less space at home, where the whole family being present in the same room, reported a distracting learning environment (Son et al., 2020a). An interrupted atmosphere at home did not allow them to cope up with the online classes, eventually added stress and anxiety levels (Son et al., 2020b).

Poor internet connectivity

In the age of virtual learning, inadequate internet access and a lack of high-speed internet are the major socio-psychological concerns (Asio et al., 2021). A reliable internet connection was a significant problem in many countries. Particularly in developing countries, a low internet bandwidth along with lesser access points made online learning very challenging (Pokhrel and Chhetri, 2021). Studies have reported the issues of tackling with poor internet connectivity by those coming from underprivileged families (Aristovnik et al., 2020). According to a student survey done in 2020, 7% of students in the UK reported insufficient access to the internet where the figure rises to 12% when it comes to those from lower socioeconomic households. Similarly, in Ireland, 21% of third-level students showed their dissatisfaction toward reliable Wi-Fi, indicating the biggest hurdle in acquiring online learning (Cullinan et al., 2021). Studies have shown that apart from underprivileged or poor students of India, 50% of those of urban private schools had reported issues with internet signal and speed (Today, 2021). A report by Federal Communications commission revealed that 97% of Americans of urban areas had a high-speed reliable internet access, however this figure drops to 65% for rural areas and 60% for tribal lands. On the global viewpoint, the data given by International Telecommunication Union is even more awful stating the internet penetration rate in developed countries is 87%, only 47% in developing countries, and merely 19% in the least developed countries (*COVID-19 Exposed the Digital Divide*, n.d.). Poor internet access and an incompatible gadget caused workload on students. Instead of focusing on studies, the students were more stressed about internet connectivity. Most of the students felt almost left out, when they were not able to attend online classes just because of the internet. Paused videos while attending live classes because of server issue was very common and by the time they resumed, one has missed out on the live session. This situation is worse for those from remote, hilly, and rural areas, where students had to walk miles to study in fully networked zones. Therefore, digital divide and poor internet connectivity proved a hassle for many students resulting in mental and psychological health issues.

Virtual learning fatigue

Although, during trying times of pandemic when educational institutions were shut due to lockdown and social distancing protocols, the online platform Zoom proved to be a new reliable medium for the mentors and mentees to communicate. However, an increment in transition from face-to-face learning to e-learning conspicuously developed a new kind of problem among students and teachers called mental fatigue or zoom fatigue (Amponsah et al., 2021). It basically arises on spending long hours on Zoom sessions without interacting with the colleagues on the other side of the camera (Salim et al., 2022). Long-time video interactions mentally drain the learners as brains are unable to process information in the way it's accustomed to. In offline classes, our brain processes a number of nonverbal cues like facial expressions, pitch and tone of voice, body language, and eye contact, which are absent in virtual learning, therefore monotonous learning results in mental fatigue. Factors like silence during zooming and amount of time spent on online contribute to Zoom fatigue. This fatigue has diverse risk factors including impact on the sleep quality and mental health (Ramachandran, 2021). Furthermore, virtual conferencing requires a constant gaze from all attendees regardless of the presenter which triggers negative physiological impacts on the learners (Lee, 2020).

Physical impacts

Virtual schools affect not only the mental and psychological health but also the physical health of the mentees. Pandemic restrictions of staying at home resulted in reduced daily walks, exercises, physical activity, diet changes, obesity, mood swings, increased TV time, and online studies. The health concerns significantly magnified with the shift to online schooling, where students were required to spend up to 6–7 hours a day in front of a digital screen. Sitting at one place and staring at computer screens distressed them both physically and mentally. It is even been connected to obesity, anxiety, and depression. Eye strain, headaches, and fatigue are among the common physical health issues experienced while e-learning.

Diet changes and obesity

Numerous studies have claimed an increased body weight and BMI among children and adolescents learners worldwide during the lockdown period due to reduced physical activity, more binging on junk food, and so on (Chang et al., 2021). More time spent at home while virtual education enhanced the hyper caloric diets, including increased meal sizes and greater snack quantity and size (Gallo et al., 2020). This sudden change in diet resulted in metabolic problems among students. Initially, they tried to maintain their meal times very well, but with the increase in time lapse of lockdown and all-day online lectures, the whole meal time changed. They had no proper time of eating food, and the stress of online classes caused students to lose interest in their daily food intake. Numerous studies have claimed that less physical activities, binge eating, and easy availability of junk food at home made them obese. For instance, research in China suggests prevalence of obesity among high school and college students hiked from 10.5% to 12.6% (Jia et al., 2021). As per study conducted in the United States, the obesity prevalence increased from 13.7% to 15.4% in 2020 (*Children and Teens Saw Significant Weight Gain During the Pandemic, CDC Says _ Coronavirus Updates _ NPR*, n.d.; Jenssen et al., 2021). In Greece, 35% of parents reported an increase in body weight among their children (Androutsos et al., 2021).

Back pain concerns

Unlike physical classrooms, in virtual classes, the learners are not supposed to adopt good ergonomics. Attending classes while sitting on sofas/bed is a very common reason that can be attributed to recent rise in back pains or fibromyalgic pains. To accomplish schoolwork, students spent many hours in front of a laptop or desktop computer in a day, however most of them were unaware of the ill effects of this practice on their health. As a result, back pain, pain on shoulders, and neck muscles, and headaches are common complaints from them because of slouching for long periods of time (Idris et al., 2021). Some of them even faced problems like stress, tingling sensations, muscle fatigue, and decreased performance because of bad posture (*Effect of Online Classes on Physical and Mental Well-Being of Students during COVID-19 Sharma M, Sharma P – Indian J Phys Ther Res*, n.d.; Health, 2020).

Eye strain and noise-induced deafness

One of the major concerns of e-learning is eye strain. The more time spent online, the fiercer eye strain will happen. Back-to-back continuous classes left no break time to the eyes during e-learning in pandemic. Numerous studies have reported severe eye strain issues among students while acquiring online education during this period (Aldukhayel et al., 2022; *How Too Much Screen Time Affects Kids' Eyes: Tips to Prevent Eye Strain | Children's Hospital of Philadelphia, n.d.*; *Online Classes, Increased Screen Time Leading to Eye Conditions in Kids_ Doctors*, n.d.; Mohan et al., 2021; Rajanbir Singh, 2020). Some children were even more deprived, and their financial status did not allow them for regular check-ups, and hence their parents could not identify the signs of eye strain. For better voice quality, use of ear phones is very common, and continuous long-hour online schools enabled students to prolonged use of ear-piece, leading to noise-induced deafness (Mazlan et al., 2002; *Online Classes: Students Complain of Eye and Ear Problems – The Hindu*, n.d.; *Work from Home, Online Classes Causing Eye and Ear Problems in Children, Adults, Say Gurugram Doctor-Edexlive, n.d.*).

Best practices toward psychological support

To curb the spread of the deadly coronavirus, physical classes were suspended worldwide in 2020. However, the teaching–learning process did not stop, where the academic institutions worked ceaselessly to ensure regular learning for their students. Despite the prevalence of numerous infrastructural and technological limitations, alternative means of education viz. blended mode (Chung et al., 2020; Scull et al., 2020) synchronous/asynchronous e-learning were explored by educational institutions across the globe to reduce the fear of academic loss among students. Nations already having options for online educations improved their facilities, and others took some time for building and launching online learning platforms for the better learning of the students which eventually relieved them from the fear of academic loss mentally. To illustrate, in countries like India, additional reading materials were provided through already running online education portals like National Repository of Open Educational Resources, SWAYAM, and SWAYAM Prabha (Mishra et al., 2020). Besides, for enhancing the quality of e-content, programs like VidyaDaan 2.0 were launched where field experts and educationists from various areas had opportunity to contribute toward digital learning for the betterment of the students (Sarif, 2020). On the other hand, in the countries of Eastern Mediterranean region, new e-learning platforms were developed and launched. For example, online education platforms like Idrak, Jo Academy, Darsak, and Abwab were introduced in Jordan (Guermazi, 2021). In Egypt, e-portals for teacher–students communications were launched, where students had the facility to submit their work online and get remarks from their teachers (Partner and Commercial, 2020). In China, to ensure a continuous learning, programs like Disrupted Classes and Undisrupted Learning were initiated (Huang et al., 2020).

The universities of Philippines and South Africa facilitated e-learning through LMS (learning management systems) to conduit the gap between students and teachers during the lockdown period (Joaquin et al., 2020; Mpungose, 2020). However, it was realized that LMS were not appropriate for the complete virtual classes. So significant changes in education systems were introduced in these countries as per their resources and capabilities. To facilitate digital learning and networking among students, projects like "E-Buddy – events on the screen to break the quarantine" were initiated in Italy (Agasisti and Soncin, 2021).

Many higher educational institutions also contributed to e-learning via delivering digital content through available platforms viz. Webex, Microsoft Teams, Zoom, YouTube, Skype, Google Meet, and Google Classroom (Agasisti and Soncin, 2021; Mishra et al., 2020). Additionally, launching of massive open online courses' platforms like edX, Udemy, and Coursera had helped enormously in smooth learning for the students during these periods and made them mentally relaxed from the loss of education (Mishra et al., 2020).

Apart from online learning, considering the mental health of the students, educational institutions also offered counseling sessions and tools for their students. Virtual communities have been set up with the help of academics to remain in touch with their students and for fostering international research networks. Universities helped the students in many ways during unanticipated pandemic crisis; by extending deadlines for fee submission, by ensuring hostel accommodation reimbursements, and by providing laptops including internet connections (El Masri and Sabzalieva, 2020 to make them stress free about their expenditures.

Various programs focusing on social and mental well-being of the students were initiated by academic institutions (Kumar and Rewari, 2022). To reduce psychological stress of paying accommodation fee during the Covid-19 pandemic, myriads of academic institutions particularly of the UK came forward to support their students by waiving or reducing the accommodation fee during the pandemic (*No Academic Fee, Concessions In Hostel Fee For Students Who Lost Both Parents To Covid_ Allahabad University, n.d.*). For example, Staffordshire University, UK, waived the accommodation fees for the students who returned back to their homes, and for those who stayed in hostels, fees were reduced by 30%, as owing to lockdown situation the opportunities to earn money for them were minimized (*About – Office for Students*, n.d.). University of Leeds, UK, provided accommodation to the students even during holidays.

Some academic institutions supported the students by providing self-isolation rooms along with daily essential items including food stuff (*About – Office for Students*, n.d.; *How to Support Students Who Are Isolating in Student Accommodation – QS*, n.d.). The University of Greenwich, UK, organized a range of online events, games, and other interventions for students staying in halls to keep them busy. Also, the facility of pastoral phone calls was arranged to check in with residents, to help them with the queries, providing assurance and assistance if needed (*About – Office for Students*, n.d.). The University of Hull, UK, provided support related to academic issues, mental health, financial issues etc. to all the students, whether on or off campus via telephone calls, videoconferencing, and live chat. Dudley College of Technology, UK, made sure to connect with their students throughout the lockdown period to make them feel encouraged and reduce loneliness. Psychological support centers were opened by the University of Gdańsk, Poland for their students during the time of crisis (Rudnik et al., 2021).

Cardif University, UK, ensured to remain in touch with their students during the testing period of pandemic to prevent detachment from the university and loneliness. Online individual as well as group counseling along with mental health support were provided by King's College London's Counselling and Mental Health Service and the University of Oxford to their students. The University of Liverpool, UK, offered video and phone appointments for students with coronavirus symptoms, frequently checking in with them and offering required support (*About – Office for Students*, n.d.).

International students were likely to be most affected during the pandemic as they experienced the precarious living situations, isolation, and financial insecurities. Numerous universities and colleges responded quickly to the requirements of international students during the pandemic. For instance, the International Student Support Office Staff of Bangor University, UK, was available for providing support and advice to their international students through emails and personal video chat appointments. De Montfort University, UK, and universities of China had set up an international hardship fund to support the pandemic-affected international students (*International Students – Office for Students*, n.d.; Nurunnabi et al., 2020).

Conclusion and suggestions

E-learning resulted in substantial transformations in the lives of both students and teachers during the Covid-19 pandemic. Among students, psychological, mental, and physical health issues are becoming a severe problem. Even after shifting to partial offline mode, anxiety, sadness, stress, clinginess, and fear of academic syllabi continue to influence students. Literature studies have shown that mostly the academic institutions of the UK supported their students financially, mentally, and psychologically. However, very scarce information is available about the support from universities/colleges of other countries worldwide. Therefore, educational institutions, families, health officials, and community leaders should come forward as a team, analyze the issues faced by both teachers and students during the pandemic, and look for better strategies in future for such kind of pandemics. We must understand that learning is not only about reading books but also about the physical, emotional, social, and mental well-being of the student.

Virtual platforms could be used for helping the students to overcome the psychological and mental health-related issues by organizing webinars on topics like stress reduction, enhancing mental health, importance of physical activities, and so on. Parents should help and support their wards by listening to them patiently, talking to them, and eating with them to relieve the already burdened brains. Virtual sessions must be integrated with activity-based learning to break the monotony of the class and to keep the students' mind busy and active. Concepts like breakout rooms should be introduced where they may get opportunities to interact with their peers during classes. Educational institutions must include wellness programmes for students like physical and breathing exercises, talk about something of your interest, and share your thoughts and talents to make the e-learning more interesting and to lessen the stress among them. The mental pressure of not interacting with their mentors may be reduced by administering student–teacher talking time.

Governments should start schemes where disadvantaged children may be helped by providing digital devices, such as laptops, tablets, and smartphones, necessary to acquire e-learning. Uninterrupted network and strong Wi-Fi may be ensured even in rural areas to decrease anxiety and stress level of losing live sessions because of server issues. Online courses must be designed by considering all these factors and issues faced by students during current time to avoid detrimental effects on students' academic development in future. Impacts on physical health can be relieved by encouraging learners to take breaks from screen time in regular intervals. To avoid ear-related issues external speakers instead of earpiece may be used. Students should be motivated and advised to adopt the right posture while attending online classes to avoid muscle pain in the neck, shoulder, and back areas. Therefore, collaborative efforts may be helpful in reducing mental stress, psychotic impacts, and physical effects on students while acquiring virtual learning.

References

Abidjan, and Côte d'Ivoire. (2021). Potential Country Responses 1 Extend the School Day Extend the School Week. April, 1–5.

About – Office for Students. (n.d.). Retrieved from https://www.officeforstudents.org.uk/about/

Agasisti, T., and Soncin, M. (2021). Higher education in troubled times: on the impact of Covid-19 in Italy. *Studies in Higher Education*, *46*(1), 86–95. doi:10.1080/03075079.2020.1859689.

Aldukhayel, A., Baqar, S. M., Almeathem, F. K., Alsultan, F. S., and AlHarbi, G. A. (2022). Digital Eye Strain Caused by Online Education Among Children in Qassim Region, Saudi Arabia: A Cross-Sectional Study. *Cureus*. doi:10.7759/cureus.23813.

Amir, L. R., Tanti, I., Maharani, D. A., Wimardhani, Y. S., Julia, V., Sulijaya, B., and Puspitawati, R. (2020). Student perspective of classroom and distance learning during COVID-19 pandemic in the undergraduate dental study program Universitas Indonesia. *BMC Medical Education*, *20*(1), 1–8. doi:10.1186/s12909-020-02312-0.

Amponsah, S., Van Wyk, M. M., and Kolugu, M. K. (2021). Academic experiences of "zoom-Fatigue" as a virtual streaming phenomenon during the COVID-19 Pandemic. *International Journal of Web-Based Learning and Teaching Technologies*, *17*(6). doi:10.4018/IJWLTT.287555.

Androutsos, O., Perperidi, M., Georgiou, C., and Chouliaras, G. (2021). Lifestyle changes and determinants of children's and adolescents' body weight increase during the first COVID-19 lockdown in Greece: The COV-EAT study. *Nutrients*, *13*(3), 1–11. doi:10.3390/nu13030930.

Aristovnik, A., Keržič, D., Ravšelj, D., Tomaževič, N., and Umek, L. (2020). Aristovnik. *Sustainability (Switzerland)*, *12*(20), 1–34.

Asio, J. M. R., Gadia, E., Abarintos, E., Paguio, D., and Balce, M. (2021). Internet Connection and Learning Device Availability of College Students: Basis for Institutionalizing Flexible Learning in the New Normal. *Studies in Humanities and Education*, 2(1), 56–69. doi:10.48185/she.v2i1.224.

Balasopoulou, A., Kokkinos, P., Pagoulatos, D., Plotas, P., Makri, O. E., Georgakopoulos, C. D., Vantarakis, A., Li, Y., Liu, J. J., Qi, P., Rapoport, Y., Wayman, L. L., Chomsky, A. S., Joshi, R. S., Press, D., Rung, L., Ademola-popoola, D., Africa, S., Article, O., . . . Loukovaara, S. (2017). Symposium Recent advances and challenges in the management of retinoblastoma Globe - saving Treatments. *BMC Ophthalmology*, *17*(1), 1. doi:10.4103/ijo.IJO.

Bast, F. (2021). Perception of online learning among students from india set against the pandemic. *Frontiers in Education*, 6(August), 1–8. doi:10.3389/feduc.2021.705013.

Baumeister, R. F., and Leary, M. R. (1995). The Need to Belong: Desire for Interpersonal Attachments as a Fundamental Human Motivation. *Psychological Bulletin*, 117(3), 497–529). doi:10.1037/0033-2909.117.3.497.

Bhardwaj, A., and Kumar, V. (2022). A Framework for Enhancing Privacy in Online Collaboration. *International Journal of Electronic Security and Digital Forensics (IJESDF)*, *14*(4), 413–432.

Bhardwaj, A., and Kumar, V. (2023). Social Media as an Enabler to Combat Misinformation. In *Pandemics in the Age of Social Media: Information and Misinformation in Developing Nations*. Routledge: New York (USA), pp. 1–15.

Boda, Z., Elmer, T., Vörös, A., and Stadtfeld, C. (2020). Short-term and long-term effects of a social network intervention on friendships among university students. *Scientific Reports*, *10*(1), 1–12. doi:10.1038/s41598-020-59594-z.

Chang, T. H., Chen, Y. C., Chen, W. Y., Chen, C. Y., Hsu, W. Y., Chou, Y., and Chang, Y. H. (2021). Weight gain associated with covid-19 lockdown in children

and adolescents: A systematic review and meta-analysis. *Nutrients*, *13*(10), 1–10. doi:10.3390/nu13103668.
Children and Teens Saw Significant Weight Gain During the Pandemic, CDC Says _ Coronavirus Updates _ NPR. (n.d.). Retrieved from https://www.usnews.com/news/health-news/articles/2021-09-17/children-and-teens-saw-significant-weight-gain-during-pandemic-cdc-says, accessed 22 February 2024.
Chowdhury, U., Suvro, M. A. H., Farhan, S. M. D., and Uddin, M. J. (2022). Depression and stress regarding future career among university students during COVID-19 pandemic. PLoS ONE, *17*(4 April), 1–14. doi:10.1371/journal.pone.0266686.
Chung, E., Subramaniam, G., and Dass, L. C. (2020). Online learning readiness among university students in Malaysia amidst Covid-19. *Asian Journal of University Education*, *16*(2), 45–58. doi:10.24191/AJUE.V16I2.10294.
COVID-19 exposed the digital divide. (n.d.).
COVID-19 Pandemic_ Reopening of Schools Causing Anxiety Among Kids_ Here's How You Can Help Them. (n.d.).
Crooks, C. V., Smith, A. C. G., Robinson-Link, N., Orenstein, S., and Hoover, S. (2020). Psychosocial interventions in schools with newcomers: A structured conceptualization of system, design, and individual needs. *Children and Youth Services Review*, *112*(March), 104894. doi:10.1016/j.childyouth.2020.104894.
Cullinan, J., Flannery, D., Harold, J., Lyons, S., and Palcic, D. (2021). The disconnected: COVID-19 and disparities in access to quality broadband for higher education students. *International Journal of Educational Technology in Higher Education*, *18*(1), 1–21. doi:10.1186/s41239-021-00262-1.
Doreian, P., and Conti, N. (2012). Social context, spatial structure and social network structure. *Social Networks*, *34*(1), 32–46. doi:10.1016/j.socnet.2010.09.002.
Dorn, E., Hancock, B., Sarakatsannis, J., and Viruleg, E. (2021). COVID-19 and education: The lingering effects of unfinished learning US states and districts have the opportunity to not only help students catch up on unfinished learning from the pandemic but also tackle long-standing historical inequities in education. July.
Effect of online classes on physical and mental well-being of students during COVID-19 Sharma M, Sharma P – Indian J Phys Ther Res. (n.d.).
El Masri, A., and Sabzalieva, E. (2020). Dealing with disruption, rethinking recovery: Policy responses to the COVID-19 pandemic in higher education. *Policy Design and Practice*, *3*(3), 312–333. doi:10.1080/25741292.2020.1813359.
Elmer, T., Mepham, K., and Stadtfeld, C. (2020). Students under lockdown: Comparisons of students' social networks and mental health before and during the COVID-19 crisis in Switzerland. *PLoS ONE*, *15*(7 July), 1–22. doi:10.1371/journal.pone.0236337.
Gallo, L. A., Gallo, T. F., Young, S. L., Moritz, K. M., and Akison, L. K. (2020). The impact of isolation measures due to covid-19 on energy intake and physical activity levels in Australian university students. *Nutrients*, *12*(6), 1–14. doi:10.3390/nu12061865.
Guermazi, B. (2021). *Digital Transformation in the Time of COVID-19: The Case of MENA*. World Bank Blogs. Retrieved from https://blogs.worldbank.org/arabvoices/digital-transformation-time-covid-19-case-mena
Health, N. (2020). Effect of Online Classes on Children's physical health | Narayana Health (pp. 4–5). Retrieved from https://www.narayanahealth.org/blog/effect-of-online-classes-on-childrens-physical-health/
Hopkins, J. (n.d.). Closure of.
How coronavirus changed college for over 14 million students. (n.d.). Retrieved from https://www.cnbc.com/2020/03/26/how-coronavirus-changed-college-for-over-14-million-students.html

How to Support Students who are Isolating in Student Accommodation – QS. (n.d.).
How Too Much Screen Time Affects Kids' Eyes: Tips to Prevent Eye Strain | Children's Hospital of Philadelphia. (n.d.). Retrieved from https://www.chop.edu/news/health-tip/how-too-much-screen-time-affects-kids-eyes
Huang, R., Tlili, A., Yang, J., and Chang, T.-W. (2020). Handbook on facilitating flexible learning during educational disruption: The Chinese experience in maintaining undisrupted learning in COVID-19 outbreak learning personalization into MOOCs view project Educational Robots Project: Call For Chapters View p. Retrieved from https://www.researchgate.net/publication/339939064
Idris, F., Zulkipli, I. N., Abdul-Mumin, K. H., Ahmad, S. R., Mitha, S., Rahman, H. A., Rajabalaya, R., David, S. R., and Naing, L. (2021). Academic experiences, physical and mental health impact of COVID-19 pandemic on students and lecturers in health care education. *BMC Medical Education*, *21*(1), 1–13. doi:10.1186/s12909-021-02968-2.
Mazlan, R., Saim, L., Thomas, A., Said, R., and Liyab, B. (2002). Ear infection and hearing loss amongst headphone users. *The Malaysian Journal of Medical Sciences: MJMS*, *9*(2), 17–22.
International students – Office for Students. (n.d.).
Jenssen, B. P., Kelly, M. K., Powell, M., Bouchelle, Z., Mayne, S. L., and Fiks, A. G. (2021). Covid-19 and changes in child obesity. *Pediatrics*, *147*(5), 2019–2021. doi:10.1542/peds.2021-050123.
Jia, P., Zhang, L., Yu, W., Yu, B., Liu, M., Zhang, D., and Yang, S. (2021). Impact of COVID-19 lockdown on activity patterns and weight status among youths in China: the COVID-19 Impact on Lifestyle Change Survey (COINLICS). *International Journal of Obesity*, *45*(3), 695–699. doi:10.1038/s41366-020-00710-4.
Jiang, S. (2020). Psychological well-being and distress in adolescents: An investigation into associations with poverty, peer victimization, and self-esteem. *Children and Youth Services Review*, 111. doi:10.1016/j.childyouth.2020.104824.
Jiao, W. Y., Wang, L. N., Liu, J., Fang, S. F., Jiao, F. Y., Pettoello-Mantovani, M., and Somekh, E. (2020). Behavioral and emotional disorders in children during the COVID-19 epidemic. *Journal of Pediatrics*, *221*, 264–266.e1. doi:10.1016/j.jpeds.2020.03.013.
Joaquin, J. J. B., Biana, H. T., and Dacela, M. A. (2020). The Philippine Higher Education Sector in the Time of COVID-19. *Frontiers in Education*, *5*(October), 1–6. doi:10.3389/feduc.2020.576371.
Kritika, S. (2020). *In India, Over 32 Crore Students Hit by Covid-19 as Schools and Colleges Are Shut: UNESCO*. The Print. Retrieved from https://theprint.in/india/education/in-india-over-32-crore-students-hit-by-covid-19-as-schools-and-colleges-are-shut-unesco/402889/
Kovid, R. K., and Kumar, V. (Eds) (2022). *Cases on Emerging Markets Responses to the COVID-19 Pandemic*. IGI – Global Publications: USA (ISBN13: 978-16-6843-504-5, DOI: 10.4018/978-1-6684-3504-5).
Kumar, V., and Gupta, G. (Eds) (2021). *Strategic Management During a Pandemic*. Routledge: Taylor & Francis Group: USA (ISBN 9780367646479).
Kumar, V., and Malhotra, G. (Eds) (2021). *Stakeholder Strategies for Reducing the Impact of Global Health Crises*. Hershey, Pennsylvania, USA: IGI – Global Publications (ISBN13: 978-17-9987-495-9, doi: 10.4018/978-1-7998-7495-9).
Kumar, V., and Nanda, P. (2020). Social Media as a Tool in Higher Education: A Pedagogical Perspective. In *Handbook of Research on Diverse Teaching Strategies for the Technology-Rich Classroom*. IGI Global, pp. 239–253. (ISBN 9781799802389).
Kumar, V., and Rewari, M. (2022). A Responsible Approach to Higher Education Curriculum Design, *International Journal of Educational Reform (IJER)*, *31*(4), 422–441.

Lata, M., and Gupta, A. (2021). Education During the Pandemic: Technology-Based Solutions. In *Stakeholder Strategies for Reducing the Impact of Global Health Crises*. IGI Global, pp. 209–224.

Lee, J. (2020). A neuropsychological exploration of Zoom fatigue. *Psychiatric Times*, 37(11), 38–39.

Mahmud, M. S., Talukder, M. U., and Rahman, S. M. (2021). Does 'Fear of COVID-19' trigger future career anxiety? An empirical investigation considering depression from COVID-19 as a mediator. *International Journal of Social Psychiatry*, *67*(1), 35–45. doi:10.1177/0020764020935488.

Mali, D., and Lim, H. (2021). How do students perceive face-to-face/blended learning as a result of the Covid-19 pandemic? *International Journal of Management Education*, *19*(3), 100552. doi:10.1016/j.ijme.2021.100552.

Manage Screen Time in the Age of Online Learning – Oxford Learning. (n.d.).

Maqableh, M., and Alia, M. (2021). Evaluation online learning of undergraduate students under lockdown amidst COVID-19 Pandemic: The online learning experience and students' satisfaction. *Children and Youth Services Review*, *128*(January), 106160. doi:10.1016/j.childyouth.2021.106160.

Marques, G., Drissi, N., Díez, I. de la T., de Abajo, B. S., and Ouhbi, S. (2021). Impact of COVID-19 on the psychological health of university students in Spain and their attitudes toward Mobile mental health solutions. *International Journal of Medical Informatics*, *147*(November 2020), 104369. doi:10.1016/j.ijmedinf.2020.104369.

McCarthy, N. (2020). This chart shows how much COVID-19 has impacted education | World Economic Forum. In World Economic Forum. Retrieved from https://www.weforum.org/agenda/2020/03/infographic-covid19-coronavirus-impact-global-education-health-schools/%0Ahttps://www.weforum.org/agenda/2020/03/infographic-covid19-coronavirus-impact-global-education-health-schools/?fbclid=IwAR1pT6y9HmCWVIcUwl3kOg

Meier, M., and Hoppe, E. (2020). Inequality in learning opportunities during Covid-19: Evidence from library takeout. Research in Social Stratification and Mobility, January.

Mishra, L., Gupta, T., and Shree, A. (2020). Online teaching-learning in higher education during lockdown period of COVID-19 pandemic. *International Journal of Educational Research Open*, *1*, 100012. doi:10.1016/j.ijedro.2020.100012.

Mohan, A., Sen, P., Shah, C., Jain, E., and Jain, S. (2021). Expedited Publication – Original Article Prevalence and risk factor assessment of digital eye strain among children using online e - learning during the COVID - 19 pandemic: Digital eye strain among kids (DESK study - 1). Retrieved from https://doi.org/10.4103/ijo.IJO

Mpungose, C. B. (2020). Emergent transition from face-to-face to online learning in a South African University in the context of the Coronavirus pandemic. *Humanities and Social Sciences Communications*, 7(1), 1–9. doi:10.1057/s41599-020-00603-x.

Nayar, K. B., and Kumar, V. (2018). Cost benefit analysis of cloud computing in education. *International Journal of Business Information Systems (IJBIS)*, *27*(2), 205–221.

New academic year postponed by up to three months. (n.d.).

No Academic Fee, Concessions In Hostel Fee For Students Who Lost Both Parents To Covid_ Allahabad University. (n.d.).

Nurunnabi, M., Hossain, S. F. A. H., Chinna, K., Sundarasen, S., Khoshaim, H. B., Kamaludin, K., Baloch, G. M., Sukayt, A., and Shan, X. (2020). Coping strategies of students for anxiety during the COVID-19 pandemic in China: A cross-sectional study. *F1000Research*, *9*, 1–16. doi:10.12688/f1000research.25557.1

O'Hagan, C. (2020). Startling digital divides in distance learning emerge. In UNESCO. Retrieved from https://en.unesco.org/news/startling-digital-divides-distance-learning-emerge

Online classes, increased screen time leading to eye conditions in kids_ Doctors. (n.d.).
Online classes: students complain of eye and ear problems – The Hindu. (n.d.). Retrieved from https://www.thehindu.com/news/national/andhra-pradesh/online-classes-students-complain-of-eye-and-ear-problems/article31863501.ece
Partner, E. T., and Commercial, C. (2020). Impact of COVID-19 on education in Egypt: a new world order in the.
Pokhrel, S., and Chhetri, R. (2021). A literature review on impact of COVID-19 pandemic on teaching and learning. *Higher Education for the Future*, *8*(1), 133–141. doi:10.1177/2347631120983481.
Procentese, F., Capone, V., Caso, D., Donizzetti, A. R., and Gatti, F. (2020). Academic community in the face of emergency situations: Sense of responsible togetherness and sense of belonging as protective factors against academic stress during covid-19 outbreak. *Sustainability (Switzerland)*, *12*(22), 1–12. doi:10.3390/su12229718.
Singh, R. (2020). Online classes leading to stress, eye problems in children, say parents. In *Chandigarh News* (p. 2). Retrieved from https://www.hindustantimes.com/chandigarh/online-classes-leading-to-stress-eye-problems-in-children-say-parents/story-y4a8cnLKqHN8oCqozZ0psN.html
Ramachandran, V. (2021). Four causes for 'Zoom fatigue' and their solutions | Stanford News. In *Stanford News*. Retrieved from https://news.stanford.edu/2021/02/23/four-causes-zoom-fatigue-solutions/
Realyvásquez-Vargas, A., Maldonado-Macías, A. A., Arredondo-Soto, K. C., Baez-Lopez, Y., Carrillo-Gutiérrez, T., and Hernández-Escobedo, G. (2020). The impact of environmental factors on academic performance of university students taking online classes during the COVID-19 pandemic in Mexico. *Sustainability (Switzerland)*, *12*(21), 1–22. doi:10.3390/su12219194.
Rudnik, A., Anikiej-Wiczenbach, P., Szulman-Wardal, A., Conway, P., and Bidzan, M. (2021). Offering psychological support to university students in poland during the COVID-19 pandemic: Lessons learned from an initial evaluation. *Frontiers in Psychology*, *12*(39).
Sahu, P. (2020). Closure of Universities Due to Coronavirus Disease 2019 (COVID-19): Impact on Education and Mental Health of Students and Academic Staff. *Cureus*, *2019*(4), 4–9. doi:10.7759/cureus.7541.
Salim, J., Tandy, S., Arnindita, J. N., Wibisono, J. J., Haryanto, M. R., and Wibisono, M. G. (2022). Zoom fatigue and its risk factors in online learning during the COVID-19 pandemic. *Medical Journal of Indonesia*, *31*(1), 1–7. doi:10.13181/mji.oa.225703.
Sarif, N. (2020). Revisiting the discourse on online and face-to-face classes amidst Covid-19 lockdown: Digital outreach, strength-weakness analysis, and constructivist view – South Asia Journal. *South Asia Journal*, Vol. Online ed. http://southasiajournal.net/revisiting-the-discourse-on-online-and-face-to-face-classes-amidst-covid-19-lockdown-digital-outreach-strength-weakness-analysis-and-constructivist-view/
School not so easy after two years – The Hindu. (n.d.).
Scull, J., Phillips, M., Sharma, U., and Garnier, K. (2020). Innovations in teacher education at the time of COVID19: an Australian perspective. *Journal of Education for Teaching*, 46(4), 497–506). doi:10.1080/02607476.2020.1802701.
Singh, J., and Kumar, V. (2022). Combating the Pandemic with ICT Based Learning tools and applications: A case of Indian Higher Education. *International Journal of Virtual and Personal Learning Environments (IJVPLE) Platforms (IJVPLE)*, *12*(1), 1–21.
Singh, S., Roy, D., Sinha, K., Parveen, S., Sharma, G., and Joshi, G. (2020). Impact of COVID-19 and lockdown on mental health of children and adolescents:

A narrative review with recommendations. *Psychiatry Research*, *293*(May), 113429. doi:10.1016/j.psychres.2020.113429.
Social anxiety in the New Normal_ Not everyone is ready to go back to campus – Telegraph India. (n.d.).
Son, C., Hegde, S., Smith, A., Wang, X., and Sasangohar, F. (2020a). Effects of COVID-19 on college students' mental health in the United States: Interview survey study. *Journal of Medical Internet Research*, 22(9). doi:10.2196/21279.
Son, C., Hegde, S., Smith, A., Wang, X., and Sasangohar, F. (2020b). Effects of COVID-19 on college students' mental health in the United States: Interview survey study. *Journal of Medical Internet Research*, *22*(9), 1–14. doi:10.2196/21279.
Stadtfeld, C., Vörös, A., Elmer, T., Boda, Z., and Raabe, I. J. (2019). Integration in emerging social networks explains academic failure and success. *Proceedings of the National Academy of Sciences of the United States of America*, *116*(3), 792–797. doi:10.1073/pnas.1811388115.
Students are more comfortable with self-learning via online. (n.d.).
Today, I. (2021). 60% students do not have internet access in India: Report – Education Today News. India Today. Retrieved from https://www.indiatoday.in/education-today/news/story/60-students-do-not-have-internet-access-1876720-2021-11-15
Torsheim, T., Eriksson, L., Schnohr, C. W., Hansen, F., Bjarnason, T., and Välimaa, R. (2010). Screen-based activities and physical complaints among adolescents from the Nordic countries. *BMC Public Health*, *10*. doi:10.1186/1471-2458-10-324.
UNESCO IESALC. (2020). COVID-19 and higher education: Today and tomorrow. Impact analysis, policy responses and recommendations. *Unesco Iesalc*, 1–46. Retrieved from http://www.iesalc.unesco.org/en/wp-content/uploads/2020/04/COVID-19-EN-090420-2.pdf
UNICEF. (2021). COVID-19: Schools for more than 168 million children globally have been completely closed for almost a full year. In Press Release (Issue March, pp. 1–8). Retrieved from https://www.unicef.org/india/press-releases/covid-19-schools-more-168-million-children-globally-have-been-completely-closed%0Ahttps://www.unicef.org/rosa/press-releases/covid-19-schools-more-168-million-children-globally-have-been-completely-closed%0Ahttp
Wave of online learning & its impact on holistic development of children. (n.d.).
Work from home, online classes causing eye and ear problems in children, adults, say Gurugram doctor-Edexlive. (n.d.).
Zurlo, M. C., Cattaneo Della Volta, M. F., and Vallone, F. (2020). COVID-19 student stress questionnaire: Development and validation of a questionnaire to evaluate students' stressors related to the coronavirus pandemic lockdown. *Frontiers in Psychology*, *11*(March), 1–11. doi:10.3389/fpsyg.2020.576758.

8 Engineering education during the pandemic

Challenges and best practices

Divya Siwach and Anu Gupta

Introduction

The engineering stream acts as an interface that connects science with society and organizes technological changes sublimely. Engineering education is based on understanding, analysing, application, evaluation, and creation (Barak, 2013). Due to neoliberalism, the focus of private technical education has shifted towards making profit that has resulted in degraded education quality with low placements (Bhardwaj and Kumar, 2022a). To add to the existing problems, the outbreak of Covid-19 in December 2019 in Wuhan, China, caused an unprecedented effect on mankind and all countries were affected (Kovid and Kumar, 2022). The virus spread internationally in March 2020, and an enormous number of deaths were reported globally by the second week of April (Kumar and Gupta, 2021). To restrict the further spread of Covid-19 virus, most countries imposed lockdowns and closed educational institutes affecting students' education all around the globe (Kumar and Malhotra, 2021). All activities were shut down along with regular face-to-face classes posing a threat to the continuity of education. This pandemic distracted everything and also affected various sectors like academic, social, and commercial around the globe (Alqurshi, 2020). Academics suffered intensively, and education was pushed towards online learning. Practically, distance learning was the only option available for students of engineering, science, technology, and medicine where distance learning was never a preferred mode of teaching due to their technical and practical aspects (Pintarič and Kravanja, 2020).

Due to sudden outbreak of the pandemic, the engineering stream suffered intensive interruptions as institutes were not primarily prepared that resulted in unplanned and forced transition towards online study (Yasmin, 2022). Moreover, the situation was even more challenging because of the dependence of engineering curriculum on practical work, laboratory experiments, and direction interaction with instruments. According to statistics, approximately 60.9% enrolled students of about one billion were affected (Thakker et al., 2021). The period of lockdown affected not only students but teachers as well depending on their responsibilities and goals (Nogales-Delgado

DOI: 10.4324/9781003491712-8

et al., 2020). The extent of disruption to education varies with region and country, depending on their development status, availability, and training regarding usage of technology in education sector. Transition from regular to online classes requires training and knowledge of ICT (information and computer technologies) (Bhardwaj and Kumar, 2023). Closure of institutes, lack of training, cultural problems, and several other issues have resulted in the difficult shift to the online education (Singh and Kumar, 2022).

As technology is advancing with time, institutes are adopting means and technologies to address the special needs of students to provide qualitative online learning experience that will accompany face-to-face classes in future (Ruiperez-Valiente et al., 2021). There are certain additional efforts required to enhance learning system, such as resources, skilled teachers, and technical facilities (Sharma and Kumar, 2017). Online learning is specifically challenging for engineering curriculum as concepts need validation through lab experiments. This practical knowledge helps in developing problem-solving skills in the real world (Qadir and Al-fuqaha, 2020).

In engineering stream, practical knowledge is vital in addition to theoretical knowledge. Computations, lab experiments, computer programs, and assignments form a crucial part of the stream. Pandemic inhibited the usage of laboratories, instruments, and specific tools (Arroio, 2020) that affected the streams of STEM (Kumar and Sharma, 2017). Streams like chemical engineering are increasingly interdisciplinary and demands experiment to be carried out in laboratories. Other streams like civil and mechanical engineering require exploration and hands-on experience of instruments that was not possible during the period of quarantine. Moreover, online education was confusing at first, and its quality was also affected as compared to the primitive mode because teachers were not ready for the sudden change of the education system. Study programmes were teacher-centric and lacked student-centric aspect of teaching approach (Granjo and Rasteiro, 2018). Furthermore, online multimedia material and assessment methods were also not prepared. As distant learning and platforms are not the best options for studying an interdisciplinary curriculum like engineering, alternative solutions are required. Many researchers have worked to elicit themes for understanding the challenges that halted the effective working of manpower. They have tried to highlight problems that were encountered by students and teachers during the delivery of online classes.

However, teachers worked restlessly to ensure that the process of learning can be made more efficient with the active interaction and participation of students with their teachers (Schophuizen et al., 2017). Learning aided by technology can be termed as online, blended, hybrid, or distance learning depending on the inclusion of technology. The last two decades have witnessed exponential increase in the transition of old educational practices towards online learning resulting in exploration of a new mode of education (Nayar and Kumar, 2015). Prevalent gaps in the education system due to unequal socio-economic status should be bridged (Zhao, 2016).

After the Covid-19 pandemic, education system was left with only two possibilities. One, return to primitive education system and second, proceed towards enhanced and transformed education. Both methods come with their own set of advantages and disadvantages. In traditional class set-up, the level and quality of physical interaction are high in comparison to virtual classrooms. Moreover, curriculum like engineering requires practical set-up and utilization of laboratory equipment for validation of concepts that don't go well with distance learning. Flow of knowledge, participation of students, and assessment of their learning and performance are easy to evaluate in traditional classrooms rather than online classes where there is passive participation of students and methods of assessment are not satisfactory. Designing of virtual classrooms and learning experiences for students are very time-consuming processes. However, there are various advantages of online learning also. As students are attending classes from the comfort of their homes, timings and learning would be flexible, and the problem of absenteeism can be avoided (Kumar and Bhardwaj, 2020). Various technological tools can be incorporated in the pedagogical design that would enrich the learning experience of students (Kumar and Nanda, 2020). Students can also learn anytime at their own pace with the help of recorded classes and online material available. In addition, geographical barrier between teacher and student can be reduced with online learning, and mutual cooperation of students of different countries would increase (Bhardwaj and Kumar, 2022b).

Transformation requires professional capital and finding ways of developing technical knowledge and skills of teachers as well as parents (McPhee and Söderström, 2012). Inclusion of teachers and parents in the decision-making process is required to make an efficient transformation.

Challenges in engineering education

The Covid-19 pandemic spread worldwide within few months after its outbreak in December 2019 in China. Soon after, WHO (World Health Organization) declared the virus outbreak as an international pandemic with public health emergency. Most of the countries adopted preventive measures, strict isolation strategies, and medical precautions. These mobility restrictions caused cancellation of classes and closing of higher educational institutes (HEIs). This resulted in shifting of face-to-face classes to online classes that created a lot of problems for engineering students as their curriculum is based on testing theoretical concepts with practical applications (Jacques et al., 2021). Distance learning was never a part of the engineering curriculum before the pandemic (Pintarič and Kravanja, 2020). A possible reason could be the requirement of practical exercises on computers and involvement of laboratory work that needed physical contact. Physical contact is needed on social grounds for better cooperation among students and intergenerational assistance. But due to the Covid-19 lockdown, online education started immediately that required some minor or major changes. Furthermore, there were certain challenges faced by education community that somehow disrupted the efforts and outcomes.

Personal barriers

One of the major barriers in front of tutors and learners was the lack of prior knowledge, experience, and understanding of technicalities in online education. Teachers were not prepared for the extreme situation and lacked adequate pedagogical skills. There was also some resistance on part of teachers in adopting new technology due to lack of interest, training, and cooperation from their respective institutes (Englund et al., 2017). Several teachers preferred age-old methods of education system and resisted to modify their prevalent teaching methods due to a lack of familiarity with technical tools and software (Lapitan et al., 2021). Teachers felt burdened in preparing and delivering lectures in which required practical aspect of engineering studies was missing. Maintenance of discipline along with student's attention were also very difficult that demoralized tutors.

Moreover, the goal of teaching and learning outcomes failed miserably on the part of students also. Investigations and research have concluded that students were not prepared for a sudden transition from face-to-face classes to online mode of education that affected their mental health and caused problems like stress, anxiety, disturbed sleeping patterns, and loneliness (Aslan et al., 2020). Students lacked motivation due to their passive role in the learning process with minimal engagement during online lectures. This resulted in declined attention span and interest towards the course leading to reduced productivity. Due to reduced face-to-face interaction between students and teachers, the concentration of the students declined in online classes and difficulties in group discussions were experienced especially during projects (Ghasem and Ghannam, 2021). Students felt a lack of connection with fellow mates and missed direct in-person contact during lockdown. Communication was also perceived more complicated than regular mode of classes (Al-Balas et al., 2020).

Non-classroom environment also took away the spirit of completing work on time that resulted in depression during isolation period. Students were also dissatisfied with the provided teacher support, assessment tools, and increased perceived workload (Dinh and Nguyen, 2020).

Technical barriers

Technology plays a crucial role in online education as it is the mere source of communication between tutors and students. There were a lot of technical challenges faced by students in online learning during the pandemic. Issues confronted in obtaining education and establishing communication were unavailability of devices (mobiles, computers, laptops etc.), a lack of adequate internet accessibility, connectivity interruptions and unstable connection by service providers, and a lack of knowledge about internet specifications (Santana et al., 2020). Technical barriers were majorly faced by underdeveloped and developing countries (Nayar and Kumar, 2018). Out of all the technical problems, inappropriate internet connectivity was the major one on the part of students as well as teachers, and high-speed connectivity was missing in rural and remote areas (Jones, 2015).

Engineering curriculum consists of theoretical concepts, tutorial, and practical. Theory and tutorial parts were delivered by teachers with the help of videoconferencing, but no specific application was offered to explore the practical aspect involving instruments. Furthermore, due to lockdown restrictions, movement was prohibited, and hence access to laboratory instruments halted the practical skill development.

Also, there were certain security issues encountered in digital classrooms like hijacking that disrupted the regular proceedings (Lata and Kumar, 2022). Cyberbullying was also noticed in the form of negative, racist, and inappropriate comments and content. Instances of data breaches by illegal logins were also noticed, requiring strict and enhanced security features by platforms.

Institutional barriers

Lack of support from the respective institutes was also a constraint on successful delivery of classes. Dependence on technology for online classes increased the hurdles of teachers while using software and reconstructing course design. Absence of prior training of technological knowledge resulted in inefficient communication of ideas and declined course outcomes. Furthermore, poorly structured pedagogical design led to multiple problems and inappropriate delivery of lectures leaving teachers as well as students dissatisfied.

There was also a loophole in the usage of platforms for specific work. Institutes don't prefer using specifically designed proctoring applications. Hence, examinations conducted without utilizing proctoring applications resulted in opting unjust and unfair means (Nguyen, 2015). But proctoring requires switching on the cameras that create lags. Furthermore, there was lack of conceptual questions in evaluation tests, and students also faced difficulties in submitting their tests and assignments (Ripoll et al., 2020).

Social barriers

The pandemic forced the political leaders for taking drastic measures of implementation of social distancing (Anderson et al., 2020). These measures slowed down the spread of virus but affected the mental and psychological health of students. Students felt pressurized to perform well that affected their mental well-being. Students studying in isolated rooms were unable to develop motivation for learning and proceeded towards depression. It was difficult for students of engineering stream to find any study partner that left them more isolated (Elmer et al., 2020). Socialization and face-to-face contact are part and parcel of students of colleges and universities. During the lockdown, absence of social contact affected their academic development as well as self-efficacy (Luan et al., 2020). The quarantine situation created a feeling of uncertainty and boredom in students leading to psychological and emotional disturbances.

Not only this, due to no face-to-face interaction and eye contact among teachers and students, teachers were not able to study the body language and responses of students. The low level of association left teachers frustrated and halted the learning process of students (Muuro et al., 2014). Assessing students' learning and performance was difficult for teachers that defeated the overall purpose of teaching–learning. As teachers were unable to receive instant feedback from students due to lack of socialization, they were unable to modify their teaching methods accordingly.

Best practices opted by institutes

Learning practical skills in engineering education is a challenging task with limited physical encounter due to the pandemic. But it is changing dynamically to adopt new and innovative technologies to overcome the challenges. Recent technology and platforms are not the best for studying holistic curriculum, that is theory and practical. Several countries with prior encounter with pandemic and appropriate availability of technology dealt wisely with disrupted educational practices. One way of harnessing the efficiency and effectiveness of technology is through its utilization in the education sector. Globally, higher education institutes have undertaken several steps to improvise the quality of education with provisions of online learning (Kumar and Rewari, 2022). Students also valued this concept and efforts that facilitated them to access education remotely. This technological inclusion enabled their engagement in collaborative as well as interactive learning (Alexander and Golja, 2007).

Microsoft Teams and Zoom were the best platforms utilized in India for delivering online classes (Thakker et al., 2021). Both the platforms supported live videoconferencing and offered 67 and 44 features respectively for proper conduct of lectures. These two tools were highly used for study purposes with additional features. Microsoft Teams offered calling, dating, chatting, and built-in features of Microsoft Office. The quality of communication was also superior in Microsoft Teams. In addition, Zoom is a cloud-based platform that offered audio–video conferencing, chatting, collaborating, and organization of webinars. These videoconferencing platforms maintained the continuity of classes during the pandemic with quality communication. Both of the platforms are easy to operate and convenient to use that helped students during the pandemic. Online platforms facilitated teachers in educating learners and enhancing their teaching pedagogies that can be carried forward in future also. Research has shown that students' learning and involvement towards curriculum was enhanced resulting in improvisation of classroom dynamics (Heggart and Yoo, 2018).

Indian government also encouraged the use of MOOC (Massive Open Online Course) platform during the Covid-19 pandemic. It is a web-based platform that provided unlimited opportunities to students for distance learning from best institutes around the globe (Mahajan et al., 2019). The platform under the guidance of Indian government provided open resources such as online libraries, repositories, e-books, media files, and so on. The material was open to everybody and reached maximum learners. The platform offered around 200 courses free of cost to the students of higher education around the globe (Biswas, 2020). It satisfied the educational needs of students and maintained its continuity. Students were assessed through quizzes, formative and summative exams for certification purposes. New learning goals for students were built and delivered with the help of MOOCs.

At Chitkara University Institute of Engineering and Technology (Punjab, India), teachers utilized augmented reality (AR) technology that combines the structures of virtual and real objects with 3D graphics to generate a real-life set-up (Singh et al., 2019). An augmented reality learning environment (ARLE) was developed by programmers and researchers of the university for exploring the effect of technology on students' learning. Students were able to operate instruments virtually with AR that provided prior knowledge and hands-on experience of the instrument. Tutors were also able to design content in presentable forms. The learning system was targeted towards accessing training, learning, and retention of concepts. Students responded positively towards this system with increased attention, learning, understanding, and motivation.

In the United Arab Emirates University, virtual classes were conducted with the help of Blackboard Collaborate Ultra (Ghasem and Ghannam, 2021). The tutors were prepared beforehand with the help of Continuous Education, Teaching and Learning (CETL) centre. Through this centre, lectures regarding pedagogy, quality education, and improved teaching styles were provided to instructors. Blended teaching and problem-centred learning were also emphasized that resulted in enhanced teaching–learning outcomes. With the outbreak of the pandemic and imposition of lockdown, these activities helped the students and tutors to fully adapt to online mode of teaching and master the use of Blackboard Collaborate Ultra. These activities enabled tutors to deliver lectures efficiently and prepare tests, quizzes, and exams for evaluation without compromising much on the quality of education.

In the University of Santo Tomas (Manila, Philippines), a blended strategy (including synchronous and asynchronous modes) was implemented for teaching and learning goals that facilitated smooth transition from traditional to online learning (Lapitan et al., 2021). The university adopted a five-component strategy named DLPCA (Discover, Learn, Practice, Collaborate and Assess). These components were reinforced as *discovering* available material on University Blackboard Learning Management System; *learning* concepts from pre-recorded material; *practising* from what they have learnt; *collaborating* actively with classmates and teachers; and *assessing* exam and understanding outcomes. This strategy resulted in students' engagement, satisfaction, and attainment of learning outcomes.

In the universities of Spain, a game-based learning platform called "Kahoot!" was used (Martín-S´omer et al., 2021). The platform got popular during the pandemic and was utilized for reviewing students' knowledge and evaluating formative assessment. The platform was a student response system that combined student responses, role-playing, and audiovisual aids. The primary goal of Kahoot! was increasing motivation, concentration, engagement, and knowledge of students towards curriculum. Quiz tests conducted with the help of Kahoot! at the end of each session resulted in reinforcement of the concepts with maximum engagement of students. Effectiveness of the platform was reflected in the final examinations, where students scored better marks in comparison to previous classes of traditional origin.

At Complutense University of Madrid (Spain), a dynamic software "Mentimeter" was used for promoting participation and facilitating collaborative learning (Pichardo et al., 2021). The software involves the joint participation of both the students and teachers. The software was used for preparing interactive presentations and providing real-time experience that enhanced students' participation and interest towards the learning process. The software is easy to use and provides great flexibility and functions for exploration. Improved results and study patterns were observed with the help of this software as concentration and interest of students are crucial for improved results.

At Alioune Diop University of Bambey, a classical university in Senegal, an open learning platform named MOODLE was utilized involving partners from various countries like Europe, the UK, Asia-Pacific region, Africa, and America (Lamine Ba et al., 2019). "Moodle" stands for Modular Object-Oriented Dynamic Learning Environment. It is a user-friendly platform that is freely accessible. The platform also provided various activities like online chat, forums, submission of documents, and practice exercises. The learning became comfortable due to assistance of pictures and videos in addition to text content. The university adopted the model of pooling the cross-cutting courses depending on the level of classes and then mitigating the pooled courses in online learning. The model resulted in optimized resource distribution, flexibility in courses with increased positive impact on students as compared to traditional classrooms.

For addressing the challenges towards learning practical skills, the concept of virtual labs was also utilized in various universities to provide familiarity of instruments and procedures to students (Glassey and Magalhães, 2020). Furthermore, virtual reality-based training was also provided to students as an interactive, 3D computer simulation to deliver the content. There are less chances of encountering unexpected hazards in these training (Kumar et al., 2021).

Future directions

As the pandemic is easing over time, and educational institutes are running at their own pace, nothing can be predicted for future. But the pandemic has shown an innovative way of studying and learning that can be implemented even after the pandemic. Despite the havoc caused by the pandemic, various positive impacts on education system can be forwarded for betterment. As the sudden outbreak of the pandemic forced engineering students towards online learning, this can be seen as an opportunity for analysing experiences and learning outcomes of students. The data would direct the designing of suitable learning pathways and desired curriculum for maximum understanding. The courses can be made more accessible. The effect of pandemic and its scope are unclear currently for coming years, therefore actions and alternative learning tools are required for proper and efficient continuation of studies. Exploiting technology for the purpose of learning will be considered as its potential. With extension of its application, it can surpass the formal borders of countries and bring students of different origins and cultures together. Hence, new aspects of teaching and learning patterns can be created.

Blended pedagogy

The pandemic and its after-effects have come with uncertainty, a hybrid approach in education system in the form of blended pedagogy can address the problem (Kumar and Nanda, 2019). Blended learning facilitates customization of information, communication, manipulation, and entertainment content creation that can promote interactivity among students and can compensate with the traditional ways of human interaction (Sun and Hsu, 2013). Interactivity can help change perceptions and exchange experiences that influence performance and learning. Usage of interactive videos and collaboration can influence intrinsic motivation with the help of game-based learning environment (Liao et al., 2019).

Transition between face-to-face classes and online learning with the help of digital collaborative techniques can lay down the foundations for new learning objectives. Virtual classrooms that incorporate innovative methodologies can aid in successful acquisition of useful and practical skills. Artificial intelligence can act as a connecting link in digital education that can provide pedagogical and technical assistance.

Cost-effectiveness

Online learning can be more cost-effective and efficient with the establishment of equality of opportunities. It is within reach of every person and organization. Educators, with the help of online teaching, can enhance students' success and play a vital role in attaining the teaching outcomes of courses. It has been investigated that cost-effectiveness of resources along with flexibility and availability can have a positive impact on students' experience and learning (Yang and Cornelius, 2004). This blended learning can play a significant role that will result in sustainable education leading to holistic development of learners. Immense dissemination of educational and knowledge will take place, and students irrespective of their economic status would be able to attain it. Furthermore, online classes can support teaching methods unknown to traditional methods and can reach to a larger number of students by breaking the barriers of space and time without investing anymore resources.

Learning is an act of social interaction that can be enhanced with online collaborative learning. Higher education institutes worldwide have utilized the technique of distance learning with enhanced social interaction, teaching–learning quality, information exchange, collaborative learning, accessibility of education, flexibility of time, and innovative technologies (Farahat, 2012). All these factors can help in the preparation of self-paced and lifelong learning, reducing the overall cost of educational services.

Flexibility

Online platform provides flexibility to teachers for conducting their online courses according to their pedagogical design. The courses can be conducted remotely for an extended period of time that can be beneficial for institutes where sessions are shorter. As online courses can be accessed anytime from any geographical position providing flexibility to students, so it can result in emergence of fully online courses. Students can also learn at their own pace with minimum distractions. Integration of pedagogy and technology has the potential of facilitating flexibility, student-centric teaching, enhanced interaction, and asynchronous communication and collaboration among students and teachers.

Expansion of technical infrastructure

There are various methods, such as interactive classrooms, videos, simulations, virtual labs, and so on, that enrich learning outcomes and students' autonomy (Davis, 2020). Recordings of laboratory experiments and interpretations of derivations, proofs, and theorems can be fruitful for students. Platforms can be simplified to be useful for a wide variety of students and can be designed to inculcate the specificity of curriculum. Virtual labs can serve the purpose of a new pedagogical tool for acquisition of knowledge and enhanced understanding. The concept can pave a way towards sustainable higher education. Implementing virtual labs can overcome the shortcomings of a traditional classroom set-up by enhancing students' confidence and practical knowledge. In this way, the academic reach, training, and excellence can expand. Furthermore, computer simulations can be utilized for performing experiments that are not feasible using traditional system.

Furthermore, AR-based applications are gaining popularity recently in the education sector. These are highly potent in representing theories and concepts in an organized manner. The technique can become highly efficient in engineering curriculum for developing technical skills and enhancing cognitive abilities of students. It is an emerging technology that can be utilized for providing unique experiences of virtual laboratory experiments to students and can be incorporated as an additional form of learning in addition to face-to-face traditional learning techniques. Students will be able to improve their performance with developed spatial perception of curriculum. Inculcation of the technology is still pending in most of the universities as they are operating with their primitive methods of teaching. But this technique can pave a way towards motivated students with better mental status.

Ultimately, distance learning is the need of the hour and with recent technological advancements, students can study anytime, anywhere according to their convenience and interact with their teachers and classmates (Lassoued et al., 2020). Representative and interactive methods and content can sustain as well as prolong the outcomes of learning. It can be said that online learning is the advanced form of science and technology bringing convenience of tools. Interaction between students and teachers is crucial for better teaching and learning. Shy students will be able to ask questions and interact with teachers resulting in enhanced understanding. The problem of absenteeism can also be solved through online classes as students will be able to attend classes from the comfort of their home.

Conclusion

All the platforms available for online learning are generally sufficient but have some shortcomings regarding ever-changing educational system. The audio–video quality of these platforms is still not up to the requirements due to technological and internet-related limitations. Tools need to be more user-friendly and adaptable for effective learning. Methods for improved concentration and motivation among students should be developed for inclusive study (Roberts et al., 2018). Online courses should be designed while considering interactive mechanisms for improving and thriving learning experiences. There were certain fields and areas of engineering studies that helped in creating innovative solutions to the problem of Covid-19. The opportunity of attending lectures from home in distance learning can save effort and time of students between actual lectures, provide access to pre-recorded lectures anytime with flexibility of their schedule, and strengthen family relations. Furthermore, this results in efficient time management and increased productivity. Online content aids in developing constructive learning, promoting self-efficacy, and stimulating learner engagement. Online learning can help in reducing anxiety and fear of failure.

There was less or no significant impact of problems like internet connection and device availability in technologically developed countries. Countries having less technical resources should take into consideration the socio-technical impacts during course designing and content delivery. Impact of pandemic on academics is crucial to understand as there has been an increased trend of offering online courses in universities. However, the transition from traditional methods to online studies is still challenging in engineering. New and relevant features should be introduced keeping in mind the requirements and specificity of engineering curriculum. These alternative tools and methods that have been employed by various universities to combat the situation and deliver qualitative education online can be carried forward in future to enrich the education sector.

References

Al-Balas, M., Al-Balas, H. I., Jaber, H. M., Obeidat, K., Al-Balas, H., Aborajooh, E. A., Al-Taher, R., and Al-Balas, B. (2020). Correction to: Distance learning in clinical medical education amid COVID-19 pandemic in Jordan: current situation, challenges, and perspectives. *BMC Medical Education*, 20(1), 1–7. doi:10.1186/s12909-020-02428-3.

Alexander, S., and Golja, T. (2007). Using students' experiences to derive quality in an e-learning system: An institution's perspective. *Educational Technology and Society*, *10*(2), 17–33.

Alqurshi, A. (2020). Investigating the impact of COVID-19 lockdown on pharmaceutical education in Saudi Arabia – A call for a remote teaching contingency strategy. *Saudi Pharmaceutical Journal*, *28*(9), 1075–1083. doi:10.1016/j.jsps.2020.07.008.

Anderson, R. M., Heesterbeek, H., Klinkenberg, D., and Hollingsworth, T. D. (2020). How will country-based mitigation measures influence the course of the COVID-19 epidemic? *The Lancet*, *395*(10228), 931–934. doi:10.1016/S0140-6736(20)30567-5.

Arroio, A. (2020). The value of education in the context of Covid-19 Pandemic. *Problems of Education in the 21st Century*, *78*(3), 309–313. doi:10.33225/pec/20.78.309.

Aslan, I., Ochnik, D., and Çınar, O. (2020). Exploring perceived stress among students in Turkey during the covid-19 pandemic. *International Journal of Environmental Research and Public Health*, *17*(23), 1–17. doi:10.3390/ijerph17238961.

Barak, M. (2013). Teaching engineering and technology: Cognitive, knowledge and problem-solving taxonomies. *Journal of Engineering, Design and Technology*, *11*(3), 316–333. doi:10.1108/JEDT-04-2012-0020.

Bhardwaj, A., and Kumar, V. (2022a). A framework for enhancing privacy in online collaboration. *International Journal of Electronic Security and Digital Forensics (IJESDF)*, *14*(4), 413–432.

Bhardwaj, A., and Kumar, V. (2022b). Web and social media approach to marketing of engineering courses in India. *International Journal of Business Innovation and Research (IJBIR)*, *27*(4), 541–555.

Bhardwaj, A., and Kumar, V. (2023). Social media as an enabler to combat misinformation. In *Pandemics in the Age of Social Media: Information and Misinformation in Developing Nations*. Routledge: New York (USA), pp. 1–15.

Biswas, S. (2020). MOOC: Challenges & Prospects in Indian Higher Education. *Journal of Informational and Computational Science*, *10*(2), 1015–1024.

Davis, R. H. (2020). Improving the faculty-student experience in chemical engineering. *AIChE Journal*, *66*(5). doi:10.1002/aic.16960.

Dinh, L. P., and Nguyen, T. T. (2020). Pandemic, social distancing, and social work education: students' satisfaction with online education in Vietnam. *Social Work Education*, *39*(8), 1074–1083. doi:10.1080/02615479.2020.1823365.

Elmer, T., Mepham, K., and Stadtfeld, C. (2020). Students under lockdown: Comparisons of students' social networks and mental health before and during the COVID-19 crisis in Switzerland. *PLoS ONE, 15*(7 July), 1–22. doi:10.1371/journal.pone.0236337.

Englund, C., Olofsson, A. D., and Price, L. (2017). Teaching with technology in higher education: understanding conceptual change and development in practice. *Higher Education Research and Development, 36*(1), 73–87. doi:10.1080/07294360.2016.1171300.

Farahat, T. (2012). Applying the Technology Acceptance Model to Online Learning in the Egyptian Universities. *Procedia – Social and Behavioral Sciences, 64*, 95–104. https://doi.org/10.1016/j.sbspro.2012.11.012

Ghasem, N., and Ghannam, M. (2021). Education for Chemical Engineers Challenges, benefits & drawbacks of chemical engineering on-line teaching during Covid-19 pandemic. *Education for Chemical Engineers, 36*, 107–114. doi:10.1016/j.ece.2021.04.002.

Glassey, J., and Magalhães, F. D. (2020). Virtual labs – love them or hate them, they are likely to be used more in the future. *Education for Chemical Engineers, 33*, 76–77. doi:10.1016/j.ece.2020.07.005.

Granjo, J. F. O., and Rasteiro, M. G. (2018). LABVIRTUAL – A platform for the teaching of chemical engineering: The use of interactive videos. *Computer Applications in Engineering Education, 26*(5), 1668–1676. doi:10.1002/cae.22007.

Heggart, K. R., and Yoo, J. (2018). Getting the most from google classroom: A pedagogical framework for tertiary educators. *Australian Journal of Teacher Education, 43*(3), 140–153. doi:10.14221/ajte.2018v43n3.9.

Jacques, S., Ouahabi, A., and Lequeu, T. (2021). Remote knowledge acquisition and assessment during the covid-19 pandemic. *International Journal of Engineering Pedagogy, 10*(6), 120–138. doi:10.3991/IJEP.V10I6.16205.

Jones, S. H. (2015). Benefits and Challenges of Online Education for Clinical Social Work: Three Examples. *Clinical Social Work Journal, 43*(2), 225–235. doi:10.1007/s10615-014-0508-z.

Kovid, R. K., and Kumar V. (Eds) (2022). *Cases on Emerging Markets Responses to the COVID-19 Pandemic.* IGI – Global Publications: USA (ISBN13: 978-16-6843-504-5, DOI: 10.4018/978-1-6684–3504–5).

Kumar, V., and Bhardwaj, A. (Eds) (2020). Role of Cloud Computing in School Education. *Handbook of Research on Diverse Teaching Strategies for the Technology-Rich Classroom.* Hershey, PA: IGI Global, pp. 98–108.

Kumar, V., and Gupta, G. (Eds) (2021). *Strategic Management During a Pandemic.* Routledge, Taylor & Francis Group: USA (ISBN 9780367646479).

Kumar, V., and Nanda, P. (2019). Social media in higher education: A framework for continuous engagement. *International Journal of Information and Communication Technology Education (IJICTE), 15*(1), 109–120.

Kumar, V., and Sharma, D. (2017). Cloud computing as a catalyst in STEM education. *International Journal of Information and Communication Technology Education (IJICTE), 13*(2), 38–51.

Kumar, V. V., Carberry, D., Beenfeldt, C., Andersson, M. P., Mansouri, S. S., and Gallucci, F. (2021). Virtual reality in chemical and biochemical engineering education and training. *Education for Chemical Engineers, 36*, 143–153. doi:10.1016/j.ece.2021.05.002.

Kumar, V., and Malhotra, G. (Eds) (2021). *Stakeholder Strategies for Reducing the Impact of Global Health Crises.* IGI – Global Publications: USA (ISBN13: 978-17-9987-495-9, DOI: 10.4018/978-1-7998–7495–9).

Kumar, V., and Nanda, P. (Eds) (2020). Social media as a tool in higher education: A pedagogical perspective. *Handbook of Research on Diverse Teaching Strategies for the Technology-Rich Classroom.* Hershey, PA: IGI Global, pp. 239–253.

Kumar, V., and Rewari, M. (2022). A responsible approach to higher education curriculum design. *International Journal of Educational Reform (IJER)*, *31*(4), 422–441.

Lamine Ba, M., Gueye, B., Dahirou Gueye, A., Kassé, O., and Wassa Mballo, M. H. (2019). Impacts of the migration of cross-cutting courses of a traditional university in distance learning. *International Journal of Engineering Pedagogy*, *9*(2), 51–64. doi:10.3991/ijep.v9i2.9945.

Lapitan, L. D., Tiangco, C. E., Sumalinog, D. A. G., Sabarillo, N. S., and Diaz, J. M. (2021). An effective blended online teaching and learning strategy during the COVID-19 pandemic. *Education for Chemical Engineers*, *35*(May 2020), 116–131. doi:10.1016/j.ece.2021.01.012

Lassoued, Z., Alhendawi, M., and Bashitialshaaer, R. (2020). An exploratory study of the obstacles for achieving quality in distance learning during the covid-19 pandemic. *Education Sciences*, *10*(9), 1–13. doi:10.3390/educsci10090232.

Lata, M., and Kumar, V. (2022). Security and Privacy Issues in Fog Computing Environment. *International Journal of Electronic Security and Digital Forensics (IJESDF)*, *14*(3), 289–307.

Liao, C. W., Chen, C. H., and Shih, S. J. (2019). The interactivity of video and collaboration for learning achievement, intrinsic motivation, cognitive load, and behavior patterns in a digital game-based learning environment. *Computers and Education*, *133*, 43–55. doi:10.1016/j.compedu.2019.01.013.

Luan, L., Hong, J. C., Cao, M., Dong, Y., and Hou, X. (2020). Exploring the role of online EFL learners' perceived social support in their learning engagement: a structural equation model. *Interactive Learning Environments*, *0*(0), 1–12. doi:10.1080/10494820.2020.1855211.

Mahajan, R., Gupta, P., and Singh, T. (2019). Massive Open Online Courses: Concept and Implications. *Indian Pediatrics*, *56*(6), 489–495. doi:10.1007/s13312-019-1575-6.

Martín-S'omer, M., Moreira, J., and Casado, C. (2021). Use of Kahoot! to keep students ' motivation during online classes in the lockdown period caused by Covid 19. *Education for Chemical Engineers*, *36*(June), 154–159. doi:10.1016/j.ece.2021.05.005.

McPhee, I., and Söderström, T. (2012). Distance, online and campus higher education: Reflections on learning outcomes. *Campus-Wide Information Systems*, *29*(3), 144–155. doi:10.1108/10650741211243166.

Muuro, M. E., Wagacha, W. P., Oboko, R., and Kihoro, J. (2014). Students'perceived challenges in an online collaborative learning environment: A case of higher learning institutions in Nairobi, Kenya. *International Review of Research in Open and Distance Learning*, *15*(6), 132–161. doi:10.19173/irrodl.v15i6.1768.

Nayar, K. B., and Kumar, V. (2015). Benefits of cloud computing in education during disaster. In *Proceedings of the International Conference on Transformations in Engineering Education*. Springer, New Delhi, pp. 191–201.

Nayar, K. B., and Kumar, V. (2018). Cost benefit Analysis of Cloud Computing in Education. *International Journal of Business Information Systems (IJBIS)*, *27*(2), 205–221.

Nguyen, T. (2015). The Effectiveness of Online Learning: Beyond No Significant Difference and Future Horizons. *MERLOT Journal of Online Learning and Teaching*, *11*(2), 309–319.

Nogales-Delgado, S., Suero, S. R., and Martín, J. M. E. (2020). COVID-19 outbreak: Insights about teaching tasks in a chemical engineering laboratory. *Education Sciences*, *10*(9), 1–13. doi:10.3390/educsci10090226.

Pichardo, J. I., López-Medina, E. F., Mancha-Cáceres, O., González-Enríquez, I., Hernández-Melián, A., Blázquez-Rodríguez, M., Jiménez, V., Logares, M., Carabantes-Alarcon, D., Ramos-Toro, M., Isorna, E., Cornejo-Valle, M., and Borrás-Gené, O. (2021). Students and teachers using mentimeter: Technological innovation to face the challenges of the covid-19 pandemic and post-pandemic in higher education. *Education Sciences*, *11*(11). doi:10.3390/educsci11110667.

Pintarič, Z. N., and Kravanja, Z. (2020). The impact of the COVID-19 pandemic in 2020 on the quality of STEM higher education. *Chemical Engineering Transactions*, *81*, 1315–1320. doi:10.3303/CET2081220.

Qadir, J., and Al-fuqaha, A. (2020). A Student Primer on How to Thrive in Engineering Education during and beyond COVID-19. *Education Sciences*, doi:10.3390/educsci10090236.

Ripoll, V., Godino-Ojer, M., and Calzada, J. (2020). Teaching chemical engineering to biotechnology students in the time of COVID-19: Assessment of the adaptation to digitalization. *Education for Chemical Engineers*, *34*, 21–32. doi:10.1016/j.ece.2020.11.001.

Roberts, J., Kigotho, M., and Stagg, A. (2018). Expanding Horizons in Open and Distance Learning. *Distance Education*, *39*(1), 1–3. doi:10.1080/01587919.2018.1439367.

Ruiperez-Valiente, J. A., Gomez, M. J., Martinez, P. A., and Kim, Y. J. (2021). Ideating and Developing a Visualization Dashboard to Support Teachers Using Educational Games in the Classroom. *IEEE Access*, *9*, 83467–83481. doi:10.1109/ACCESS.2021.3086703.

Santana, H. S., de Souza, M. R. P., Lopes, M. G. M., Souza, J., Silva, R. R. O., Palma, M. S. A., Nakano, W. L. V., Lima, G. A. S., Munhoz, G., Noriler, D., Taranto, O. P., and Silva, J. L. (2020). How chemical engineers can contribute to fight the COVID-19. *Journal of the Taiwan Institute of Chemical Engineers*, *116*, 67–80. doi:10.1016/j.jtice.2020.11.024.

Schophuizen, M., Kreijns, K., Stoyanov, S., and Kalz, M. (2017). Eliciting the challenges and opportunities organizations face when delivering open online education: A group-concept mapping study. *Internet and Higher Education*, *36*, 1–12. doi:10.1016/j.iheduc.2017.08.002.

Sharma, D., and Kumar, V. (2017). A Framework for Collaborative and Convenient Learning on Cloud Computing Platforms. *International Journal of Web-Based Learning and Teaching Technologies (IJWLTT)*, *12*(2), 1–20.

Singh, J., and Kumar, V. (2022). Combating the Pandemic with ICT Based Learning tools and applications: A case of Indian Higher Education. *International Journal of Virtual and Personal Learning Environments (IJVPLE) Platforms (IJVPLE)*, *12*(1), 1–21.

Singh, G., Mantri, A., Sharma, O., Dutta, R., and Kaur, R. (2019). Evaluating the impact of the augmented reality learning environment on electronics laboratory skills of engineering students. *Computer Applications in Engineering Education*, 27(6), 1361–1375. doi:10.1002/cae.22156.

Sun, J. N., and Hsu, Y. C. (2013). Effect of interactivity on learner perceptions in Web-based instruction. *Computers in Human Behavior*, *29*(1), 171–184. doi:10.1016/j.chb.2012.08.002.

Thakker, S. V., Parab, J., and Kaisare, S. (2021). Systematic research of e-learning platforms for solving challenges faced by Indian engineering students. *Asian Association of Open Universities Journal*, *16*(1), 1–19. doi:10.1108/AAOUJ-09-2020-0078.

Yang, Y., and Cornelius, L. F. (2004). *Students' Perceptions Towards the Quality of Online Education: A Qualitative Approach*. Association for Educational Communications and Technology, 27th, Chicago, II. October, 19–23.

Yasmin, M. (2022). Online chemical engineering education during COVID-19 pandemic: Lessons learned from Pakistan. *Education for Chemical Engineers*, *39*(November 2021), 19–30. doi:10.1016/j.ece.2022.02.002.

Zhao, Y. (2016). From Deficiency to Strength: Shifting the Mindset about Education Inequality. *Journal of Social Issues*, *72*(4), 720–739. doi:10.1111/josi.12191.

9 Learning opportunities and challenges in virtual teams

Ayu Maria Lestari, Cheuk Hin Mark Ng, Danping Yu, Yang Pu, and Eko Liao

Introduction

Importance of virtual teams for modern companies

Virtual teams play an increasingly important role in enhancing the effectiveness and functionality of teamwork in modern industries, as many companies are operating from various locations and require seamless communication among their members irrespective of time and place (Singh and Kumar, 2022). Moreover, due to technological advances, individuals may choose to work for companies that are no longer situated in their city or even country (Bhardwaj and Kumar, 2023). Similar changes are taking place in education and other settings, indicating that working and learning settings must be more dynamic and responsive to the changing landscape (Kumar and Rewari, 2022). Although these trends were evident earlier, the Covid-19 pandemic has expedited them significantly, as the majority of organizations had to close or shift their operations to the remote mode to comply with the government-imposed rules aimed at curbing the spread of infection (Kumar and Gupta, 2021). Thus, in the last few years, virtual teams have had ample opportunity to demonstrate their benefits, but also drawbacks, in various industries (Kumar and Malhotra, 2021). Even though the pandemic has largely abated, many companies are continuing with a remote or hybrid work model, indicating that virtual teams are here to stay and thus require closer investigation.

Virtual teams refer to a group of individuals who work or study together by utilizing the latest information and communication technology (ICT) to achieve the common purpose or shared target irrespective of time and space. According to Choudhury et al., when collaborative ICTs are utilized effectively, virtual teamwork has the capacity to promote cooperation and efficiency among team members. Here, virtuality implies that the interaction between team members is not physical, but this extends beyond mere use of emails and other internal electronic communications that are typically adopted at the workplace (Abarca et al., 2021). Although a broad range of

DOI: 10.4324/9781003491712-9

companies relied on remote operations during the pandemic, in the conventional sense, virtual teams are formed based on project-based or function-based short- or long-term requirements (Dulebohn and Hoch, 2017). This view is also compatible with the trend of globalization, which necessitates active collaboration and communication between organizations, project teams, and individuals to conduct a wide range of tasks that can be distributed across diverse locations (Bhardwaj and Kumar, 2022).

Company needs

In the rapidly changing global business environment, companies that take advantage of virtual teams can quickly respond to the market needs, as these teams are more agile and are better able to adapt to new requirements (Kovid and Kumar, 2022). In addition, by dispensing with the need for having a workforce in one location, companies can broaden their search for talent while highly skilled individuals can take employment anywhere in the world as they can work remotely (Bergiel et al., 2008). In 2020, possibly due to the issues caused by the pandemic, 62% of employees worldwide stated that they were thinking of resigning from a colocated organization to a company that offers remote work. Because daily commuting between work and home remains a critical concern for many people, especially for the employees with heavy family responsibilities, having the ability to work remotely means that they no longer have to worry about the housing cost, or changing schools for their children, modifying their living habits, etc. Even two decades ago, given that moving is a stressful and costly undertaking, most people were reluctant to move to an area closer to their workplace even if this would advance their career (Joinson, 2002). Fortunately, technology has advanced considerably since then, and now many companies allow their staff to work some or all the time away from office. As a result, the required professionals can be hired without considering the geographic location.

In sum, to recruit and retain talented employees, companies need to provide more flexible work arrangements, one of which is a chance to work as a part of a virtual team. For example, during the pandemic, American technology giant Twitter initially announced that its employees would be working from home indefinitely, because Twitter saw the benefits to shifting to a virtual model, as it allowed its staff more autonomy and freedom while facilitating the recruitment and reducing the operational costs. Twitter Human Resources Chief Jennifer Christie appropriately assumes this, noting that they were already on this route, and the crisis only propels them towards a future state. She also observed that flexibility for workers is the "fourth industrial revolution" because it will fundamentally change the way people work. In her opinion, the future of work lies in offering employees more optionality (Dwoskin, 2020). Thus, for companies which still persisted in adopting the style of traditional face-to-face teams, it would be more challenging for them to access the talent globally.

As globalization is also one of the trends that are likely to continue into the future, and multinational companies are facing unprecedented challenges in responding to the market and shareholder needs, many see reliance on foreign-based subcontracted employees in their new geographical areas as a valid solution. Logitech is one of the companies that have effectively utilized global teaming (Schiff, 2006). Although its headquarters are located in Fremont, California, where the key functions like corporate marketing, software engineering, and quality assurance are gathered, other secondary sections are dispersed worldwide. For instance, its mechanical engineering and design are based in Ireland, electrical engineering takes place in Switzerland, tooling is situated in Taiwan, and manufacturing in China (Bergiel et al., 2008).

Project team needs

Virtual teams are also critical for the execution of various projects, although they are not suitable in all contexts. According to Bergiel et al. (2008), virtual teamwork is typically compatible with design tasks in the electronics industry because the designers are comparatively dispersed. In addition, if project teams lack the talent needed to accomplish specific objectives, recruiting quality designers from any location across the world would increase the likelihood that the specific aspect of the project would be executed correctly. This concept has given rise to new product development (NPD), which greatly benefits from virtual teams, as they are highly productive and can easily respond to the interdisciplinary nature of the work and industry trends.

Benefits for organizations, employees, and teams

As already stated, virtual teams are unaffected by the limitations of space and time and can therefore comprise members of different specialties that are located anywhere across the globe. This is cost-effective for the companies but is also very advantageous for individuals, as they are more likely to be hired on merit, and their recruitment will not be subjected to age and race discrimination. Likewise, without time-zone and geographical barriers, it is easier for organizations, especially for multinational corporations, to adopt the 7/24 support model for their customers. According to Maynard et al. (2006), virtual teams not only empower organizations to reach an extended geographical area but also keep a productive communication between employees and customers. Compared to the traditional teams, virtual teams are more cost-efficient, because the expenses associated with travel, accommodation, and other daily allowances are drastically reduced. However, to attain these benefits from a virtual workplace, effective management skills are needed, as well as greater cultural awareness, especially if staff with different backgrounds will be hired (Bergiel et al., 2008).

The role of technology advancement

Virtual settings enable real-time communication and cooperation from any location and at any time with minimal latency. Virtual teams are becoming increasingly common in industry as technology advances. The use of ICT enables the establishment of virtual teams to perform numerous activities in business, education, and personal life (Davidekova and Hvorecky, 2017). For those that are yet to implement this model, technological requirements are usually the greatest barrier (Mikkola et al., 2005). Thus, the possibility of combining synchronous and asynchronous communication enabled by the latest ICT advancements is likely to result in the growth in virtual team adoption.

The technology tools that are required for virtual teams to function effectively include meeting tools (including video and audio-conferencing tools), collaboration tools, project management tools, document storage or file sharing tools, high-end videoconferencing tools, and instant messaging tools, among others.

a The emergence and upgrade of various meeting tools like Zoom and WebEx have enabled seamless communication among virtual team members. They are also more likely to continue this communication through other means, such as social media.
b Collaboration tools are crucial to the successful management of virtual teams, as their use allows all team members to understand their responsibilities, monitor progress, and communicate in an efficient manner (Sharma and Kumar, 2017). As one of the leading collaboration tools and one major platform adopted by many local and international universities, Microsoft 365 is widely used all over the world. Its cloud-based software includes several tools that may be linked together for maximum efficiency and cooperation. Furthermore, Microsoft 365 allows users to exchange and collaborate on Word documents, Excel spreadsheets, and PowerPoint presentations, and it also includes Microsoft Teams, a strong collaboration platform. According to the available data, 10,000 people can work together on Microsoft Teams no matter where they are located in the world. Downloading an app is not required because it can support the web version. This is a major benefit for teams that need to communicate with clients that do not use Microsoft 365.
c By keeping track of all the work done by team members, such as projects, tasks, and requirements, project management tools can help virtual teams to plan their resources with maximum efficiency. They not only help virtual teams stay organized to make sure that their deadlines are met but can also increase efficiency by eliminating the need for long meetings, clogged inboxes, and repeated revisions of individual work schedules.
d Document storage and file sharing tools are also essential, as virtual team members may need to use the same resources simultaneously. They typically utilize high-grade, secure cloud software technology to support such seamless collaboration by creating one place for team members to share ideas and work together in real time.

Given these rapid technological advancements, the application and penetration rate of virtual teams is steadily increasing. In 2020, GitLab found that almost 90% of virtual team members were satisfied with the technology tools and systems that allow them to communicate and collaborate. According to Meluso et al. (2020), 64% of organizations were also planning to shift to virtual teamwork on a permanent basis even once the pandemic had ended.

Influence of pandemic on virtual teams' adoption

Due to the outbreak of the Covid-19 pandemic, social distancing was mandated in most countries around the world, necessitating that companies adopt remote working models where possible (Brooks et al., 2020). As a result, virtual teams became the norm rather than exception. In an era of rapidly evolving digital technology, organizations and teams from many industries are urged to adopt the remote work model even once all the restrictions have been lifted (Velicia-Martin et al., 2021). The concept of virtual teams initially emerged to enable collaborative discovery and innovation among global or regional professionals who do not have the time to travel to work on projects that require specialized skills. However, due to the rapid globalization, the reliance on virtual teams has grown, because this work model allows for rapid product development and innovation while facilitating access to regionally distributed skills and improving network connectivity (Taras et al., 2019). The recent Covid-19 pandemic has prompted companies that would not typically consider this model to adopt it out of necessity. As it has been proven effective across various contexts, virtual teams have become an accepted way of working and will likely remain one of the main working models going forward.

In the early stage of their adoption, virtual teams were mostly found in workplaces that required virtual learning, teleworking, virtual communities, virtual partnerships, e-marketplaces, and outsourcing or offshoring (Townsend et al., 1998, as cited in Karunathilaka, 2022). However, over time, their scope has broadened considerably, whereby virtual teams are now found in almost all settings. In particular, they have been found beneficial in enhancing learning effectiveness (Chan et al., 2003; Van den Bossche et al., 2006). Although ample body of research has been conducted on the benefits and drawbacks of virtual teams, the findings published by Ortega et al. (2010) are particularly noteworthy. These authors have found that (1) virtual teams improve performance, satisfaction, and viability; (2) some factors like psychological safety, shared beliefs about task interdependence, and collective efficacy can affect the learning behaviors of virtual team members and reinforce the use and adoption of the technological tools, which will ultimately improve team effectiveness; and (3) the behavior in the team learning process can partially mediate the relationship between beliefs about interpersonal context and the effectiveness of virtual teams learning.

When required to learn under virtual team conditions, individuals feel psychologically safe, because the virtual environment facilitates more open communication, allowing members to feel more free to ask questions, seek feedback, or discuss errors without or with little worry about being penalized or feeling embarrassed. Furthermore, task interdependence and collective efficacy are trademarks of virtual teams meaning that they need to interact and share their knowledge to each other in confidence of their ability to fulfill their goal (Handke et al., 2019; McLarnon and Woodley, 2021). These advantages apply to individual learning, increasing the knowledge obtained by the entire team.

Importance of team learning via virtual teams

Owing to the technological advances and the rapidly intensifying competition in the business world, every company must transform itself into a learning organization. The concept of learning organization was introduced by Peter Senge, in *The Fifth Discipline*, who defined it as a place where a group of people learn and expand their capabilities continually to reach their desired outcomes. In this context, learning starts at the team level, as team members are more likely to start thinking together and share their experiences, skills, knowledge, and insights with each other, allowing them to perform better. These positive changes are then expanded across the entire company, transforming it into a learning organization, capable of adapting more dynamically to the unpredictable market conditions than its competitors (Mittal and Kumar, 2019). This competitive advantage is particularly important in today's rapidly changing business environment (Garvin et al., 2008).

Those that perceive team learning as a behavioral process define it as a cyclical set of actions which consist of seeking feedback, sharing information, asking for help, discussing errors, and experimenting. These exercises help team members to strengthen their collective understanding of a problem and learn about the needs of others (Edmondson, 1999).

According to the self-regulation theory (Bandura, 1991), self-efficacy increases one's confidence in his/her ability to perform tasks. The higher the self-efficacy, the more likely an individual is to engage in tasks, especially those that are new or are deemed challenging. Consequently, self-efficacy plays an important role in the team learning process, as seeking feedback and discussing mistakes and errors is necessary in this context but can generate concerns of being judged by the others (Edmondson, 2004). According to Yoon and Kayes (2016), self-efficacy is positively related to the perception of individual learning in teams, whereby the learning process moderates the relationship between one's self-efficacy and the perception of individual learning in teams.

When team learning is seen as an outcome, it depicts the shift in common knowledge, that is information held by the team, not by a particular team member (Wiese and Burke, 2019). Team learning content needs to be constantly communicated and should ideally be documented for easy access by all members. Another type of learning outcome is shift in performance, which is typically observed on the learning curves. As learning curves are assumed to represent the consequence of team learning, changes in costs and man-hours required to complete a task can reveal if the team has effectively made use of its collective knowledge to improve its performance over a period of time.

Transitioning from traditional face-to-face learning to virtual team learning introduces additional factors that may influence the learning outcomes. For example, when interactions between members solely take place online, team performance can vary with changing team structure and the learning behavior of individual members. More than two decades ago, when virtual learning was still in its infancy, Edmondson (1999) observed that team learning behavior was affected by the physical presence/absence of the team leader. Therefore, it can be assumed that the same effects would manifest when teaching and learning are conducted through virtual collaboration and communication tools, as team leader coaching and context support will be more difficult to provide. In addition, as some team members are more independent than others, the need for supervision and support will vary.

Case study: stakeholders' perspective

By looking into the online learning environment of postgraduate students in Hong Kong, we can see both benefits and challenges of the hybrid or fully remote working model. Due to the emergence of new Covid-19 variants, the local government had imposed social distancing measures, which resulted in all postgraduate courses shifting to the distance learning mode through Microsoft Teams, Zoom, e-campus portal, etc. To ensure continuity of learning, some instructors have set new classroom rules to manage class discipline and monitor students' participation in class. For instance, students were required to turn on their front camera when attending online classes and taking tests and examinations. In general, students have to manage groups themselves to complete group assignments and be assessed by tutors under a virtual team setting. To understand their perspectives on working and learning under virtual team setting and the influences on team learning, we have conducted interviews with several postgraduate students, instructors, and facilitators from the Information Technology Center from a few local tertiary institutions. Our findings are summarized here.

Instructors' perspective

After interviewing the instructors, we can observe that teamwork between tutors under the virtual teams setting is not that difficult but has become more challenging for them to monitor students' learning progress and their group work. The commonly used collaboration tools include Microsoft

Teams, Zoom, Google Chat, Google Meet, and Cisco WebEx. The major difficulties that the instructors encountered mostly stemmed from technical issues. Apart from poor network connection and frozen screens, the hosts as well as the participants occasionally pressed the mute button by accident, and in some extreme cases this issue was not rectified for 15–20 minutes.

From our interview with one finance area instructor, he offered his perspective. Before the pandemic, he had conducted classes under virtual team settings due to social issues which prevented some students from attending face-to-face classes. When classes were conducted online, he found that having students work together became more challenging. The instructor also mentioned that motivated students would typically work in the same group while the other students were left behind. He also observed that when students work in groups under virtual settings, he has to spend more time on resolving problems and handling complaints related to groups. Common issues include lack of participation by some group members, who in most extreme cases could not be contacted at all. Comparing traditional student teams with virtual teams, the instructor finds face-to-face teaching more effective in gauging students' learning process and effectiveness. While in both face-to-face classes and virtual classes, very few students are actually active participants, in the traditional setting, the instructors can at least observe their postures and facial expressions.

Students' perspective

The most common tools that our student interviewees use are Microsoft Teams, Zoom, WhatsApp, WeChat, and Tencent Meetings. In general, the interviewees felt that team learning was more demanding under virtual team setting. Marco and Cameron are postgraduate students who enrolled in the master program at local universities. To stand out from other candidates to become an inspector under the Hong Kong Customs and Excise Department, Marco enrolled on the MSc in International Shipping and Transport Logistics programme after finishing his undergraduate study in business school. To get a relatively stable job with higher occupational mobility, Cameron has chosen the accounting pathway this semester. During the interview, both Marco and Cameron expressed their concerns on the team learning process, focusing specifically on the inadequate learning behavior by some members. In the feedback and information sharing stage, they often find it challenging to ascertain if their team members are focusing on the discussion and paying attention to others' feedback, as they are not engaged in the process. The feeling of "not being heard" and/or being misunderstood is particularly problematic when working on group assignments with other students. Although virtual team settings enabled students to carry out group discussions during the lockdown, as many classmates moved back home where they did not necessarily have good internet connection, this compromised the communication effectiveness. To tackle this issue, team members had to spend more time on clarifying concepts and making sure that everyone knows their tasks and responsibilities. In their view, the learning process is much easier in traditional student teams, as group members can sit together, raise questions, and share their thoughts simultaneously while messages in the checkbox might be ignored when they chat via online messengers.

Cameron is now working on a financial analysis project, and his team members have just completed the discussion part via WeChat. The progress was smooth, and he described it as a very successful experience. Unlike Cameron, Marco was upset by his experience with team projects conducted via virtual teams. Knowing that technical issues are common, Marco and his team members had spent extra time on practicing and running the group presentation before presenting their work to the instructors. To avoid any unforeseen issues, the team decided to give the presentation at school even though students were required to present via Microsoft Teams. Unfortunately, technical issues still occurred, and they were unable to share screen with the examiners at the beginning of their presentation. The instructor scolded the team right away, and they lost confidence in their work. As a result, the group presentation was executed poorly. This negative experience, in Marco's view, undermined the team members' confidence, which compromised their subsequent learning efficacy. He also believes that, discouraged by this unfortunate incident, the team members have become less engaged in that course. The incident demonstrated how punitive actions on behalf of the tutor and examiners adversely impacted on students' learning behavior. In his interview, Marco also described a lower team cohesiveness, and noted that relationships with team members tend to last longer in traditional student teams. As peers usually have interactions with each other either on campus after the class or through social media platforms, given that none of this is possible when working under virtual team conditions, team members may feel like strangers after completing the group assignments.

To evaluate productivity under the virtual team setting, Cameron thinks that team performance (learning process as outcome) can be evaluated by course grades, but Marco is of the view that no metric is suitable for measuring team members' productivity. When we asked the interviewees about the functionalities that they would find beneficial but the existing collaboration tools lack, Cameron mentioned that the recording function is not available in WeChat, but Microsoft Teams and Zoom can be used as suitable substitutes. He finds recording beneficial, as it can be used to review any content that would facilitate learning or for tracking each member's participation and responsiveness. However, when we asked Marco for his thoughts on this topic, he pointed out that the performance metrics are discriminative in nature. He was also of the view that such a framework might create an unfair disadvantage for the introverts who may not feel comfortable with being recorded in a learning environment.

To enhance learning effectiveness under virtual team setting, Cameron suggested drafting a progress chart to assist teams with monitoring each member's work progress. Creating a meeting outline before discussion is also beneficial, as it helps the team to stay on the right track and discuss all the important issues step by step.

Facilitators' perspective

In the interview with staff from the Information Technology Center (ITC), they also mentioned the problem of being unable to observe team members' facial expressions and small gestures. For virtual team settings, Microsoft Teams, Zoom, and WhatsApp are being used across various occasions. At the moment, these tools still lack functions such as capturing behavioral hints and facial expressions to enhance the augmentation of social interaction via working with other team members virtually. As facilitators of online learning, the frequent inquiries from teachers are on how to use certain functions and set up their own classes for specific groups of students. With increasing inquiries and issues on teaching online, the ITC has allocated two staff to address issues under the new paradigm shift. When they first started working under virtual team settings, technical issues remained as the major obstacles. Different from instructors' and students' angles, they are more tech-savvy, so things went smoothly after getting the non-technical members familiarized with the system. They often hold meetings with over 30 participants which are not possible to conduct in a physical place due to the strict social distancing policy or otherwise a time- and energy-consuming event. They see virtual teams as an alternative that proves to be beneficial in the way that different issues can be addressed simultaneously. Compared to traditional face-to-face setting, virtual teams facilitate productivity as it reduces time, manpower, and financial cost significantly especially with multitasking from a busy work schedule.

To ensure effectiveness of teamwork under virtual team settings, the supervisor emphasized on the importance of clear direction from other departments from the institution and ensured effective and frequent dyadic communication with management teams. This helps the ITC team in formulating execution plans and providing other units with the necessary technical support. Within the team, team morale is highly dependent on team members' engagement and professionalism. Learning behavior and team morale can be worse if team members go silent or even turn off their video.

Benefits and challenges of team learning via virtual team

Benefits

Virtual teams are often expected to perform in the same manner with traditional team setting in organizations, in the sense that they must adapt quickly to the need to innovate, establish inter-organizational partnerships, and respond to corporate globalization and the adoption of new information technology (Ortega et al., 2010). To achieve these ambitious objectives, all team members have to fully exert their effort, ability, intelligence, skills, and knowledge and even draw upon their private resources in some circumstances. When teams operate in a virtual setting, many benefits can be attained, but various issues may also arise. The main advantage of virtual teams stems from their ability to communicate and interact across the limitations of space and time. Moreover, virtual teams can help organizations achieve economies of scale, increase efficiency through flexible work cycles, recruit top personnel regardless of geographic location, accelerate creative product launches, and increase local expertise and presence (Collins et al., 2015, as cited in Karunathilaka, 2022). Table 9.1 shows a literature review on benefits brought by virtual teams.

Table 9.1 Benefits Associated With Virtual Teams

Benefits		*References*
Across Time and Space	Virtual teams overcome the limitations of time, space, and organizational affiliation that traditional teams face.	Piccoli et al. (2004)
	Virtual teams are increasingly being utilized by organizations because they facilitate bridging time and space.	Kanawattanachai and Yoo (2002)
	Virtual teams enable organizations to attain a broader geographic reach while maintaining effective contact with employees and customers.	Maynard et al. (2006)
Take Advantage of Global Talent	Virtual teams have emerged as one of the key management tools available to companies wishing to take advantage of the pool of global talent.	Bergiel et al. (2008)
Cost Effective	Virtual teams are usually more cost-efficient compared to synchronous face-to-face teams (that incur expenses related to travel, office space, etc.) and often provide a means for better utilization of distributed human resources.	Lipnack and Stamps (1999)
	Virtual teams drastically reduce travel time and cost, as well as the expenses associated with accommodation and various daily allowances.	Bergiel et al. (2008)
Easier to Document and Review the Performance	Performance is often easier to document and review in virtual teams because most interactions, commitments, and outcomes are archived automatically and electronically.	Gibson and Cohen (2003)
Facilitate Knowledge Sharing	The interactions within virtual teams focus around knowledge sharing and, as team members may range from novices to experts, there is a potential for training new talent.	Gannon-Leary et al. (2007)
Discourage Age and Race Discrimination	Virtual teams promote equity, as members are hired and retained based on merit, as opposed to other attributes.	Bergiel et al. (2008)

A review of related literature has revealed the following core benefits of virtual teams:

1 Unlike traditional teams, virtual teams work across geographical and temporal boundaries by utilizing information communication technologies, allowing them to feel greater control over their learning and tasks, as these can be managed more flexibly. For organizations, virtual teams are beneficial, as they increase the talent pool, which can be recruited across a wider geographical region (Ale Ebrahim et al., 2009). Owing to these advantages, companies are increasingly relying on virtual teams to strengthen their competitive advantage (Bell and Kozlowski, 2002). The recent Covid-19 pandemic has accelerated this trend, as it has demonstrated that virtual teams can function in almost any context and are particularly beneficial for the execution of projects with specific targets and deadlines.
2 As virtual teams are not colocated on the same physical premises, taking advantage of the global talent pool, which was very challenging to achieve in traditional face-to-face teams, is now attainable. As the critical resource for the organizations, talented individuals must not only be hired but also be retained, and having more flexibility as a result of the virtual team working mode is more likely to facilitate this process. Prasad and Akhilesh (2002) are also of the view that virtual teams are more dynamic and inspiring, and can be viewed as centers of excellence, allowing companies that have adopted this working model to retain the best talent regardless of location.
3 Virtual teams are cost-effective, as they eliminate the significant expenses associated with accommodation, travel, and various daily allowances (Bergiel et al., 2008). The time saved by eliminating the need for commuting to the workplace can be spent on tasks that contribute to the company goals while making the employees more satisfied with their work–life balance (Rabelo and Speller, 2005). Therefore, virtual teams can offer organizations rapid solutions at a lower cost than would be incurred by physical teams (Zhang, 2022). In the domain of education, virtual teams can be beneficial to learners, as they are able to access high-quality teaching courses irrespective of their location, which will mitigate the disparities in knowledge that arise due to differences in financial capabilities.
4 Knowledge sharing is another important benefit of virtual teams, as members can utilize the knowledge and skills others in the team possess. Moreover, the diversity is enhanced in virtual teams as their members can come from different locations, which would foster greater appreciation for different cultures, races, and languages. As virtual teams communicate via various platforms, team members can use different tools to present their innovative ideas and suggestions to the others, thereby increasing the overall team output (Hong and Vai, 2008). Most importantly, all team members can capitalize on their strengths while helping each other overcome their weaknesses.

Challenges

Although virtual teams have many advantages, some of the barriers commonly encountered in this working arrangement are outlined here. (Table 9.2 shows a literature review on potential challenges brought by virtual teams.)

Table 9.2 Challenges Associated With Virtual Teams

Challenges		*References*
Trust and Communication Barriers	Vulnerable to mistrust, communication breakdowns, conflicts, and power struggles.	Cascio (2000)
	Project management challenges may arise due to the distance between team members, irrespective of their cultural or language differences.	Badrinarayanan and Arnett (2008)
	Challenges related managing conflict.	Ocker and Fjermestad (2008)
	As cultural and functional diversity in virtual teams leads to differences in the members' thought processes, developing trust among the members can be challenging.	Badrinarayanan and Arnett (2008)
Share Less Information	Virtual team members tend to initially share less information than members of teams that work in the same physical space.	Hinds and Weisband (2003)
	Lack of knowledge among some senior, mature managers concerning advanced technological applications may hinder the effective adoption of virtual teams.	Bergiel et al. (2008)
Lack of Physical Interaction	Virtual teams' cohesion is harmed by a lack of physical encounters and informal ties.	Shin (2005)
Reduced opportunity for informal relationships and connections	Virtual teams may face difficulties when there are less possibilities for casual work- and non-work-related talks.	Furst et al. (2004)

(*Continued*)

Table 9.2 (Continued)

Challenges		*References*
	Virtual team members are more likely to treat one another formally and less likely to reciprocate requests from one another, relative to teams that share physical space.	Wong and Burton (2000)
Create Obstacles Like Technophobia	Virtual teams are challenged because they rely solely on computer-mediated communication technology for their interactions, which may hinder the development of bonds that would come more naturally in teams that share the same physical space	Hardin et al. (2007)
	Virtual teams may require complex technological applications to execute all their tasks effectively.	Badrinarayanan and Arnett (2008)
	Adoption of virtual teams may result in technophobia, as some employees who are uncomfortable with computers and other telecommunications technologies will struggle to get used to the new working model.	Johnson et al. (2001)
Lack of Supervision and Motivation	Adoption of virtual teams decreases the capacity for monitoring and controlling activities.	Pawar and Sharifi (1997)
	The dispersed nature of virtual teams makes direct supervision of team members through coaching and rewarding team performance less viable.	Bell and Kozlowski (2002)
	Extrinsic motivation is exacerbated by the physical absence of a formal leader.	Kayworth and Leidner (2001)

The major points of discussion that emerge are:

1 Trust and communication may be more difficult to establish, especially if the team members have not had the opportunity to work in the same physical space before. Moreover, if they come from vastly different cultures, their attitudes toward work and deadlines may not be aligned (Munkvold

and Zigurs, 2007). As virtual teams lack the opportunity for face-to-face interactions and feedback, they may struggle with consolidating group membership and may prefer working autonomously (Gannon-Leary and Fontainha, 2007). In addition, as all communication is conducted virtually, the potential for misinterpretation and misunderstandings is significant, because many nonverbal cues can be absent (Cramton, 2001; Gibson and Manuel, 2003). If the team atmosphere becomes unreliable and unproductive, team members will lose the sense of belonging and will exist as a team in name only.

2 According to the survey conducted by the University College of London in April 2020, the virtual team learning mode has exacerbated educational unfairness. In particular, the children who lack parental support and tutoring will fall further behind their peers who do not experience these issues. In developing or undeveloped countries or areas, the disparity between virtual team and traditional learning modes in terms of effectiveness is even more severe, as children from urban families are more inclined to adapt to the virtual team learning model compared to those from rural areas. Generally, children from rural areas tend to use computers or mobile phones for entertainment because they lack positive guidance from their parents. It is thus expected that the learning style changes brought about by the internet technologies will widen the divide between more affluent and poorer, as well as urban and rural children.

3 For both young and adult learners, reliance on virtual teams for their learning needs substantially reduces the social aspects of the learning process and may thus undermine their interest in learning. In a physical learning setting, learners have the natural opportunities to talk about some personal issues before or after the class or to have a cup of coffee together. During these informal social activities, the connections and relationships are developed. Consequently, virtual teams are particularly challenging for learners who are not self-motivated or do not have strong support at home or in their community.

Conclusion

Virtual team mode is exacerbating the polarization between different learners or organizations who adopt virtual teams' management methods. On the one hand, the great convenience and flexibility that virtual team models bring can accelerate the learners' progress, due to which the learning effectiveness and efficiency will be improved by a large margin. In the work context, organizations that possess advanced management experience or techniques are able to fully utilize the benefits of virtual team model and can convert them to competitive advantage. On the other hand, in the absence of direct supervision or physical interaction, learners who are not highly motivated to learn and manage their time effectively will face more challenges in attaining the benefits of the virtual team learning model.

Acknowledgment

The work described in this chapter was supported by a grant from the Research Grants Council of the Hong Kong Special Administrative Region, China (Project No. UGC/FDS14/B05/19).

References

Abarca, V. G., Sanchez, P. P., and Camacho, M. A. (2021). Virtual Teams in Times of Pandemic: Factors that Influence Performance. *Frontiers in Psychology, 12.* doi:10.3389/fpsyg.2021.624637.

Ale Ebrahim, N., Ahmed, S., and Taha, Z. (2009). Virtual Teams: A Literature Review. *Australian Journal of Basic and Applied Sciences, 3*(3), 2653–2669.

Badrinarayanan, V., and Arnett, D. B. (2008). Effective Virtual New Product Development Teams: An Integrated Framework. *Journal of Business & Industrial Marketing, 23*(4), 242–248. doi:10.1108/08858620810865816.

Bandura, A. (1991). Social Cognitive Theory of Self-regulation. *Organizational Behavior and Human Decision Processes, 50*(2), 248–287. doi:10.1016/0749-5978(91)90022-l.

Bell, B. S., and Kozlowski, S. W. (2002). A Typology of Virtual Teams. *Group & Organization Management, 27*(1), 14–49. doi:10.1177/1059601102027001003.

Bergiel, B. J., Bergiel, E. B., and Balsmeier, P. W. (2008). Nature of Virtual Teams: A Summary of Their Advantages and Disadvantages. *Management Research News, 31*(2), 99–110. doi:10.1108/01409170810846821.

Bhardwaj, A., and Kumar, V. (2022). A Framework for Enhancing Privacy in Online Collaboration. *International Journal of Electronic Security and Digital Forensics (IJESDF), 14*(4), 413–432.

Bhardwaj, A., and Kumar, V. (2023). Social Media as an Enabler to Combat Misinformation. In *Pandemics in the Age of Social Media: Information and Misinformation in Developing Nations*. Routledge: New York (USA), pp. 1–15.

Brooks, S. K., Webster, R. K., Smith, L. E., Woodland, L., Wessely, S., Greenberg, N., and Rubin, G. J. (2020). The psychological impact of quarantine and how to reduce it: Rapid review of the evidence. *The Lancet, 395*(10227), 912–920. doi:10.1016/s0140-6736(20)30460-8.

Cascio, W. F. (2000). Managing a Virtual Workplace. *Academy of Management Perspectives, 14*(3), 81–90. doi:10.5465/ame.2000.4468068.

Chan, C. C. A., Pearson, C., and Entrekin, L. (2003). Examining the effects of internal and external team learning on Team Performance. *Team Performance Management: An International Journal, 9*(7/8), 174–181. doi:10.1108/13527590310507426.

Collins, N., Chou, Y.-M., Warner, M., and Rowley, C. (2015). Human factors in East Asian virtual teamwork: A comparative study of Indonesia, Taiwan and Vietnam. *The International Journal of Human Resource Management, 28*(10), 1475–1498. doi:10.1080/09585192.2015.1089064.

Cramton, C. D. (2001). The mutual knowledge problem and its consequences for dispersed collaboration. *Organization Science, 12*(3), 346–371. doi:10.1287/orsc.12.3.346.10098.

Davidekova, M., and Hvorecky, J. (2017). ICT Collaboration Tools for Virtual Teams in Terms of the SECI Model. *International Journal of Engineering Pedagogy (iJEP), 7*(1), 95–116. doi:10.3991/ijep.v7i1.6502.

Dulebohn, J. H., and Hoch, J. E. (2017). Virtual Teams in Organizations. *Human Resource Management Review, 27*(4), 569–574. doi:10.1016/j.hrmr.2016.12.004.

Dwoskin, E. (2020, October 1). *Americans might never go back to the office, and Twitter is leading the charge.* The Washington Post. Retrieved from https://

www.washingtonpost.com/technology/2020/10/01/twitter-work-from-home/#:~:text=%E2%80%9CWe've%20already%20been%20on,change%20the%20way%20people%20work

Edmondson, A. (1999). Psychological Safety and Learning Behavior in Work Teams. *Administrative Science Quarterly*, *44*(2), 350–383. doi:10.2307/2666999.

Edmondson, A. C. (2004). Psychological Safety, Trust, and Learning in Organizations: A Group-Level Lens. In Kramer, R. M., and Cook, K. S. (Eds), *Trust and Distrust in Organizations: Dilemmas and Approaches*. New York, NY: Russell Sage, pp. 239–272.

Furst, S. A., Reeves, M., Rosen, B., and Blackburn, R. S. (2004). Managing the Life Cycle of Virtual Teams. *Academy of Management Perspectives*, *18*(2), 6–20. doi:10.5465/ame.2004.13837468.

Gannon-Leary, P., & Fontainha, E. (2007). Communities of Practice and virtual learning communities: benefits, barriers and success factors. *Barriers and Success Factors*. eLearning Papers, (5).

Gannon-Leary, Pat and Fontainha, Elsa, Communities of Practice and Virtual Learning Communities: Benefits, *Barriers and Success Factors*. eLearning Papers, No. 5, September 2007. Retrieved from https://ssrn.com/abstract=1018066.

Garvin, D. A., Edmondson, A. C., and Gino, F. (2008). Is Yours a Learning Organization? *Harvard Business Review*, *86*(3), 109–134.

Gibson, C. B., and Cohen, S. G. (2003). The Last Word: Conclusions and Implication. In Gibson, C. B., and Cohen, S. G. (Eds), *Virtual Teams That Work: Creating Conditions for Virtual Team Effectiveness*. San Francisco, CA: Jossey-Bass, pp. 403–421.

Gibson, C. B., and Manuel, J. A. (2003). Building Trust: Effective Multicultural Communication Processes in Virtual Teams. In Gibson, C. B., and Cohen, S. G. (Eds), *Virtual Teams That Work: Creating Conditions for Virtual Team Effectiveness*. San Francisco, CA: Jossey-Bass, pp. 59–86.

Hardin, A. M., Fuller, M. A., and Davison, R. M. (2007). I Know I Can, But Can We? *Small Group Research*, *38*(1), 130–155. doi:10.1177/1046496406297041.

Hinds, P. J., and Weisband, S. P. (Eds) (2003). Knowledge Sharing and Shared Understanding in Virtual Teams. In *Virtual Teams That Work: Creating Conditions for Virtual Team Effectiveness*, pp. 21–36.

Hong, J. F., and Vai, S. (2008). Knowledge-Sharing in Cross-Functional Virtual Teams. *Journal of General Management*, *34*(2), 21–37. doi:10.1177/030630700803400202.

Johnson, P., Heimann, V., & O'Neill, K. (2001). The "wonderland" of virtual teams. *Journal of workplace learning*. *13*(1), 24–30.

Joinson, C. (2002, June 1). *Workplace trends: Managing virtual teams*. SHRM. Retrieved from https://www.shrm.org/hr-today/news/hr-magazine/pages/0602joinson.aspx

Kanawattanachai, P., and Yoo, Y. (2002). Dynamic Nature of Trust in Virtual Teams. *The Journal of Strategic Information Systems*, *11*(3–4), 187–213. doi:10.1016/s0963-8687(02)00019-7.

Karunathilaka, G. S. (2022). Virtual team adaptation: Management perspective on individual differences. *Businesses*, *2*(2), 118–128. doi:10.3390/businesses2020008.

Kayworth, T., & Leidner, D. (2004). Organizational culture as a knowledge resource. *Handbook on Knowledge Management 1: Knowledge Matters*, 235–252.

Kumar, V., and Rewari, M. (2022). A Responsible Approach to Higher Education Curriculum Design. *International Journal of Educational Reform (IJER)*, *31*(4), 422–441.

Kumar, V., and Malhotra, G. (Eds) (2021). *Stakeholder Strategies for Reducing the Impact of Global Health Crises*. Hershey, PA, USA: IGI – Global Publications (ISBN13: 978-17-9987-495-9, DOI: 10.4018/978-1-7998-7495-9).

Kumar, V., and Gupta, G. (Eds) (2021). *Strategic Management During a Pandemic*. Routledge, Taylor & Francis Group: USA (ISBN 9780367646479).

Kovid, R. K., and Kumar, V. (Eds) (2022). *Cases on Emerging Markets Responses to the COVID-19 Pandemic.* IGI – Global Publications: USA (ISBN13: 978-16-6843-504-5, DOI: 10.4018/978-1-6684-3504-5).

Lipnack, J., and Stamps, J. (1999). Virtual Teams: The New Way to Work. *Strategy & Leadership*, *27*(1), 14–19. doi:10.1108/eb054625.

Maynard, D. C., Joseph, T. A., and Maynard, A. M. (2006). Underemployment, job attitudes, and turnover intentions. *Journal of Organizational Behavior*, *27*(4), 509–536. doi:10.1002/job.389.

McLarnon, M. J., and Woodley, H. J. (2021). Collective efficacy in virtual teams: Emergence, trajectory, and effectiveness implications. *Canadian Journal of Behavioural Science/Revue Canadienne Des Sciences Du Comportement*, *53*(2), 187–199. doi:10.1037/cbs0000233.

Meluso, J., Johnson, S., and Bagrow, J. (2020). Flexible environments for hybrid collaboration: Redesigning Virtual Work through the four orders of Design. doi:10.31235/osf.io/wehsk.

Mikkola, J. H., Maclaran, P. and Wright, S. (2005). Book reviews. *R&D Management*, *35*, 104–109.

Mittal, S., and Kumar, V. (2019). Study of knowledge management models and their relevance in organisations. *International Journal of Knowledge Management Studies*, *10*(3), 322–335.

Munkvold, B. E., and Zigurs, I. (2007). Process and technology challenges in swift-starting virtual teams. *Information & Management*, *44*(3), 287–299. doi:10.1016/j.im.2007.01.002.

Ocker, R. J., and Fjermestad, J. (2008). Communication Differences in Virtual Design Teams. *ACM SIGMIS Database: The DATABASE for Advances in Information Systems*, *39*(1), 51–67. doi:10.1145/1341971.1341977.

Ortega, A., Manzanares, M. S., Gil, F., and Rico, R. (2010). Team Learning and Effectiveness in Virtual Project Teams: The Role of Beliefs about Interpersonal Context. *The Spanish Journal of Psychology, 13*(1), 267–276. doi:10.1017/S11387 4160000384X.

Pawar, K. S., and Sharifi, S. (1997). Physical or Virtual Team Collocation: Does It Matter? *International Journal of Production Economics*, *52*(3), 283–290. doi:10.1016/s0925-5273(97)89241-9.

Piccoli, G., Powell, A., and Ives, B. (2004). Virtual Teams: Team Control Structure, Work Processes, and Team Effectiveness. *Information Technology & People*, *17*(4), 359–379. doi:10.1108/09593840410570258.

Prasad, K., and Akhilesh, K. B. (2002). Global Virtual Teams: What Impacts Their Design and Performance? *Team Performance Management: An International Journal*, *8*(5/6), 102–112. doi:10.1108/13527590210442212.

Rabelo, L., and Speller Jr, T. H. (2005). Sustaining Growth in the Modern Enterprise: A Case Study. *Journal of Engineering and Technology Management*, *22*(4), 274–290.

Schiff, D. (2006). Global Teams Rock Around the Clock. *Electronic Engineering Times*, *1435*, 12–13.

Sharma, D., and Kumar, V. (2017). A Framework for Collaborative and Convenient Learning on Cloud Computing Platforms. *International Journal of Web-Based Learning and Teaching Technologies (IJWLTT)*, *12*(2), 1–20.

Shin, Y. (2005). Conflict Resolution in Virtual Teams. *Organizational Dynamics*, *34*(4), 331–345. doi:10.1016/j.orgdyn.2005.08.002.

Singh, J., and Kumar, V. (2022). Combating the Pandemic with ICT Based Learning Tools and Applications: A Case of Indian Higher Education. *International Journal of Virtual and Personal Learning Environments (IJVPLE) Platforms (IJVPLE)*, *12*(1), 1–21.

Taras, V., Baack, D., Caprar, D., Dow, D., Froese, F., Jimenez, A., and Magnusson, P. (2019). Diverse Effects of Diversity: Disaggregating Effects of Diversity in Global Virtual Teams. *Journal of International Management*, *25*(4), Article 100689. doi:10.1016/j.intman.2019.100689.

Townsend, A. M., DeMarie, S. M., and Hendrickson, A. R. (1998). Virtual Teams: Technology and the Workplace of the Future. *Academy of Management Perspectives*, *12*(3), 17–29. doi:10.5465/ame.1998.1109047.

Van den Bossche, P., Gijselaers, W. H., Segers, M., and Kirschner, P. A. (2006). Social and Cognitive Factors Driving Teamwork in Collaborative Learning Environments: Team Learning Beliefs and Behaviors. *Small Group Research*, *37*(5), 490–521. doi:10.1177/1046496406292938.

Velicia-Martin, F., Cabrera-Sanchez, J. P., Gil-Cordero, E., and Palos-Sanchez, P. R. (2021). Researching COVID-19 Tracing App Acceptance: Incorporating Theory from the Technological Acceptance Model. *PeerJ. Computer Science*, *7*, e316. doi:10.7717/peerj-cs.316.

Wiese, C. W., and Burke, C. S. (2019). Understanding Team Learning Dynamics Over Time. *Frontiers in Psychology*, *10*, Article 1417. doi:10.3389/fpsyg.2019.01417.

Wong, S.-S., and Burton, R. M. (2000). Virtual Teams: What are their Characteristics, and Impact on Team Performance?. *Computational & Mathematical Organization Theory*, *6*(4), 339–360. doi:10.1023/a:1009654229352.

Yoon, J., and Kayes, D. C. (2016). Employees' Self-Efficacy and Perception of Individual Learning in Teams: The Cross-Level Moderating Role of Team-Learning Behavior. *Journal of Organizational Behavior*, *37*(7), 1044–1060. doi:10.1002/job.2092.

Zhang, A. (2022). The Application of Virtual Teams in the Improvement of Enterprise Management Capability from the Perspective of Knowledge Transfer. *PLOS ONE*, *17*(3). doi:10.1371/journal.pone.0264367.

10 Model for conducting online laboratory courses during the pandemic

Aashish Bhardwaj and Anu Gupta

Introduction

In today's digital world, everybody used to capture moments of joy, natural beauty, celebrations, religious processions, historical event, or any other occasion with their digital devices. These digital devices include mobile phones, cameras, tablets, smartwatches, ebooks, digital cameras, digital televisions, robotics, drones, and so on, which previously was done as a personal moment using the eyes and human mind (Kumar and Bhardwaj, 2020). This is digital transformation which has completely transformed the way humans live (Bhardwaj and Kumar, 2023). The same technology is to be used in the way teachers teach and students learn in the current scenario. Teachers are expected to integrate various learning management systems (LMS) like Blackboard Learn, Moodle, Desire2Learn, Canvas, Sakai, or many others (Kumar and Sharma, 2017). So the internet has become popular for teaching and learning spaces. Presently, teachers are acting as digital immigrants and students as digital native to new technologies (Sharma and Kumar, 2017). Also, with the outbreak of Covid-19 or corona virus from Wuhan, China, in December 2019 to the whole world and WHO declaring it as a pandemic on March 11, 2020 (Kovid and Kumar, 2022). The educational system in the world was severely affected as many governments temporarily closed the educational institutes and replacing them with online education. As per Hoffman and Miller, 2020, approximately 1.077 billion learners were affected due to the closure of educational institutions by September 2020. Also, the higher educational institutions were closed in approximately 185 countries in April 2020 itself affecting around 1,000 million students throughout world as per UNESCO (Marinoni et al., 2020). Such a closure of educational institutions throughout the world had impacted students, teachers, and their families with far-reaching social and economic consequences. The online curriculum had impacted learning pedagogy for both students and teachers in comparison to the physical format where education used to be the focus between learners and educators (Singh and Kumar, 2022). The education system has changed intensely with unique rise of e-learning where teaching is taken up remotely with the use of digital platforms. The

DOI: 10.4324/9781003491712-10

digital platforms include language apps, videoconferencing tools, online learning software, virtual tutoring, and so on. The overall market share for online learning is projected to reach US$350 billion by 2025 with dominance by the United States and China (https://www.globenewswire.com/news-release/2019/12/17/1961785/0/en/Online-Education-Market-Study-2019-World-Market-Projected-to-Reach-350-Billion-by-2025-Dominated-by-the-United-States-and-China.html).

Some of the online learning platforms used extensively during Covid-19 includes Tencent classroom which was recommended by Chinese government for their full-time students. This was the largest online movement in the history with 81% of the K-12 students attending classes through Tencent online platform (Luo et al., 2022). Also, there was a significant demand of the free online learning platforms for which many companies offer free access to their resources, like Byju's platform from Bengaluru, India. Byju's allowed free live online classes for its Think and Learn all and has seen a 200% increase in the number of learners using their products (Egielewa et al., 2022). Another such example is Lark from Singapore which started with offering of online unlimited online videoconferencing to students and teachers. It also includes capabilities of auto-translation, real-time editing, calender scheduling, and so on as important features. DingTalk, a distance learning tool from Alibaba, is also a similar solution to support large-scale remote work (Li, 2022). Clearly, the corona virus pandemic has radically transformed the education system as done for other ways of living, working, or other related activities suddenly at the universal level (Kovid and Kumar, 2022; Kumar and Malhotra, 2021). The digital technology-enabled learning provides different ways in which students can learn at their own pace and happily without burden (Kumar and Nanda, 2020). Similarly, conducting laboratory courses in online mode can lead to higher-order learning. Some of the online tools for conducting laboratory courses are shown in Figure 10.1.

In a short duration of time people from academics have converted their teaching materials and methods to online as per the current requirement imposed by the Covid-19 pandemic. This has imposed unprecendented challenges for students and teachers to reinvent themselves during the pandemic in record time (Tate and Warschauer, 2022). It was also found that there were pre-existing technologies which supported the online learning like instant messaging tools like Whatsapp, Telegram; videoconferencing tools like Zoom, Cisco Webex, Google Meet, GoToMeeting, Microsoft Teams, and educational apps like Google Classroom. Use of these digital technologies in education was very helpful as they provide multiple options of teaching such as sharing materials through presentation, slides, and videos. Delivering lectures through videoconferencing in real time; interaction through forums, chats, work groups, etc. Evaluating and supervising students in synchronous and asynchronous manner for their better involvement in teaching–learning process. Other advantages of using such online tools in education includes multi-pinning which allows teacher to pin up to multiple students at a time

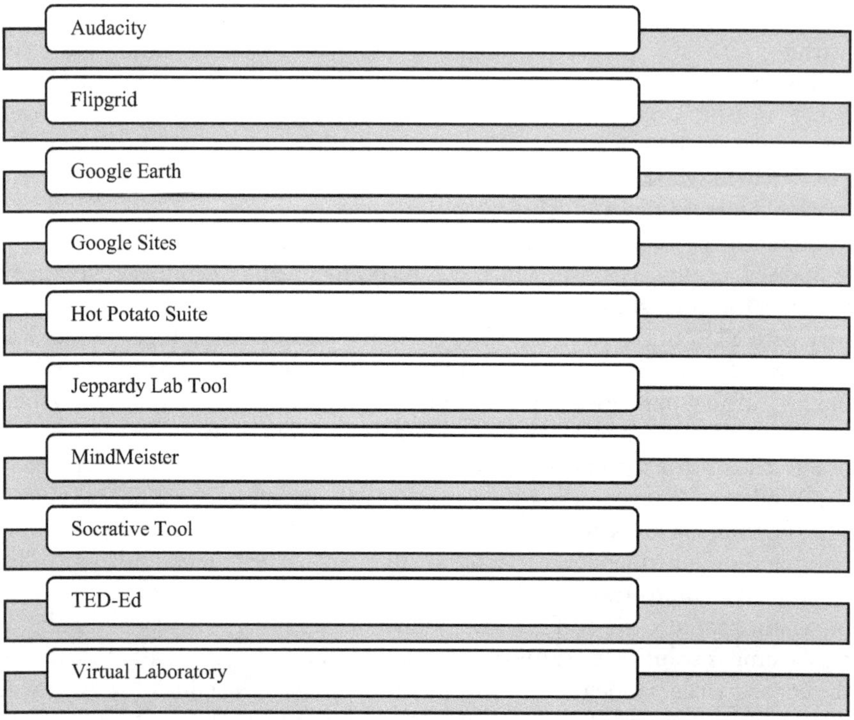

Figure 10.1 Online tools available for conducting online laboratory courses.

on screen in their custom personal view, and students can do the same with permission. Multi Spotlight which allows creating a custom-focused group view which is visible to the entire class to see and is useful for group presentation. Unmute with Consent where teachers can unmute their students only once and that permission will carry over into other classes. Video reordering which allows seeing videos of multiple participants at a time with easy drag dropping video and rearranging the order in which students appear.

- Audacity (https://www.audacityteam.org/): Audacity is audio software which is free, open-source and can be used for cross platform applications. It is a multi-track audio editor and recorder for Windows, Macintosh, Linux, and other operating systems. It allows student to apply their technology skills to create and manipulate audio. It supports collaborative communities for modifications, feedback, creativity, and experimentation (Ober, 2021; Kumar and Bhardwaj, 2020a). Its salient features include recording of live audio through microphone or mixer or other digital media. It supports import, edit, and export of files in multiple formats with sound quality of 16-bit, 24-bit, or 32-bit. It supports plug-ins of Audio Unit effect, LADSPA, LV2, Nyquist, and VST with accessibility of tracks and selection through keyboard. It also supports spectrogram view for visualizing and selecting frequency and spectrum window for analyzing frequency.

- Flipgrid (https://info.flipgrid.com/): Flipgrid is a social learning environment through video discussion where teachers and students in class support learning with fun. This application is used by millions of students from pre-primary to doctorate, teachers, and families. Using this video tool, teachers post a topic which is a video with related text and start to facilitate video discussion. Students are prompted to respond and share their responses. The response is prepared by software's camera and is posted to original topic. It is helpful in social networking and online discussion forums as well (Rinfret and Forster, 2022; Bhardwaj and Cyphert, 2020). The salient features of Flipgrid include storytelling by creating and arranging video clips, expressing the work flipped on White board with Live Inking. It also supports adding text on photos from personal camera, emoji, and stickers on video. It also applies unique filters like warm, cool, pixel, old-town, super warm, and super cool. It also provides the feature to embed video on user's websites and saving them on Microsoft One-Drive or Google Drive.
- Google Earth (https://earth.google.com/): Google Earth provides a three-dimensional rendered image of the earth primarily based on satellite imagery through its computer program. It provides a tool for earth navigation, night sky, globe of moon and mars with measuring distance between any points using desktop application. It provides two views, that is two-dimensional map and Live View for directions placed in real world. It can be used in classroom to understand concepts across the globe canvas. It provides real-time experience to students for their daily lives, community, and the whole world (Guo et al., 2022). The salient features of Google Earth include search capabilities, ability to rotate, pan, zoom, and tilt different views of the earth. It also supports tools for creating data, growing sets of layers of new data like volcanoes and terrain. Also, it doesn't require specific address, and locations are simply identified from the map by just picking them off. This provides the capability to map locations or informal locations easily without specific address.
- Google Sites (https://sites.google.com/): Google Sites is an editor suite from Google which is web based for creation of structured wiki and web pages. It also includes Google Docs, Google Sheets, Google Slides, Google Forms, Google Drawings, and Google Keep. It allows users to collaborate online in real time and also allows creating and editing files online for learning media. It is also used as online learning management for effective learning and teaching activities. It can also be used for different learning activities, preparation of lesson plans, collection of teaching resources,

and provision of learning media (Widayanti and Khasanah, 2021). The salient features of Google Sites include editor sidebar which is similar to Google Drive Addons, Embed section with automatically adding URLs, Title, and image visibility. It provides a streamline workflow by uploading files and folders directly from Google Drive. It also supports a preview mode for mobile and responsive design views and support for material design elements like motion for animation and material transition through JavaScript.

- Hot Potato Suite (https://hotpot.uvic.ca/): Hot Potato Suite is a freeware which is a classroom activity tool and includes applications for creating exercises including World Wide Web. It was created by the University of Victoria, Canada and Half-Baked Software Inc. handles the commercial aspects of the software. Mainly it includes applications like JCloze, JCross, JMatch, JMix, JQuiz, and The Masher. Kids are made to play the game for the purpose of learning as if they are handling hot potato which is real and could burn them. Also, it allows creating exercises like multiple-choice, interactive, short-answer, cross-word, jumbled-sentence, fill-in-the-blanks, matching, or ordering (Bhat et al., 2021). The salient features of Hot Potato Suite include corporate learning solution at a fast pace and provides the structure which promotes contribution to a range of different ideas. For students it allows them to think deep and more divergently for creating new ideas. The feature of changing pace of learning energizes students and keeps kinesthetic learners well involved.
- Jeopardy Lab Tool (https://jeopardylabs.com/): Jeopardy Lab tool allows building customized games to help students in understanding new concepts, getting ready for a test, review prior information or interactive application concerned with specific topic of course. Jeopardy Lab tool allows users to create jeopardy game without use of PowerPoint slides or paying registration fees. Games can be prepared by using more than 6,000 Jeopardy Templates which are readily available (Saha et al., 2021; Bhardwaj and Kumar, 2011). The salient feature of Jeopardy Lab tool includes tool through which teachers can create games for reviewing materials for students during class in jeopardy style. It also allows to create own Jeopardy board or a choice from millions of boards which are already prepared. It helps to make class interactive with input of question and answer only; other important things are assembled by Jeopardy itself.
- MindMeister (https://www.mindmeister.com/): MindMeister is an online mind mapping tool that allows students and teachers to share, present, and envisage their thoughts through cloud computing technology. It allows creating mind maps, brainstorming ideas, and collaborating within groups or class. Such activities help students to gain higher-order thinking skills such as critical thinking, creative thinking, and problem-solving required for twenty-first-century knowledge society. MindMeister also helps to create new ideas through its paragraph formation tool (Hursen, 2021; Bhardwaj and Kumar, 2022b). The salient features of MindMeister

include beautiful themes to add colors and styles to improve readability, map layouts to display contents like mind map view, org chart, and list. It supports a lot of mind map templates for every occasion of human life and provides key shortcuts to add topics, format text, or arranging map easily without even using mouse to click. Also, it supports the feature of connections between mind map topics with customized style, shape, and endpoints.

- Socrative Tool (https://www.socrative.com/): Socrative is an online student response system developed using cloud technologies which allow teachers to create simple tests. Students can check their skills on these tests using smartphones, laptops, or tablets. The Socrative provides an online platform to conduct assessments, facilitate understanding and feedbacks. It helps to improve the learning environment in classroom, with increased motivation and more engaged students. It has also worked in minimizing learning disruptions during the outbreak of Covid-19 pandemic (Raman et al., 2021; Bhardwaj and Kumar, 2022). The salient feature of socrative tool includes its support for cognitivism and connectivism types of learning which enable students to become computational thinkers and global collaborators. Also, it provides an SAMR model which is substitution, augmentation, modification, and redefinition. It provides display of results in real time, comparison of outcomes with online communities, access to reports across time, and seamless score keeping and tabulation of results. Also, the learning activities which it supports include arithmetic, health, and community organizing.
- TED-Ed (https://ed.ted.com/): TED-Ed is a web-based platform that offers video contents which are stored primarily on YouTube which can be easily shared and integrated with Google Classroom. It provides lessons organized by different subjects, age, collection of video-based lessons on altered theme, feature of exploration with other organizations, and blog for reading articles and updates. TED-Ed videos could also foster vocabulary learning through its different input and output modalities (Rashtchi et al., 2021; Bhardwaj and Kumar, 2014). The TED-Ed has a salient feature of wider platform engagement which helps students to create Ted talks which encourages research, discovery, presentation, and exploration. It also supports universal themes for simple and universal talk, provides catch phrases which attract students and forces them to think. It also provides a feature of supporting evidence which makes talk memorable and easy to understand. Also, TED-ED uses memorable models like the rule of reciprocal affinity in marketing, the cool factors, powerful visuals, emotional connections, low point, twist moment, and authenticity.
- Virtual Laboratory (https://www.vlab.co.in/): Virtual Laboratory is an initiative under Ministry of Education, Government of India to provide remote access to simulation-based labs and permit students to conduct different experiments. This project provides access to online labs, training, and upgradation of skill sets through workshops. It provides students and

teachers a learning management system for various tools including video-lectures, web-resources, demonstrations, and evaluations (Kachari et al., 2021; Bhardwaj and Kumar, 2022a). The salient features of virtual laboratory include access to top-notch equipment of laboratory to students in virtual mode, virtual aid for complex teaching concepts, safety of students, and engagement of students at different levels of learning. Also, it provides an affordable solution to physical laboratory, allows flexibility in learning as per the pace of student, and offers instant feedback from an expert teacher.

The social analysis of the aforementioned online tools to examine the socio-cultural, administrative, and influential context of operations is presented in Table 10.1.

The social analysis of online tools discussed also presents the process which aims to identify the social dimensions on different platforms like Facebook, Twitter, and YouTube. This also aims to identify the perspectives of different stakeholders and their priorities (Bhardwaj and Kumar, 2021). The task has been performed by Emplifi social marketing cloud which is an end-to-end cloud for modern enterprises (Zha et al., 2022). The Emplifi perfectly manages the multi-channel strategies for optimizing trends and analysing performance (Yang et al., 2022). Usage of online tools in laboratory courses also provides an opportunity for developing and strengthening LMS.

Opportunity for developing and strengthening LMS

An LMS is a software application which provides a framework to handle different aspects of learning process, learning activities, and learning experience. There are many advantages of using LMS like cost savings, consistency of trainings, improving performance, tracking of learner progress, and

Table 10.1 Social Analysis of Different Tools Using Emplifi Social Marketing Cloud

S. No.	*Name of the Tool*	*Facebook Fans*	*Twitter Followers*	*YouTube Subscribers*
1	Audacity	12,431	3,312	9,580
2	Flipgrid	21,164	164,014	12,600
3	Google Earth	118,029	1,100,714	212,000
4	Google Sites	2,066	32,216	3
5	Hot Potato Suite	3,902	1,332	6,400
6	Jeopardy Lab Tool	1,120,506	332,550	1,780
7	MindMeister	17,352	22,341	10,500
8	Socrative Tool	12,140	66,294	2,040
9	TED-Ed	6,370,855	540,990	16,000,000
10	Virtual Laboratory	611	12	17

matching regulatory compliance. The use of online laboratory courses augments the development and strengthens the LMS in the following ways:

- Prepares a learning catalog which allows publishing of documents in common formats, videos, and audio materials with e-learning courses as well.
- Manages the learning materials library with study materials, notes of concerned subject by teachers, last year question papers, and assignments.
- Manages enrollment requests on learning by approving or rejecting requests, analyzing history and feedback of students and result obtained.
- Creates compound courses by combining documents online training, multimedia materials, e-courses, and on-site training for better learning experience.
- Follows a learner-centric approach where each student obtains a personal set of learning materials, assignments, and role during online laboratory courses.

Some of the LMS like SAP Litmos, Violet LMS, talent LMS, and eFront are shown in Figure 10.2.

SAP Litmos provides an online learning for every segment of business, such as sales, services, support, operations, compliance, customers, and employees. It is used by top companies of the world like IBM, YouTube, Fitbit, Pepsico, Mercedez-Benz, and so on. All the data used in the platform is encrypted and accessed only through firewall. It uses HTTPS for transfers of data, has a private certificate, and is GDPR (General Data Protection

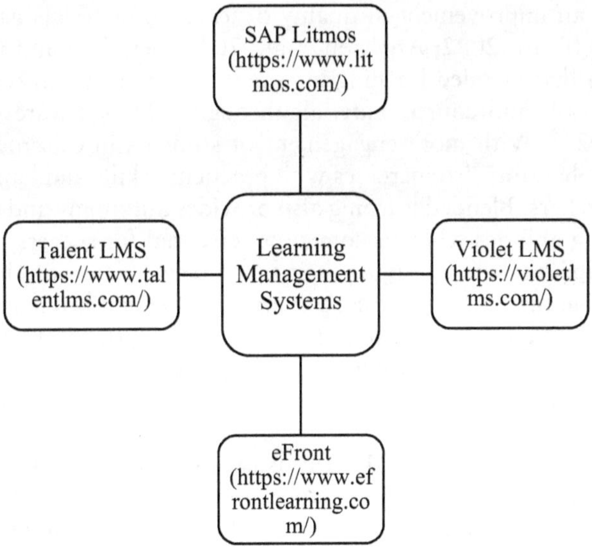

Figure 10.2 Examples of LMS.

Regulation) compliance (Ciobanu and Zaharia, 2022). Talent LMS is an online, cloud-based LMS which is free to operate on desktops or any mobile device with existing operating systems or connection stability. The platform allow users to build courses from scratch or use the present material already available (Qin et al., 2022). Users can host training sessions on the platform with integration through videoconferencing tools like Zoom, Webex, and so on. eFront is an enterprise learning management system which supports most challenging and multifaceted learning environments. It is used by organizations like Blue-chip, American Water College, University of South Carolina, Schneider Electric, Honeywell, and so on. It has a unique option of customization through which enterprises can access the source code and build learning platform as per their requirements. It provides a variety of security features like data encryption, access control, audit logs, and two-factor authentication for platform safety (Alia, 2022). Violet LMS is a prominent learning management platform with more than three lakh users. It provides an artificial intelligence-based learning with automated and relevant course recommendations. It also provides a simulated learning experience with interactive coursework and videos. The learning experience is also augmented with mobile app which can be accessed anytime and anywhere. The platform is hosted on SaaS (Software as a Service) which stores data on cloud and upgrades to current demands of organizations (Cadapan et al., 2022).

The learning management systems have provided new opportunities and are strengthening online laboratory courses in different ways. Like, a new format of blended learning has started which combines digital learning tools with traditional classroom practices of face-to-face teaching (Islam et al., 2022). This is bringing transparency in academics through LMS, which has pushed an improvement in quality of learning materials used in teaching. Studies (Prifti, 2022; Argyriou et al., 2022; Bergdahl and Bond, 2022) have shown that blended learning improves student engagement by providing digital tools and course materials through video software (Kumar and Sharma, 2021). With more engagement of students in classroom sessions, their comprehension also increases with practicing skills and hands-on training from teachers. Blended learning also provides autonomy and control over their learning abilities which is sometimes essential for success. This type of teaching helps teachers by saving their time outside classroom in traditional administrative tasks like printing handouts, uploading attendance, grading assignments, and so on. The use of digital tools helps to analyze student's data in more effective ways which can help students to succeed (Greener, 2022). Blended learning was also effective for teaching and learning during social restrictions imposed throughout the world due to the Covid-19 pandemic (Kumar and Gupta, 2021). This is because blended learning programs require only a few in-person attendance, and institutions can create realistically a safe social distancing environment (Megahed and Ghoneim, 2022).

The advantages of using LMS are numerous as they are an integral part of online learning design and development (Al-Handhali et al., 2020). Some of the advantages include organization of online learning resources in one location, which is normally cloud instead of different hard disks or other storage devices (Nayar and Kumar, 2015). This helps in easily creating the teaching courses and further reduces the risk of losing important data. LMS provides unlimited access of online resources with access through any devices, any time and free from locations. This reduces the restrictions related to locations where global students can access resources with different time zones (Al-khresheh, 2022). LMS very efficiently provides ability to track learner's performance and different checks for attainment of personal milestones. Teachers can also provide with supplementary notes, classes, or tutorials for helping students in attaining their goals. This is possible due the presence of analytics and reporting features available in most of the learning management systems (Simon and Randall, 2022). LMS helps in reducing the learning material costs like printing of assignments, lecture notes, attendance sheets, travel costs, learning site rentals, and so on. LMS makes the colleges up-to-date with respect to different regulatory compliances of national (National Assessment and Accreditation Council) or international levels (National Board of Accreditation). Expansion of online courses can be done easily when colleges use LMS for teaching–learning process (Lata and Gupta, 2021). LMS also provides easy linkage with social learning like links to include Twitter or Facebook pages, LinkedIn groups, or online forms. Such things are helpful of colleges as they can market their courses socially with ripple advantages to students as well (Ye and Pennisi, 2022).

One of the most important advantages of using LMS for online laboratory courses is related to flipped classrooms. Learning management systems can support teaching and lead to enhanced personalized learning for students. This can lead to flipped classrooms with the integration of video-conferencing. The free use of online videoconferencing has created a new opportunity for collaborative teaching and learning which can even be monetized (Bailey et al., 2022). Teachers can deliver online courses to students of even competing schools and colleges across the nation to benefit each other. Some of the videoconferencing platforms like Zoom, Cisco Webex, Microsoft Teams, and GoToMeeting have philanthropically allowed features to be used for free. This act has remarkably formed ideal learning experience in classroom especially during Covid-19 pandemic (Nguyen, 2022). Other advantages of using videoconferencing in the classroom includes easy and quick connection with experts. For example, business leaders can deliver their talks from boardrooms, and scientists can show performance of equipment from their labs for better understanding (Riedl, 2022). Students can go to virtual field trips like visit to world-renowned museums, zoos, monuments, and House of Commons without worrying about additional funds. Videoconferencing boosts work collaboration globally which increases joint activities and reduces cultural barriers. Schools can instill connection with classrooms all over the world and work collaboratively to form a global society (Owens and Hite, 2022). Teachers can use videoconferencing in classrooms to take students for a virtual trip to visit active volcano with Operation Montserrat (Kumar and Bhardwaj, 2018). Teaching subjects like geography or culture can become interesting with the integration of games like Mystery Skype. Also, the teachers can deliver lectures to other schools around the world, create common assessments, and even create review sessions (Schröder and Kohl, 2022). A model for conducting online laboratory classes is presented in the next section.

Model for online laboratory courses

The model for conducting online laboratory courses is designed to provide learning experience using interactive MOOC (Massive Open Online Course) to students enrolled in particular courses (Tseng et al., 2022). Teachers act as facilitators for students to complete their learning tasks in a computer lab which is accommodated physically in the school or college (Unsworth and Posner, 2022). The model for online laboratory classes is presented in Figure 10.3.

The model provides an understanding of infusing online technologies into instructions during laboratory classes. The model helps to connect content to context during laboratory classes teaching learning process as per the requirements of the course. The first step in the model for conducting online laboratory classes includes the enrollment of students in the laboratory class of different disciplines like computer science, electronics, electrical, mechanical, and so on. These laboratory classes are used for in-house professional students where the host is a teacher of the course (Colthorpe and Ainscough, 2021). This is arranged in a normal working day of the school or college with predefined objectives and debriefing outcomes. The main objective of getting students enrolled in laboratory classes is to enhance their understanding of specific scientific concepts and facts (Zhu and Zhang, 2022). The next step

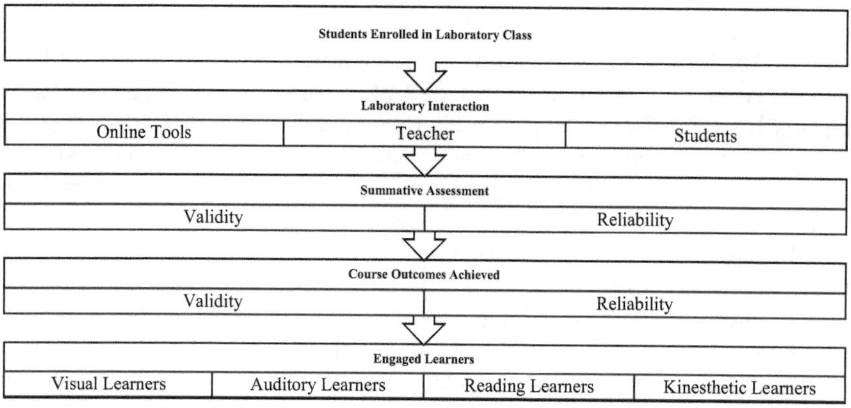

Figure 10.3 Model for conducting online laboratory courses.

in the model includes laboratory interaction with online tools like Audacity, Flipgrid, Socrative tool, Jeopardy, and so on of teachers and students. Laboratory interaction includes online tools with content type of course management system, course structure, interactive tools available, and focus on interaction. The teachers are required to be technology savvy, capable of good writing style or tone, engagement or presence, instructional designs, activities, assignments, and motivation. Students are considered to be motivated and equipped with learning styles (Picciano, 2021). Use of such online tools allows students to work on real-time case studies, perform experiments, interaction with lab equipment, and learning with theory queries (Warfvinge et al., 2022). Some of the tools even allow users to build their own digital models to enhance the learning experience. The next step in the model is summative assessment to evaluate learning of students by comparing standard laboratory outcomes and the online laboratory outcomes (Iannone and Simpson, 2022). These summative assessments are of high stake like midterm examination, a minor or major project with a high value of marks. This includes reliability and validity where reliability is the consistency of scores across administration of similar assessment instruments (Hill et al., 2022). Validity is the degree to which evidence and theory support the interpretation of evaluation scores and proposed uses of assessment instruments (Ryan et al., 2022). The next, course outcome is central to the online laboratory course which helps students to articulate the reason of pursuing the course. These also help them to identify what they will be able to achieve after the completion of course (Gregory et al., 2022). The course outcomes are a well-defined assessment pattern, an item bank as per assessment pattern, a defined instrument for a chosen difficulty level with syllabus of the course communicated to students (Flores et al., 2022). The next step in the model for conducting online laboratory courses is to engage different types of learners which include visual learners, auditory learners, reading learners, and kinesthetic learners (Zapalska, 2022). The model is capable of helping students to remember information efficiently through making notes, diagrams, listening to lectures at their own pace while studying. All four types are including in this model as there is no learning style which fits for all the students as they learn new information. These four types of learners are a part of VARK (visual learners, auditory learners, reading learners, and kinesthetic learners) system, which presents the best teaching methods and activities to match the learning styles and preferences of students (Pérez-Marín et al., 2022).

The model for online laboratory courses can strengthen the teaching–learning process in numerous ways:

- The model adds flexibility in the time for conducting the experiments by teachers, which helps in self-pace of understanding and learning by students.
- The model presents better time management for students to complete assignments, actively participate with teachers in the classroom and do future planning efficiently.

- It can be used to organize a large number of conferences, seminars, and academic meetings, which in present-day situation have moved online and has reduced travel overhead expenditures and computing times.
- The model helps students to become self-motivated for completing the course which is an important employability skill and is known to employers as well.
- It helps students to develop their virtual communication and collaboration skills which are essential these days to become efficient leaders capable to make best decisions.
- The students can log in from anywhere in the world without any restrictions of location or time zones, hence the model provides a broader perspective of learning.
- It allows students to plan their activities for every day, which plays an important role in every type of education system.
- The model equips students with new technical skills, which are a definite augmentation to job seekers as their familiarization with such skills can solve many common issues quickly.

Conclusions

The model for conducting online laboratory courses is very useful to students as well as teachers. This is going to be an essential requirement during the Covid-19 pandemic. Students can perform laboratory experiments at their personal time and can schedule accordingly. Students can learn at their own pace, spend less time in traditional classroom activities, and can create customized learning environment. This will help students in technology enabled for online laboratory courses and lifelong self-learning. These online laboratory courses encourage collaborative use of virtual reality models, simulations, and animations. Such things are much better than real laboratory experiments, which are mostly based on data acquisition systems. All these require the teachers to become more technology savvy for which appropriate online training needs to be imparted to the teachers. The proposed model for conducting online laboratory courses helps the all different types of learners like visual learners, auditory learners, reading learners, and kinesthetic learners.

References

Al-Handhali, B. A., Al-Rasbi, A. T., and Sherimon, P. C. (2020). Advantages and disadvantages of earning Management System (LMS) at AOU Oman. *International Journal of Technology*, *1*(2), 222–228.

Alia, A. A. H. (2022). The Analysis of a Learning Management System from a Design and Development Perspective. *International Journal of Information and Education Technology*, *12*(4), 280–289.

Al-khresheh, M. H. (2022). Revisiting the effectiveness of blackboard learning management system in Teaching English in the Era of COVID-19. *World*, *12*(1), 1–14.

Argyriou, P., Benamar, K., and Nikolajeva, M. (2022). What to Blend? Exploring the Relationship Between Student Engagement and Academic Achievement via a Blended Learning Approach. *Psychology Learning & Teaching*, *21*(2), 126–137.

Bailey, D. R., Almusharraf, N., and Almusharraf, A. (2022). Video conferencing in the e-learning context: explaining learning outcome with the technology acceptance model. *Education and Information Technologies*, 1–20.

Bergdahl, N., and Bond, M. (2022). Negotiating (dis-) engagement in K-12 blended learning. *Education and Information Technologies*, *27*(2), 2635–2660.

Bhardwaj, A., and Cyphert, D. (2020). Direct Benefit Transfer Using Aadhaar: Improving Transparency and Reducing Corruption. In *Examining the Roles of IT and Social Media in Democratic Development and Social Change*. IGI Global, pp. 185–210.

Bhardwaj, A., and Kumar, V. (2011). Cloud security assessment and identity management. In *14th International Conference on Computer and Information Technology (ICCIT 2011)*. IEEE, pp. 387–392.

Bhardwaj, A., and Kumar, V. (2014). Identity management practices in cloud computing environments. *International Journal of Cloud Computing*, *3*(2), 143–157.

Bhardwaj, A., and Kumar, V. (2021). Electronic Healthcare Records: Indian vs. International Perspective on Standards and Privacy. *International Journal of Service Science, Management, Engineering, and Technology (IJSSMET)*, *12*(2), 44–58.

Bhardwaj, A., and Kumar, V. (2022). A framework for enhancing privacy in online collaboration. *International Journal of Electronic Security and Digital Forensics*, *14*(4), 413–432.

Bhardwaj, A., and Kumar, V. (2022a). Web and social media approach to marketing of engineering courses in India. *International Journal of Business Innovation and Research*, *27*(4), 541–555.

Bhardwaj, A., and Kumar, V. (2022b). Privacy and Healthcare During COVID-19. In *Cybersecurity Crisis Management and Lessons Learned From the COVID-19 Pandemic*. IGI Global, pp. 82–96.

Bhardwaj, A., and Kumar, V. (2023). Social Media as an Enabler to Combat Misinformation. In *Pandemics in the Age of Social Media: Information and Misinformation in Developing Nations*. Routledge: New York (USA), pp. 1–15.

Bhat, A. Z., Singh, B., and Fadhil, T. (2021). Role of Cloud Computing to Support Big Data and Big Data Analytics for Education Par Excellence. In *Applications of Artificial Intelligence in Engineering*. Springer, Singapore, pp. 327–337.

Cadapan, R. R., Tindowen, D. J., Mendezabal, M. J., and Quilang, P. (2022). Graduate school students' self-efficacy toward online learning in the midst of the COVID-19 pandemic. *International Journal of Evaluation and Research in Education*, *11*(2), 555–564.

Ciobanu, R. C., and Zaharia, A. V. (2022). Opportunities and Disadvantages of Using Mobile Technologies Based on Cloud in Learning. In *Education, Research and Business Technologies*. Springer: Singapore, pp. 55–63.

Colthorpe, K., and Ainscough, L. (2021). Do-it-yourself physiology labs: Can hands-on laboratory classes be effectively replicated online?. *Advances in Physiology Education*, *45*(1), 95–102.

Egielewa, P., Idogho, P. O., Iyalomhe, F. O., and Cirella, G. T. (2022). COVID-19 and digitized education: Analysis of online learning in Nigerian higher education. *E-Learning and Digital Media*, *19*(1), 19–35.

Flores, M. A., Barros, A., Simão, A. M. V., Pereira, D., Flores, P., Fernandes, E., and Ferreira, P. C. (2022). Portuguese higher education students' adaptation to online teaching and learning in times of the COVID-19 pandemic: personal and contextual factors. *Higher Education*, *83*(6), 1389–1408.

Greener, S. (2022). The tensions of student engagement with technology. *Interactive Learning Environments*, *30*(3), 397–399.

Gregory, D. D., Tomes, H. E., Panasiuk, S. L., and Andersen, A. J. (2022). Building an online field course using digital and physical tools including VR field sites and virtual core logging. *Journal of Geoscience Education*, *70*(1), 85–100.

Guo, Y., Xia, H., Pan, L., Zhao, X., and Li, R. (2022). Mapping the northern limit of double cropping using a phenology-based algorithm and Google Earth Engine. *Remote Sensing*, *14*(4), 1004.

Hill, A. E., Bartle, E., Copley, J. A., Olson, R., Dunwoodie, R., Barnett, T., and Zuber, A. (2022). The VOTIS, part 1: development and pilot trial of a tool to assess students' interprofessional skill development using video-reflexive ethnography. *Journal of Interprofessional Care*, 1–9.

Hoffman, J. A., and Miller, E. A. (2020). Addressing the Consequences of School Closure Due to COVID-19 on Children's Physical and Mental Well-Being. *World Medical & Health Policy*, *12*(3), 300–310. https://doi.org/10.1002/wmh3.365

Hursen, C. (2021). The effect of problem-based learning method supported by web 2.0 tools on academic achievement and critical thinking skills in teacher education. *Technology, Knowledge and Learning*, *26*(3), 515–533.

Iannone, P., and Simpson, A. (2022). How we assess mathematics degrees: the summative assessment diet a decade on. *Teaching Mathematics and its Applications: An International Journal of the IMA*, *41*(1), 22–31.

Islam, M. K., Sarker, M. F. H., and Islam, M. S. (2022). Promoting student-centred blended learning in higher education: A model. *E-Learning and Digital Media*, *19*(1), 36–54.

Kachari, N. A., Biswas, S., and Deka, J. K. (2021). Conversion of Virtual Lab Experiments using FOSS: A Case Study of Virtual Labs by NMEICT. In *2021 IEEE International Conference on Engineering, Technology & Education (TALE)*. IEEE, pp. 318–324.

Kovid, R. K, and Kumar V. (Eds) (2022). *Cases on Emerging Markets Responses to the COVID-19 Pandemic*. IGI – Global Publications: USA (ISBN13: 978-16-6843-504-5, DOI: 10.4018/978-1-6684-3504-5).

Kumar, V., and Bhardwaj, A. (2018). Identity Management Systems: A Comparative Analysis. *International Journal of Strategic Decision Sciences (IJSDS)*, *9*(1), 63–78.

Kumar, V., and Bhardwaj, A. (2020). Deploying Cloud-Based Healthcare Services: A Holistic Approach. *International Journal of Service Science, Management, Engineering, and Technology (IJSSMET)*, *11*(4), 87–100.

Kumar, V., and Bhardwaj, A. (2020a). Role of cloud computing in school education. *Handbook of Research on Diverse Teaching Strategies for the Technology-Rich Classroom*, 98–108.

Kumar, V., and Gupta G. (Eds) (2021). *Strategic Management During a Pandemic*. Routledge, Taylor & Francis Group: USA (ISBN 9780367646479).

Kumar, V., and Malhotra, G. (Eds) (2021). *Stakeholder Strategies for Reducing the Impact of Global Health Crises*. Hershey, PA, USA: IGI – Global Publications (ISBN13: 978-17-9987-495-9, DOI: 10.4018/978-1-7998-7495-9).

Kumar, V., and Nanda, P. (2020). Social Media as a Tool in Higher Education: A Pedagogical Perspective. In *Handbook of Research on Diverse Teaching Strategies for the Technology-Rich Classroom*. IGI Global, pp. 239–253.

Kumar, V., and Sharma, D. (2017). Cloud computing as a catalyst in STEM education. *International Journal of Information and Communication Technology Education (IJICTE)*, *13*(2), 38–51.

Kumar, V., and Sharma, D. (2021). E-Learning Theories, Components and Cloud Computing Based Learning Platforms. *International Journal of Web-Based Learning and Teaching Technologies*, *16*(3), 1–16.

Lata, M., and Gupta, A. (2021). Education During the Pandemic: Technology-Based Solutions. In *Stakeholder Strategies for Reducing the Impact of Global Health Crises*. IGI Global, pp. 209–224.

Li, D. (2022). The Shift to Online Classes during the COVID-19 pandemic: Benefits, Challenges, and Required Improvements from the Students' Perspective. *Electronic Journal of e-Learning*, *20*(1), 1–18.

Luo, Y., Yao, L., Hu, L., Zhou, L., Yuan, F., and Zhong, X. (2022). Urban and rural disparities of personal health behaviors and the influencing factors during the COVID-19 outbreak in China: based on an extended IMB model. *Disaster Medicine and Public Health Preparedness*, *16*(3), 880–884.

Marinoni, G., Van't Land, H., and Jensen, T. (2020). The impact of Covid-19 on higher education around the world. *IAU global survey report*, *23*.

Megahed, N., and Ghoneim, E. (2022). Blended learning: the new normal for post-Covid-19 pedagogy. *International Journal of Mobile and Blended Learning (IJMBL)*, *14*(1), 1–15.

Nayar, K. B., and Kumar, V. (2015). Benefits of cloud computing in education during disaster. In *Proceedings of the International Conference on Transformations in Engineering Education*. Springer: New Delhi, pp. 191–201.

Nguyen, T. H. (2022). Non-English-major students' Attitudes toward English Learning and Teaching via Video Conferencing. *International Journal of TESOL & Education*, 2(1), 296–309.

Ober, J. (2021). 1. I, Socrates . . . The Performative Audacity of Isocrates' Antidosis. In *Isocrates and Civic Education*. University of Texas Press, pp. 21–43.

Qin, S., Orchakova, L., Liu, Z. Y., Smirnova, Y., and Tokareva, E. (2022). Using the Learning Management System" Modular Object-Oriented Dynamic Learning Environment" in Multilingual Education. *International Journal of Emerging Technologies in Learning (iJET)*, *17*(3), 173–191.

Owens, A. D., and Hite, R. L. (2022). Enhancing student communication competencies in STEM using virtual global collaboration project based learning. *Research in Science & Technological Education*, *40*(1), 76–102.

Pérez-Marín, D., Paredes-Velasco, M., and Pizarro, C. (2022). Multi-mode Digital Teaching and Learning of Human-Computer Interaction (HCI) using the VARK Model during COVID-19. *Educational Technology & Society*, *25*(1), 78–91.

Picciano, A. G. (2021). Theories and Frameworks for Online Education: Seeking an Integrated Model. In *A Guide to Administering Distance Learning*. Hershey, PA: Brill, pp. 79–103.

Prifti, R. (2022). Self–efficacy and student satisfaction in the context of blended learning courses. *Open Learning: The Journal of Open, Distance and e-Learning*, *37*(2), 111–125.

Rashtchi, M., Khoshnevisan, B., and Shirvani, M. (2021). Integration of Audiovisual Input via TED-ED Videos and Language Skills to Enhance Vocabulary Learning. *MEXTESOL Journal*, *45*(1), n1.

Riedl, R. (2022). On the stress potential of videoconferencing: definition and root causes of Zoom fatigue. *Electronic Markets*, *32*(1), 153–177.

Rinfret, S. R., and Forster, E. (2022). FlipGrid: Re-imagining online discussion forums for the public administration classroom. *Journal of Public Affairs Education*, 1–15.

Roman, C., Delgado, M. A., and García-Morales, M. (2021). Socrative, a powerful digital tool for enriching the teaching–learning process and promoting interactive learning in Chemistry and Chemical Engineering studies. *Computer Applications in Engineering Education*, *29*(6), 1542–1553.

Ryan, J. F., Mador, B., Lai, K., Campbell, S., Hyakutake, M., and Turner, S. R. (2022). Validity Evidence for Procedure-specific Competence Assessment Tools in General Surgery: A Scoping Review. *Annals of Surgery*, *275*(3), 482–487.

Saha, P., Bose, S., Srivastava, A. K., Chaudhary, A. A., Lall, R., and Prasad, S. (2021). Jeopardy of COVID-19: Rechecking the Perks of Phytotherapeutic Interventions. *Molecules*, *26*(22), 6783.

Schröder, K., and Kohl, S. (2022). Vicon-towards understanding visual support systems in collaborative video conferencing. In *International Conference on Human-Computer Interaction*. Springer: Cham, pp. 278–288.

Sharma, D., and Kumar, V. (2017). A Framework for Collaborative and Convenient Learning on Cloud Computing Platforms. *International Journal of Web-Based Learning and Teaching Technologies (IJWLTT)*, *12*(2), 1–20.
Simon, J. R., and Randall, J. G. (2022). Predictors and consequences of typical and "addictive" LMS use. *Education and Information Technologies*, 1–29.
Singh, J., and Kumar, V. (2022). Combating the Pandemic with ICT Based Learning tools and applications: A case of Indian Higher Education. *International Journal of Virtual and Personal Learning Environments (IJVPLE) Platforms (IJVPLE)*, *12*(1), 1–21.
Tate, T., and Warschauer, M. (2022). Equity in online learning. *Educational Psychologist*, *57*(3), 192–206.
Tseng, T. H., Lin, S., Wang, Y. S., and Liu, H. X. (2022). Investigating teachers' adoption of MOOCs: the perspective of UTAUT2. *Interactive Learning Environments*, *30*(4), 635–650.
Unsworth, A. J., and Posner, M. G. (2022). Case Study: Using H5P to design and deliver interactive laboratory practicals. *Essays in Biochemistry*, *66*(1), 19–27.
Warfvinge, P., Löfgreen, J., Andersson, K., Roxå, T., and Åkerman, C. (2022). The rapid transition from campus to online teaching–how are students' perception of learning experiences affected?. *European Journal of Engineering Education*, *47*(2), 211–229.
Widayanti, F. D., and Khasanah, R. (2021). Online Learning Management Using Google Sites In Covid-19 Pandemic Era. *Jurnal Aplikasi Manajemen*, *19*(2).
Yang, W. C., Jain, A., De Raedt, L., and Meert, W. (2022, April). Parameter Learning in ProbLog with Annotated Disjunctions. In *International Symposium on Intelligent Data Analysis*. Springer: Cham, pp. 378–391.
Ye, D., and Pennisi, S. (2022). Analysing interactions in online discussions through social network analysis. *Journal of Computer Assisted Learning*, *38*(3), 784–796.
Zapalska, A. (2022). Enhancing Students Learning in an Undergraduate Engineering Economics Course During the COVID-19 Pandemic. *Interdisciplinary Education and Psychology*, *3*(1), 2.
Zha, D., Foroudi, P., Jin, Z., and Melewar, T. C. (2022). Making sense of sensory brand experience: Constructing an integrative framework for future research. *International Journal of Management Reviews*, *24*(1), 130–167.
Zhu, M., and Zhang, Y. (2022). Medical and public health instructors' perceptions of online teaching: A qualitative study using the Technology Acceptance Model 2. *Education and Information Technologies*, *27*(2), 2385–2405.

11 Futuristic outlook of online learning

The post-pandemic era

Sandhya Rai and Manju Lata

Introduction

Online learning or e-learning can be defined as the delivery of training or learning content with the help of digital resources (Kumar and Sharma, 2021). It is rapidly gaining pace due to the flexibility that it offers for the learner. Ranging from university-based self-paced learning courses to independent study courses to instructor-led workshops, seminars, tutorials, corporate trainings, it is gaining acceptability everywhere. Due to the advancement of the technology, it has become part of many institutions. Though online learning had shown significant growth pre-Covid-19, it had taken a leap during Covid-19 (Kovid and Kumar, 2022). Covid-19 had made online learning more centric in people's life (Kumar and Gupta, 2021). Pandemic had forced institutions (schools, universities, corporates) to work remotely, and this booms the usage of digital platforms and online learning (Lata and Gupta, 2021). There are multiple learning platforms in the market, like Coursera, Udemy, EdX, Udacity, Skillshare, and Great Learning, to name a few. Along with these platforms many top-tier institutions and universities are also offering their courses via online. Indian Institute of Management (IIM), Indian Institute of technology (IIT), Harvard University, and Stanford University are offering online courses. Though every platform or university caters to their niche market, for example Coursera gives access to university courses, whereas Udemy has experts offering their own courses and focuses on latest skill set requirement. Universities are offering courses in their stream of expertise like sciences, mathematics, engineering, computer science, personal development; Skillshare offers courses in creativity like painting, animation, and photography. The emergence of a new platform every day shows the demand for these courses. These platforms are providing a means to the learner to upgrade their skill that too with complete flexibility of time and location of study. As per the data shared by Coursera, one of the online learning platforms, the number of registered users has increased from 21 million in the year 2016 to 92 million by the year 2021. Not only this, the enrollment across the courses has increased from 26 million in the year 2016 to 189 million in the year

DOI: 10.4324/9781003491712-11

2021. This is an indication of the popularity of online learning platforms. The region-wise analysis indicates that the highest chunk of students are coming from the Asia-Pacific region. Not only this, the education technology sector is expected to grow to US$680 million by 2027; this will happen majorly due to advancement in the mobile technology, cloud services, and virtual reality (Bhardwaj and Kumar, 2023).

Stages of online learning

According to Salmon (2004, 2022), there are five stages in e-learning or online learning; these include access and motivation, online socialization, information exchange, knowledge construction, and development.

Stage 1: access and motivation

Access and motivation is the first stage of the online learning. In the beginning, students are new to the system of online education, and at times they need technical support to access the material, login to the portal, and navigate between the resources. At times this can be demotivating if they are not able to do it properly, and here comes the role of the technical support team. They need to be available to help the student navigate and find what he/she is looking for. From student's side a deep motivation to learn and stay in the course should be there, else the progress will be lost. At this stage, it is important to help students settle in the system and make him/her comfortable with the learning environment and technology adopted by the institution. One can create a short video/audio or course/training to help students understand the learning environment.

Stage 2: online socialization

Once the students are comfortable with the learning environment, the next stage is to make them develop connections with the peers and course instructor. For this, online socialization is encouraged (Kumar and Nanda, 2019). Students are made to participate on the discussion forum, they are encouraged to read and enjoy the comments and feedback of other contributors and share their opinion and queries on the forum. This will help them become comfortable with the online community, and they will be open to the queries and ideas in a better manner. It is important to ensure that these discussion forums promote mutual respect and handle conflicts and differences in a dignified manner. At this stage, students learn to share their thoughts and opinions on the platform and learn to express.

Stage 3: information exchange

At this stage, students have become familiar with the platform and peers and have started interacting. Learning has started, and they have tasted the benefit of quick access to content and have become comfortable in sharing feedback or posting comments. This stage is all about information exchange, and by this stage, students have become comfortable in sharing information (Kumar and Nanda, 2020). For better grasping of content, the students may be encouraged to summarize about their learning before moving to the next stage.

Stage 4: knowledge construction

This is the stage where new knowledge is built based on what is learnt in the previous stage and with social collaboration. Students are encouraged to share their ideas with one another. This can be done by posting open-ended online discussion questions. Knowledge construction is an important aspect of the knowledge management in organizations (Mittal and Kumar, 2019)

Stage 5: development

This is the stage of student's reflection of their learning and evaluating the same. The aim is to make them understand their attainment level and help them understand the achievement of the goal. Participants began to explore their own thinking and knowledge building process. By this stage, learners become responsible for their own learning, and they require little-to-no support beyond the available one. These learners also become guide to people who are new to online learning or are less experienced peer and help them improve the learning process.

Technologies in online education

There are multiple technologies that help in making teaching–learning process more interactive and user-friendly. In the past, we have seen the use of course management system (CMS) or learning management system (LMS), e-books, kindles, and audio books, video and podcast being used in place of physical books. A course management system is a tool that can be used to manage all information related to a course. It is a place where entire course details can be uploaded and the same can be used to offer a course. It is also useful in case one is planning to offer online courses and need the same to be integrated with the website. A course management system also facilitates secure online payment and enrollment. A CMS along with helping in managing resources on the web also helps in managing task and course activities (Tan, 2004). WebBoard, WebCT, Blackboard are a few examples of a subscription-based CMS, whereas Sakai and Moodle are open source. According to Dahlstrom, almost all the universities around the world have adopted an LMS to improve the learning environment and facilitate learning (Dahlstrom, 2014). The web-based online course management systems are more popular in education as they make information and resources available in real time (MacPhee et al., 2003; Rosato et al., 2007; Blankley et al.,

2019). An LMS enables institutions to run e-learning for the students. LMS can be used to upload the content for the enrolled students and give freedom to students to access the content from anywhere. It also offers the facility of offering self-pace courses and flexible assessment. Another new trend which is becoming very popular nowadays among students is preference of audio and video format of study materials over the readable one. Another format added to the audio material is podcast, a multimedia audio file where the material is usually shared in the form of a themed series. These are new formats of offering study material and make learning fun and engaging. With the growing trend of blogs and dedicated website for every field and institutions offering their own channels for knowledge sharing, the format of books has also changed. There is an increase in the trend of adopting e-books. Every publisher is now offering both the hard copy and e-book formats of their publications. In addition to this, the Kindle editions of books are also being offered by many publishers.

The impact of these resources and platforms is further enhanced by artificial intelligence, augmented, virtual and mix reality, big data, wearable devices, videoconferencing tools like Zoom, Google Meet, and other communication platforms such as Microsoft Teams and Cisco WebEx.

Artificial intelligence

Artificial intelligence (AI) refers to the intelligence displayed by a machine/digital computer/computer-controlled robots as opposed to the intelligence displayed by human beings and animals (Lata and Kumar, 2021). It is usually applied to the task of developing a system capable of reasoning, generalizing, discover meaning, or learn from past experiences (Copeland, 2022). AI has the potential to revolutionize the whole learning experience. It can play a great role in identifying the area of improvement and assists students in focusing on one that is important or the one in which they are lagging. Not only this, it can facilitate learning by helping students find multiple ways to solve the same problem, thus facilitating learning in a more comprehensive manner which otherwise is not feasible in a traditional classroom. It can also help in creating more realistic experiences by taking examples from one's interest area and suggesting reading and materials from that field rather than offering a pre-programmed lesson. Not only in learning but AI can also help in assessment and grading. With the help of available answer keys, it can grade students; not only this it has the potential to compile the result and publish the grade sheet and report cards. The role doesn't end here, it is also helpful in providing feedback and tracking the same to support the student. It can go to the extent of finding the trend in the incorrect answers and suggest the topics to be revised or content to be read, so that students can clear the concept. This way it will not be a mere feedback but a meaningful feedback. AI can help in better content delivery and student engagement at all stages, be it university level, corporate trainings, or at school level. Merlyn, an AI-powered digital assistance for teachers developed by "Merlyn-Mind" a US-based company has already been deployed in some schools and is helping teachers in presenting their lectures and in class management (Smith, 2021).

Augmented reality

Augmented reality (AR) is a technology that enhances a user's real-world views by incorporating computer-generated images on the user's real world thus providing a composite experience. It can also play a major role in online learning by making it more interesting and easier to understand. For example, while discussing the assembly line model of manufacturing, the class can have a virtual tour of an automobile factory, and students can see real cars getting assembled. Few examples of application of AR in education include apps like "Catchy Words AR" in which students walk around the classroom and find out the letters and guess the right word. This app is useful for students attending kindergartens and is useful to make them learn new words. Another app that has found application in schools is "Quiver masks", the app allows student to create masks of their choice, these masks or characters can be used by them for narrating stories. Apps like "Arloon Gemoetry" allow students to explore 2D (two dimensional) and 3D (three dimensional) shapes, and "Merge Cube" app allows students to transform any object into a 3D item, and with the help of touchable AR, they can explore the inside and out. This is very useful for science classes.

Virtual reality

Virtual reality (VR) is the use of computer modeling and simulation that enables a person to interact with an artificial three-dimensional (3D) visual or another sensory environment (Lowood, 2021). With the help of headsets or HMD (head mount devices), the user is immersed into a computer-generated environment that feels real. It is this feature of VR that has made it popular in academics and e-learning. It is already being used in fields that are too expensive or dangerous for life. It has already found huge applications in health care, architecture, pharma, sports, entertainment, and physics to name a few. Those areas where there is danger and a training or sensitization is required, VR does it well; from training fighter pilots to surgeons, to space travelers, it allows one to take virtual risk and learn rather than diving onto the real risk. With the advancement of technologies, the cost of VR devices is going down, they are becoming faster, wireless, and more sophisticated. In future, one would see a frequent use of these devices in academics, especially in online learning. It can give a feel of being a part of the class, and not only this, one can immerse in the topic of discussion as well. Once used in online classroom, it will be engaging, there will be no boredom, one does not have to be confined to the books and its pages and the bullets and illustrations; education would be experiential. With decrease in the cost of device we will see more applications coming up. At present, there are three main categories of virtual reality, these are non-immersive virtual reality, semi-immersive virtual reality, and fully immersive virtual reality. Non-immersive virtual reality is a computer-generated virtual environment where the user remains aware and controlled by the physical environment (Bardi, 2022), for example video games. However, semi-immersed virtual reality provides an experience partially based on virtual reality, for example flight simulator. The fully immersed virtual reality provides a realistic simulation experience. They have everything, sound motion, light, and every possible effect. One of the simplest examples of fully immersive virtual reality is car racing games. An example of the application of virtual reality in education is "TheVirtual-Speech" app, which allows students to practice public speaking with virtual assistance. Similarly, "VR Expedition" app allows the teachers to expose students to 360 different cities via providing virtual field trips. Another example of VR application in education is "Labster" a simulation-based science laboratory that allows the students to perform experiments without actual risk and costly mistakes.

Mixed reality

Mixed reality (MR) is merging of real and virtual world experience to produce a new environment and visualization. It does not exclusively happen in virtual or physical world but in a hybrid manner, that is a mix of virtual and physical (Milgram and Kishino, 1994). With the help of MR any environment can be created, for example while discussing the world war and its impact, students can be immersed in a mixed reality experience and be a part of the war field of the world war, the learning and experience would be totally different. These can be used across courses, be it science, social studies, or literature; one can see the complex system of human body to planets, chemical reactions in plants and animals to the one in the oil refineries, the battlefield of history to the romance of the literature with equal ease. It can help understand complicated concepts in a simple manner and has the potential to be used in all subjects alike.

Big data

"Data is the new gold and one who know how to mine it will be the winner". With multiple technologies around the corner and their adoption rate, everyone is creating huge volumes of data every second, this data is called big data. Oracle India defines big data as a data that consists of huge variety and is constantly getting added up at high velocity and is generated in multiple forms; volume, velocity, and variety are three popular Vs of big data. This huge volume of data if analyzed can give a great insight about the learner, learning attainment level, and suitable learning method. The data in education mainly includes students' roll number or enrollment/registration number, course details, year of enrollment, examination grades, and marks obtained in individual subjects. This data once analyzed can be very crucial in giving direction to learning and career. It can help in enhancing students' result by providing details about the time taken by the students to respond to the questions. The additional information like the question missed and the question successfully answered can indicate the strong and the weak areas of learning. Also, a close look at the sources used by the students to educate themselves can help in understanding the reason for missing concept/learning. The comprehensive analysis of the grades can help in understanding the area where the students fair well and the one that needs reinforcement; also, it indicates the area of student's interest. This helps in better content planning and class scheduling. There are many applications which can help in analyzing the attention span of the students by analyzing their heart rate and facial expression and thus help in course planning. All these together can help in better learning and may also help in reducing the dropouts. All these information can be used further to customize the learning resources or create customized training programs.

Wearable devices

Another technology trend that has the potential to disrupt online learning is wearable devices. Wearable devices are smart electronic devices that can be worn on the body as accessories, implanted in user's body, embedded in clothing, or tattooed on the skin (Adam Hayes, 2022). The credit to the growth of wearable devices goes to the internet or internet-based technologies (Internet of Things: IOT) (Lata and Kumar, 2022). The journey begins with the popularity of fitness activity trackers, which has now added web-enabled glasses, Bluetooth, smartwatches, AR, and VR headsets. These devices are already being used in the medical field to track the health of patients or to identify the potential patient; for example, a device set up by AIR Louisville in Louisville is used to monitor air quality, pollutants, and identify the hotspot for respiratory challenges; smart tattoos containing flexible electronic sensors are being developed to monitor sleep disorder, brain activity, and muscle functions in patients. Not only in medical filed, but these devices also have a great potential to be used in education; these can be used as a great training tool, they can help to keep in contact with the learner and take learning and simulations to the next level. Smartwatches when used by learners to receive feedback about the pronunciation of words helped in improving the same and facilitating learning (Shadiev et al., 2018). The wearable devices can be used to learn about the body; students can analyze the temperature of the body in response to an exercise and record the same using a smartwatch. The same can be used to learn about the body (Lee et al., 2015). The brain sensor devices can be used to check the state of the brain and signal stress or anxiety. Brain sensor devices like Muse can be used to train students about ways to relax their mind (Attallah and Ilagure, 2018). The same helps in learning how to relax the brain and focus on learning.

Chatbots

Artificial intelligence-based chatbots are another technology trend which is gaining popularity in education. They act as virtual teaching assistants and are capable of helping students and teacher in getting answers to queries like finding course modules, scholarship, assignment details, hostel facilities, and access to calendar events. Not only this they can also help students with the admission process, finding answers to queries, and connecting students with the right department. Overall, they provide instant support to students; be it getting information regarding the courses to be opted for or connecting with the right faculty or campus update, chatbots helped. Not only this, they are also helpful in getting instant feedbacks and conducting assessment and increasing students' engagement by personalized chats. This is also very helpful for faculty as they do not have to explain the same concepts to different students again and again. It is also very helpful in conducting assessment and in grading and results generation. Teachers can also send updates with the help of chatbots and manage day-to-day activities like course notification and assignment reminders. Chatbots can also be used very effectively in administrative activities to handle frequently asked questions like infrastructure details, contact number/mailing address of different departments, library information, hostel and mess information, and bank account information for fee submission. In future, AI-based chatbots will not only facilitate the learning process by making it more interacting but will also ease the work of teachers and administrative staff. Soon, chatbots will become an integrated part of classroom connect. Many universities have started using chatbots for different purposes like Qassim University of Saudi Arabia, which uses chatbots for student engagement and support over social media and website. The chatbot is used for handling students queries about scholarships, admission process, facilities, and communities. Similarly, Podar education uses chatbots to scale parent outreach. The University of Rochester is using chatbots for helping students and faculty access mental well-being facility (Engati Team, 2022).

Apps

Learning is a continuous process, and there is no end to what you can learn, there is always a scope to learn something new. It becomes more convenient and attractive if you can access the material anytime, anywhere; and mobile apps help in this. They have made the access to information and all kind of material at the fingertip. They have made a lot of tasks easy; one does not have to go to the library in search of books or have to carry bulky books all the time; a single app can accommodate thousands of books and can be easily installed in a mobile phone that fits in a pocket. Not only this, it gives flexibility to access the book in the form of audio as well as video, and one can also look for meaning and antonyms and synonyms, that is in many cases there is an inbuilt dictionary as well, this makes learning fun and effective.

The apps also come with the function of connecting to teacher, sharing a query, sending feedback, which helps in better communication between parents, teachers, and students. This makes communication faster and helps in reducing the communication gap as one can refer to the information at any point of time. These apps are also useful when the student has lots of leisure time, the same can be utilized in learning something new. There are many apps like MentalUP Educational Games and LogicLike that provide game-based learning, making learning fun. These apps also save a lot of parent's time as they do not have to stand in a queue to make the payment of fee or any other payment, it can very well be done using the app; also, the school is able to communicate notices, schedule, and announcements to the students using these apps. Apps are an integral part of modern-day learning, and their scope is going to grow.

Web-based information services (WBIS)

During the Covid-19 pandemic, the world witnessed a closing of physical classes for students (Singh and Kumar, 2022). In this situation, when people were restricted to move out and interact, the education sector also witnessed many adaptations like moving to online classes, replacing exams with online quizzes, sending pdf for reading, and so on. One of the most important support in this situation was the WBIS or videoconferencing tools like Zoom, Google Meet, Microsoft Teams, Cisco WebEx to name a few (Bhardwaj and Kumar, 2022). These tools brought the school into every home, and teachers started delivering sessions using them. This was an effort to avoid wastage of academic year and keep learning going on; what started as a videoconferencing tool in 2020 has now grown into a full-fledged classroom; these WBIS has white board to write, they have waiting room to restrict the movement of students and participants, they have the facility to record and stop the recording of the lectures. Facilities like breakout room, pooling facility, and virtual background make the classroom interesting. Facilities like meeting report that provides the list of attendees are useful tools for attendance management. Creating recurring meeting or automatic scheduling of meetings and attaching the same with Google Calendar help in maintaining timetable. Microsoft Teams has gone a step further and along with the aforementioned facility, they also provide the facility to create teams/classes, conduct quizzes, submit assignments, send calendar invites and reminders, and connect everything. These WBIS are constantly improving their products and services and coming with added features, like zoom have introduced "translate it" feature, which can translate the text into different languages; Wikipedia search feature allows the search of Wikipedia from Zoom chat and share them. Google Meet comes with features like embedding live video into google docs, sheet and slides, auto-transcribing of the Google Meet video, livestreaming of the Meet video to name a few. Microsoft Teams has come up with features like "Together Mode", where the whole class can be seen in one go, the "insight" feature helps in getting students data, "Assignment", "Track", and "Class grade" features help in keeping a track on the student's performance. Students can also view what assignment is pending from their side or if the teacher has shared any feedback and returned the assignment; do they need to rework on the same or not. All these WBIS have bought the school inside every household and with impact of Covid-19 diminishing and world returning to physical working and physical schooling, the things are going to change. But it will never be the same as what it was before Covid-19; the new world will continue to use these technology tools as they give them the flexibility to conduct classes from anywhere, and students will be able to attend it from the place of their choice. New features will get added up, and it would be the hybrid classes, which will be the new normal. These WBIS will be continued to be used for guest lectures, projects, conferences, conducting classes, and with new feature getting added up, they will be more interactive.

Futuristic trends in online learning

The Covid-19 pandemic forced the education sector to experiment new ways of teaching and learning. Technology came to the aid when everyone was feeling helpless and lost. We all saw how institutions started using Zoom, Google Meet, Microsoft Teams, and other platforms like Cisco WebX for conducting classes and assessments. This has changed the whole process of teaching and learning, and now the institutions are looking for a hybrid model. There is an increase in the instance of use of platforms like virtual tutoring, videoconferencing technologies, language programs, and online learning software. Main reason for the popularity of online learning is that it provides flexibility of time and location to the teachers and students. Along with the economy of scale, the videos can be translated into multiple languages and can be accessed by thousands of students worldwide, which is not possible in a regular physical class. This brings down the cost of education and we can make education from best places, from best faculty accessible to the entire world at a very cost-effective rate. The other major trend in the online learning includes the following.

Learn from world-class experts

With the online learning, it has now become easy to learn from the world-class expert. They need not visit the places to deliver their lectures but can simply broadcast their recorded lectures

Rise in MOOCs

Post pandemic, we are seeing a rising trend in the offering of online learning programs in the higher education. Many higher educational institutions are offering online or blended learning courses. This had led to the availability of a variety and quality of courses in the online education. There is also a rise in the demand for MOOC courses for students and employees.

AI in education

Educational institutions have started integrating AI (Artificial Intelligence) into education system to bring personalization. It is being used for recommending courses and content for assessment. Based on the profile, behavior, and performance of the students, these contents are being offered. It is also being used to optimize operations and enrolments.

Adoption of LMS (learning management system)

With the growth of online education, there is an upward trend in the adoption of learning management system (Kumar and Sharma, 2017). Institutes have started appreciating the role of data and data analytics for measuring learning outcomes and hence have started adopting LMS to track students' performance and offer courses. LMS has also been found useful in generation of course report and creating metrics like course completion rate, pass percentage, and so on. Such information helps in designing better quality courses and study material and also helps in identifying the area of improvement (Sharma and Kumar, 2017).

Video-based learning

There is a saying that people remember 20% of what they read and 80% of what they see. To increase the retention of the content and provide better learning experiences, universities and other educational institutions have started using video as a mode of learning. These interactive videos have quizzes, embedded questions, key words, and notes to keep the student engaged. A study by Pearson concluded that Gen Z accepted YouTube as a preferred mode of learning (Pearson, 2018).

Open educational resource (OER)

Due to their cost-efficiency and compactness, open educational resources are steadily going to replace the printed textbooks. Digital OERs are finding acceptance among faculty and students and are going to become the mainstream in future as they are easy to carry and provide the flexibility to access from anywhere. These e-contents are available in the form of PDF and audio books and are gaining popularity. As per Acumen Research (2022), the audiobook market is expected to reach at US$33,538 million by 2030, registering a CAGR of 26.5%. This is due to increase in the number of adult and young listeners.

Gamification of learning

Gamification of learning is another trend which the education sector is witnessing. Technology is assisting not in supplementing the learning but in complementing the same with new classroom experiences. Strategies like scorecards, leaderboards, and badges encourage the students to perform better and have positive effect on learning. Gamification also increases cognitive abilities, engagement, and motivation to learn.

Online communities are the new classrooms

There is a growing trend of community creation. There are online communities all over the internet and consists of like-minded people (Nanda and Kumar, 2021). This provides a platform to interact with like-minded people and learn from them. They help in connecting with peers of the same level and peers who are more experienced. They foster relationship and motivate peer learning. These communities act like virtual campus of people with similar goals.

Conclusion

Online learning is the future of learning. With the advancement of technology and increasing access to the internet and best universities entering into it, increasing numbers of students are opting for the same. Larning is now going beyond the school boundaries, and students from any part of the world have access to the best professors in the world. Technologies like artificial intelligence, machine learning, big data, and augmented and virtual realities are going to give a far better experience, and the need for the physical classes will not be felt. One may visit the professor just for a chitchat or to socialize (though the same will happen more over online community) and have a cup of coffee.

The online learning will be technology-driven and from the entry stage to the exit stage, everything will be mapped to provide personalized learning experience. At the entry stage, the data will be captured about the past performance, interests, and why one is doing the course, the objective of enrollment and the motivation to study. This data will be later used for the mapping of the achievement of learning goals. Once the students had been enrolled for a course and starts going through the resources, augmented and virtual reality can help him/her learn the content better. They will provide the opportunity to immerse in the situation and understand it. Machine learning will help in identifying further courses that the students can go through based on his/her interest. In this way, the whole learning will be very engaging, and one will not feel lost or misplaced in the system. To facilitate further, there will be big data-based analysis that will help student understand his/her strength and weaknesses and work on improving what is missing. The assessment will all be online and graded using artificial intelligence technologies; immediate scores will be released, and there will be feedback as well. The technology may go further and suggest immediate topics which require attention or relook. This way, the whole learning process will be fast, self-paced, and free from locational constraints.

References

Acumen Research. (2022). *Audiobooks Market Analysis – Global Industry Size, Share, Trends and Forecast 2022 – 2030*. Retrieved from https://www.acumenresearchandconsulting.com/audiobooks-market#:~:text=Audiobooks%20Market%20Analysis%20%2D%20Global%20Industry,Trends%20and%20Forecast%202022%20%2D%202030&text=The%20Global%20Audiobooks%20Market%20size,Period%20from%202022%20to%202030, accessed 2, February 2024.

Attallah, B., and Ilagure, Z. (2018). Wearable technology: Facilitating or complexing education. *International Journal of Information and Education Technology*, *8*(6), 433–444.

Bardi, J. What Is Virtual Reality: Definitions, Devices, and Examples. Retrieved August 04, 2022, from https://www.marxentlabs.com/what-is-virtual-reality/#:~:text=Virtual%20reality%20is%20the%20use,and%20interact%20with%203D%20worlds. Published: 03/26/2019 | Updated: 05/13/2022.

Bhardwaj, A., and Kumar, V. (2022). A framework for enhancing privacy in online collaboration. *International Journal of Electronic Security and Digital Forensics*, *14*(4), 413–432.

Bhardwaj, A., and Kumar, V. (2023). Social Media as an Enabler to Combat Misinformation. In *Pandemics in the Age of Social Media: Information and Misinformation in Developing Nations*. Routledge: New York (USA), pp. 1–15.

Blankley, A., Kerr, D., and Wiggins, C. (2019). An Examination and analysis of technologies employed by accounting educators. *The Accounting Educators' Journal*, *28*.

Copeland, B. (2022, March 18). Artificial intelligence. Encyclopedia Britannica. Retrieved from https://www.britannica.com/technology/artificial-intelligence

Dahlstrom, E., Brooks, D. C., and Bichsel, J. (2014). The current ecosystem of learning management systems in higher education: Student, faculty, and IT perspectives.

Engati Team. (2022, June). *Education Chatbot: 10 Powerful Applications for 2022*. Retrieved from https://www.engati.com/blog/chatbot-applications-in-educationn, retrieve on 10 sept 2022 https://www.globenewswire.com/news-release/2022/07/20/2483053/0/en/Massive-Open-Online-Courses-MOOC-Market-Is-Likely-to-Rise-USD-64034-37-Million-with-Highest-CAGR-of-36-7-by-2029.html

Hayes, A. (2022, July). *Wearable Technology*. Retrieved from https://www.investopedia.com/terms/w/wearable-technology.asp#:~:text=What%20Is%20Wearable%20Technology%3F,even%20tattooed%20on%20the%20skin

Kovid, R. K., and Kumar V. (Eds) (2022). *Cases on Emerging Markets Responses to the COVID-19 Pandemic*. IGI – Global Publications: USA (ISBN13: 978-16-6843-504-5, DOI: 10.4018/978-1-6684-3504-5).

Kumar, V., and Gupta G. (Eds) (2021). *Strategic Management During a Pandemic*. New York: Routledge, Taylor & Francis Group (ISBN 9780367646479).

Kumar, V., and Nanda, P. (2019). Social Media in Higher Education: A Framework for Continuous Engagement. *International Journal of Information and Communication Technology Education (IJICTE)*, *15*(1), 109–120.

Kumar, V., and Nanda, P. (2020). Social Media as a Tool in Higher Education: A Pedagogical Perspective. In *Handbook of Research on Diverse Teaching Strategies for the Technology-Rich Classroom*. Hershey, PA: IGI Global, pp. 239–253.

Kumar, V., and Sharma, D. (2017). Cloud Computing as a Catalyst in STEM Education. *International Journal of Information and Communication Technology Education (IJICTE)*, *13*(2), 38–51.

Kumar, V., and Sharma, D. (2021). E-Learning Theories, Components and Cloud Computing Based Learning Platforms. *International Journal of Web-Based Learning and Teaching Technologies*, *16*(3), 1–16.

Lata, M., and Gupta, A. (2021). Education During the Pandemic: Technology-Based Solutions. In *Stakeholder Strategies for Reducing the Impact of Global Health Crises*. Hershey, PA: IGI Global, pp. 209–224.

Lata, M., and Kumar, V. (2021). Standards and Regulatory compliances for IoT. *International Journal of Service Science Management, Engineering and Technology (IJSSMET)*, *12*(5), 133–147.

Lata, M., and Kumar. (2022). IoT Networks Security in Smart Home. In *Cybersecurity for Smart Home*. ISTE-WILEY Publications, pp. 155–176.

Lee, V. R., Drake, J., and Williamson, K. (2015). Let's get physical: K-12 students using wearable devices to obtain and learn about data from physical activities. *TechTrends*, *59*(4), 46–53.

Lowood, H. E. (2021, May 13). virtual reality. Encyclopedia Britannica. Retrieved from https://www.britannica.com/technology/virtual-reality

MacPhee, L., Shelley, E., and Karcz, G. (2003). *How Can a Course Management System (CMS) Enhance Myonline (or Faceto-Face) Course*. Portland: Center for Technology Enhanced Learning.

Milgram, P., and Kishino, F. (1994). A Taxonomy of Mixed Reality Visual Displays. *IEICE Trans. Information Systems*, *E77-D*(12), 1321–1329.

Mittal, S., and Kumar, V. (2019) 'Study of knowledge management models and their relevance in organisations'. *International Journal of Knowledge Management Studies*, *10*(3), 322–335

Nanda, P., and Kumar, V. (2021). Social Media Analytics: Tools, Techniques and Present Day Practices. *International Journal of Services Operations and Informatics (IJSOI)*, *11*(4), 422–436.

Oracle India. "What is Big Data?". Retrieved from https://www.oracle.com/in/big-data/what-is-big-data/

Pearson. "Beyond Millennials: The Next Generation of Learners, https://plc.pearson.com/en-US/news/new-research-finds-youtube-video-drives-generation-z-learning-preference, 08 Aug 2018. Retrieved from https://plc.pearson.com/en-US/news/new-research-finds-youtube-video-drives-generation-z-learning-preference

Rosato, J., Dodds, C., and Laughlin, S. (2007). *Usability of Course Management Systems by Students*. Duluth: Department of Computer Information Systems/Computer Science, College of Scholastica.

Salmon, G. (2004). *E-Moderating: The Key to Teaching and Learning Online* (2nd ed.). London: Routledge. Retrieved from www.e-moderating.com.

Salmon, G. (2022). *5 stage model for 2022 and beyond*. Retrieved from https://www.gillysalmon.com/five-stage-model.html, accessed 10, September 2022.

Shadiev, R., Hwang, W. Y., Huang, Y. M., and Liu, T. Y. (2018). Facilitating application of language skills in authentic environments with a mobile learning system. *Journal of Computer Assisted Learning*, *34*(1), 42–52. doi:10.1111/jcal.12212.

Sharma, D., and Kumar, V. (2017). A Framework for Collaborative and Convenient Learning on Cloud Computing Platforms. *International Journal of Web-Based Learning and Teaching Technologies (IJWLTT)*, *12*(2), 1–20.

Singh, J., and Kumar, V. (2022). Combating the Pandemic with ICT Based Learning tools and applications: A case of Indian Higher Education. *International Journal*

of Virtual and Personal Learning Environments (IJVPLE) Platforms (IJVPLE), *12*(1), 1–21.
Smith, J. E. Meet Merlyn, the world's first digital assistant for teachers (June 2021). Retrieved from https://www.fenews.co.uk/skills/meet-merlyn-the-world-s-first-digital-assistant-for-teachers/, viewed on 10.09.22.
Tan, V. (2004). Using IVLE to teach large classes – a personal experience. In TLHE 2004 Proceedings, pp. 443–448.

Index